The Pico C API
Functionary

The Dictionary of the Pico C API Functions

Special thanks to
American Distributors Inc.
and
Tidal Engineering

The Pico C API
Functionary

The Dictionary of the Pico C API Functions

Written and Compiled by
Donald D. Dienst

Hackettstown, New Jersey

FIRST EDITION
ISBN: 979-8-853-25693-4
Library of Congress Control Number: 2023942634

Published by DienstNet LLC
3 The Trail North
Hackettstown, NJ 07840
info@DienstNet.com
www.DienstNet.com

Printed on demand by
Amazon KDP Independent Publisher

TABLE OF CONTENTS

PREFACE

Welcome to the world of the Pico C SDK, a dynamic platform that empowers developers to create exceptional applications and unleash the true potential of their projects. As you hold this book in your hands, you embark on a journey to explore the intricate depths of this remarkable software development kit, guided by a unique resource—a functionary.

A functionary, in the context of this book, is a meticulously organized function dictionary, designed to be a comprehensive reference for developers working with the Pico C SDK. Just as a dictionary provides definitions and explanations for words, this functionary serves as your compass in navigating the vast landscape of functions and their applications within the SDK.

In an era dominated by the vast expanse of online resources, some may wonder why a printed reference like this functionary exists. It's true that the digital landscape is replete with information, readily accessible with just a few clicks. Yet, there is a timeless allure to the tangible, the feeling of flipping through pages and discovering knowledge within the printed word. For those who relish the tactile experience and appreciate having a dependable reference at their fingertips, this functionary seeks to fill that gap.

As you embark on your coding endeavors, this book, valid up to release 1.5.0, will serve as your trusted ally, demystifying complex functions and illuminating the path to unlocking new possibilities.

SCOPE OF THE BOOK

It is important to establish the scope of this functionary to ensure a clear understanding of its contents and limitations. This book primarily focuses on providing in-depth coverage of functions, their supporting macros, and data type definitions within the Pico C SDK, up to its release 1.5.1.

While the Pico C SDK offers a vast array of features and capabilities, it is essential to note that this book does not venture into the concepts of compiler or library setup, support, or features targeted at custom RP2040 boards other than the Pico and the Pico-W. The book is specifically tailored to serve developers working with the Pico and Pico-W boards, providing them with a comprehensive reference for understanding and utilizing the functions and related elements available in the SDK.

It is our intention to provide clarity and focus on the core aspects directly relevant to the Pico C SDK's functionality. By maintaining this scope, we aim to ensure that the information presented within these pages remains concise, practical, and specifically applicable to the supported boards.

We understand that the Pico C SDK is part of a larger ecosystem, and there may be instances where you require guidance beyond the functions and their supporting macros and data type definitions. For such cases, we encourage you to explore the official documentation

I

and resources provided by the Raspberry Pi Foundation and the wider RP2040 community, where you will find valuable insights into compiler setup, library support, and additional features for different boards and configurations.

By acknowledging and respecting the boundaries of this functionary's scope, we aim to provide you with a focused and invaluable resource, ensuring that you can swiftly find the information you need to work effectively with the Pico and Pico-W boards within the context of the Pico C SDK.

Let the pages ahead be your guide to navigating the realm of functions, macros, and data types, empowering you to unleash the full potential of your Pico C SDK projects on these specific boards.

HOW TO USE THIS BOOK

To make the most of this functionary and efficiently harness its wealth of knowledge, it is essential to understand its structure and organization. This section will guide you on how to effectively use this book to locate the information you need within its pages.

The API documentation in this functionary is divided into sections, each focusing on a specific aspect of the Pico C SDK. These sections progress from language-level functionality to low-level hardware interactions and then to high-level features. Each of these sections is further divided into specific topics. The organization of these sections ensures that you can easily locate the relevant information.

Each topic is divided into its elements—macros, defines, data types and structures, and functions, each item within these elements is listed alphabetically. This alphabetical arrangement enables quick reference and ensures a systematic approach to finding the desired information.

Every listed API element is accompanied by informative descriptions that provide a clear understanding of its functionality, purpose, and usage. These descriptions also include details about the parameters that each API element accepts, as well as the information it returns.

It is important to note that not all sections will include every type of API element. The presence of macros, defines, data types and structures, and functions within each section will vary based on the nature of the topic being covered. Rest assured, however, that all relevant elements are included as needed to provide a comprehensive and cohesive reference.

To quickly locate the information you need, we recommend utilizing the table of contents located at the beginning or the alphabetical index at end of the book. These indexes serve as a handy reference points, allowing you to jump directly to the desired API element or section.

As you navigate through this functionary, we encourage you to explore the sections that align with your development requirements. By delving into each API element, reading their descriptions, and understanding their usage, you will gain a deeper understanding of the Pico

C SDK's capabilities and how to effectively leverage them in your projects.

OTHER SOURCES AVAILABLE ONLINE

While this functionary serves as a comprehensive reference for the Pico C SDK, there are numerous online sources that can further enhance your Pico development journey. Here, we have compiled a list of valuable resources that provide additional insights, tutorials, and community support for Pico development. We encourage you to explore these sources to expand your knowledge and connect with fellow developers.

Raspberry Pi Foundation Pico Documentation:
Website: *https://datasheets.raspberrypi.com*
This official documentation from the Raspberry Pi Foundation provides detailed information on the Pico board, including technical specifications, GPIO pinouts, and programming guides.

Raspberry Pi Pico Forum:
Website: *https://forums.raspberrypi.com/*
The Pico Forum is a vibrant community where developers can ask questions, share ideas, and seek assistance related to Pico development. It's a great place to connect with like-minded individuals and benefit from their collective knowledge and experience.

Pico C/C++ SDK Repository on GitHub:
Repository: *https://github.com/raspberrypi/pico-sdk*
The official Pico C/C++ SDK repository on GitHub provides access to the SDK source code, examples, and documentation. It serves as a valuable resource for exploring the SDK internals, understanding its implementation details, and accessing the latest updates and bug fixes.

Pico C/C++ SDK Examples Repository on GitHub:
Repository: *https://github.com/raspberrypi/pico-examples*
The Pico C/C++ SDK Examples repository hosts a wide range of code examples that demonstrate various functionalities and applications of the Pico board. It's an excellent resource for learning through practical hands-on experiences and gaining inspiration for your own projects.

These online resources, along with this functionary, provide a rich tapestry of knowledge and support for your Pico development endeavors. We encourage you to dive into these sources, engage with the community, and leverage the collective wisdom to unleash the full potential of your Pico projects.

Happy exploring and happy coding!

Support Level (Runtime)

This section is dedicated to exploring the support level functionality of the Pico SDK, which corresponds to the runtime section of the online API documentation.

Within these pages, you will discover a treasure trove of functions that play a vital role in the execution and management of your Pico applications. Here, you will find an extensive collection of functions tailored to various language and system support tasks. These functions are carefully organized to cover a wide range of essential functionalities, including input/output operations, memory management, system configuration, and more. Each function is accompanied by informative descriptions, parameter details, and return information, giving you a clear understanding of its purpose and how to use it effectively.

Enumerations

pico_error_codes

```
enum pico_error_codes
```

PICO_OK = 0
PICO_ERROR_NONE = 0
PICO_ERROR_TIMEOUT = -1
PICO_ERROR_GENERIC = -2
PICO_ERROR_NO_DATA = -3
PICO_ERROR_NOT_PERMITTED = -4
PICO_ERROR_INVALID_ARG = -5
PICO_ERROR_IO = -6
PICO_ERROR_BADAUTH = -7
PICO_ERROR_CONNECT_FAILED = -8

The above enumeration lists the standard pico error code responses given by a variety of functions in the API. They are listed above along with their numerical value for reference. When a function or operation in the Pico SDK encounters an error, it typically returns a value of the "pico_error_codes" enumeration type, indicating the specific error condition. By inspecting the returned error code, developers can take appropriate actions based on the nature of the error and implement error handling strategies to gracefully handle exceptional scenarios in their Pico applications.

For example, if a function returns the error code "PICO_ERROR_GENERIC", it signifies a general or unspecified error condition. This code can serve as a catch-all for errors that do not fit into any specific category. On the other hand, error codes such as "PICO_ERROR_INVALID_ARG" or "PICO_ERROR_TIMEOUT" point to more specific issues related to invalid input arguments or timeouts, respectively.

PORTABILITY DATA TYPES

int16_t - Signed 16-bit integer type

int32_t - Signed 32-bit integer type

int64_t - Signed 64-bit integer type

int8_t - Signed 8-bit integer type

size_t - Type used for sizes and counts (platform-dependent)

uint16_t - Unsigned 16-bit integer type

uint32_t - Unsigned 32-bit integer type

uint64_t - Unsigned 64-bit integer type

uint8_t - Unsigned 8-bit integer type

The use of a portability data type is not necessary when programming for the Pico however, it is a good idea and the SDK examples make extensive use of them. They are used to ensure consistent representation and behavior of fundamental data types across different platforms and architectures. They are specifically designed to be independent of the underlying hardware and compiler implementation, making them reliable and predictable across various environments.

The purpose of portability data types is to address potential differences in data type sizes and representations among different systems. This is particularly crucial when developing applications that need to work seamlessly on multiple platforms or when handling data that requires a specific size or behavior regardless of the underlying system.

Boot ROM

pico_bootrom

```
#include "pico/bootrom.h"
```

The bootrom functions in the Pico SDK serve as an interface to access and utilize the functionalities provided by the BootROM (Boot Read-Only Memory) of the Raspberry Pi Pico microcontroller. These functions allow developers to interact with and control various aspects of the boot process and BootROM functionality.

The bootrom functions provide a way to perform specific operations related to the BootROM, enabling developers to customize the boot behavior, handle low-level system operations, and access essential boot-related information. They offer a high-level interface to interact with the underlying BootROM code and leverage its capabilities within their Pico applications.

Macros

ROM_TABLE_CODE (c1, c2)

```
#define ROM_TABLE_CODE (c1, c2)
```

Return a bootrom lookup code based on two ASCII characters. These codes are used to lookup data or function addresses in the bootrom

Parameters

c1   the first character
c2   the second character

Returns

The 'code' to use in rom_func_lookup() or rom_data_lookup()

FUNCTIONS

reset_usb_boot()   **Inline Static**

```
static void reset_usb_boot (uint32_t
       usb_activity_gpio_pin_mask, uint32_t
       disable_interface_mask)
```

Reboot the device into BOOTSEL mode. This function reboots the device into the BOOTSEL mode ('usb boot"). Facilities are provided to enable an "activity light" via GPIO attached LED for the USB Mass Storage Device, and to limit the USB interfaces exposed.

Parameters

usb_activity_gpio_pin_mask

0 = No pins are used as per a cold boot. Otherwise a single bit set indicating which GPIO pin should be set to output and raised whenever there is mass storage activity from the host.

disable_interface_mask

The value to control exposed interfaces

0 = To enable both interfaces (as per a cold boot)

1 = To disable the USB Mass Storage Interface

2 = To disable the USB PICOBOOT Interface

rom_data_lookup()

```
void *rom_data_lookup (uint32_t code)
```

Lookup a bootrom address by code.

Parameters

code

The code to lookup.

Returns

A pointer to the data, or NULL if the code does not match any bootrom function.

rom_func_lookup()

```
void *rom_func_lookup (uint32_t code)
```

Lookup a bootrom function by code.

Parameters

code
> The code to lookup.

Returns

> A pointer to the function, or NULL if the code does not match any bootrom function.

rom_func_lookup_inline()   Inline Static

```
Static __force_inline void *rom_func_lookup_inline
        (uint32_t code)
```

Lookup a bootrom function by code. This method is forcibly inlined into the caller for FLASH/RAM sensitive code usage.

Parameters

code
> The code to lookup.

Returns

> A pointer to the function, or NULL if the code does not match any bootrom function.

rom_funcs_lookup()

```
bool rom_funcs_lookup (uint32_t *table, unsigned int
        count)
```

This is a helper function to lookup the addresses of multiple bootrom functions. This method looks up the 'codes' in the table, and convert each table entry to the looked up function pointer, if there is a function for that code in the bootrom.

Parameters

table

An IN/OUT array, elements are codes on input, function pointers on success.

count

The number of elements in the table.

Returns

True if all the codes were found, and converted to function pointers,

false otherwise.

rom_table_code()   Inline Static

```
static uint32_t rom_table_code (uint8_t c1, uint8_t c2)
```

Return a bootrom lookup code based on two ASCII characters. These codes are uses to lookup data or function addresses in the bootrom.

Parameters

c1   the first character

c2   the second character

Returns

The 'code' to use in rom_func_lookup() or rom_data_lookup().

MATH

pico_bit_ops   pico_divider

In addition to the regular C math functions, the Pico SDK introduces a unique set of math and bit manipulation functions specifically tailored for the Pico platform. These functions offer optimized implementations that are designed to enhance performance and efficiency on the Pico hardware.

While the regular C math functions are not covered, it's important to note that many of them have been overridden in the Pico SDK to provide optimized versions specifically tailored for the Pico platform. These optimized implementations take advantage of the unique features and capabilities of the Pico hardware, resulting in improved performance and efficiency.

The focus of this section is on the unique math and bit manipulation functions that are provided by the Pico SDK.

__rev

```
uint32_t __rev (uint32_t bits)
```

`#include bit_ops.h`

Reverse the bits in a 32 bit word.

Parameters

bits   A 32 bit input.

Returns

The 32 input bits reversed.

__revll

```
uint64_t __revll (uint64_t bits)
```

`#include bit_ops.h`

Reverse the bits in a 64 bit double word.

Parameters

bits   64 bit input

Returns

The 64 input bits reversed.

div_s32s32()

```
int32_t div_s32s32 (int32_t a, int32_t b)
```

`#include divider.h`

Integer divide of two signed 32-bit values.

Parameters

a = Dividend
b = Divisor

Returns

Quotient

div_s32s32_unsafe()

```
int32_t div_s32s32_unsafe (int32_t a, int32_t b)
```

`#include divider.h`

Unsafe integer divide of two signed 32-bit values. Do not use in interrupts.

Parameters

a = Dividend
b = Divisor

Returns

Quotient

div_s64s64()

```
int64_t div_s64s64 (int64_t a, int64_t b )
```

`#include divider.h`

Integer divide of two signed 64-bit values.

Parameters

a = Dividend
b = Divisor

Returns

Quotient

div_s64s64_unsafe()

```
int64_t div_s64s64_unsafe (int64_t a, int64_t b)
```

`#include divider.h`

Unsafe integer divide of two signed 64-bit values. Do not use in interrupts.

Parameters

> **a** = Dividend
> **b** = Divisor

Returns

> Quotient

div_u32u32()

```
uint32_t div_u32u32 (uint32_t a, uint32_t b)
```

`#include divider.h`

Integer divide of two unsigned 32-bit values.

Parameters

> **a** = Dividend
> **b** = Divisor

Returns

> Quotient

div_u32u32_unsafe()

```
uint32_t div_u32u32_unsafe (uint32_t a, uint32_t b)
```

`#include divider.h`

Unsafe integer divide of two unsigned 32-bit values. Do not use in interrupts.

Parameters

a = Dividend
b = Divisor

Returns

Quotient

div_u64u64()

```
uint64_t div_u64u64 (uint64_t a, uint64_t b)
```

`#include divider.h`

Integer divide of two unsigned 64-bit values.

Parameters

a = Dividend
b = Divisor

Returns

Quotient

div_u64u64_unsafe()

```
uint64_t div_u64u64_unsafe (uint64_t a, uint64_t b)
```

`#include divider.h`

Unsafe integer divide of two unsigned 64-bit values. Do not use in interrupts.

Parameters

a = Dividend
b = Divisor

Returns

Quotient

divmod_s32s32()

```
divmod_result_t divmod_s32s32 (int32_t a, int32_t b)
```

`#include divider.h`

Integer divide of two signed 32-bit values.

Parameters

a = Dividend
b = Divisor

Returns

Quotient in low word/r0, remainder in high word/r1.

divmod_s32s32_rem()

```
static int32_t divmod_s32s32_rem (int32_t a, int32_t b,
        int32_t *rem)
```

`#include divider.h`

Integer divide of two signed 32-bit values, with remainder.

Parameters

a = Dividend
b = Divisor
[output] rem = The remainder of dividend/divisor

Returns

Quotient result of dividend/divisor.

divmod_s32s32_rem_unsafe()

```
int32_t divmod_s32s32_rem_unsafe (int32_t a,
        int32_t b, int32_t *rem)
```

`#include divider.h`

Unsafe integer divide of two signed 32-bit values, with remainder. Do not use in interrupts.

Parameters

a = Dividend
b = Divisor
[output] rem = The remainder of dividend/divisor

Returns

Quotient result of dividend/divisor.

divmod_s32s32_unsafe()

```
int64_t divmod_s32s32_unsafe (int32_t a, int32_t b)
```

`#include divider.h`

Unsafe integer divide of two unsigned 32-bit values. Do not use in interrupts.

Parameters

a = Dividend
b = Divisor

Returns

Quotient in low word/r0, remainder in high word/r1.

divmod_s64s64()

```
int64_t divmod_s64s64 (int64_t  a, int64_t b)
```

`#include divider.h`

Integer divide of two signed 64-bit values.

Parameters

a = Dividend
b = Divisor

Returns

Quotient in result (r0,r1), remainder in regs (r2, r3).

divmod_s64s64_rem()

```
int64_t divmod_s64s64_rem (int64_t a, int64_t   b, int64_t
    *rem)
```

`#include divider.h`

Integer divide of two signed 64-bit values, with remainder.

Parameters

a = Dividend
b = Divisor
[output] rem = The remainder of dividend/divisor

Returns

Quotient result of dividend/divisor.

divmod_s64s64_rem_unsafe()

```
int64_t divmod_s64s64_rem_unsafe (int64_t a, int64_t
    b, int64_t *rem)
```

`#include divider.h`

Unsafe integer divide of two signed 64-bit values, with remainder. Do not use in interrupts.

Parameters

a = Dividend
b = Divisor
[output] rem = The remainder of dividend/divisor

Returns

Quotient result of dividend/divisor.

divmod_s64s64_unsafe()

```
int64_t divmod_s64s64_unsafe (int64_t a, int64_t b)
```

`#include divider.h`

Unsafe integer divide of two signed 64-bit values. Do not use in interrupts.

Parameters

> **a** = Dividend
> **b** = Divisor

Returns

> Quotient in result (r0,r1), remainder in regs (r2, r3).

divmod_u32u32()

```
divmod_result_t divmod_u32u32 (uint32_t a, uint32_t b)
```

`#include divider.h`

Integer divide of two unsigned 32-bit values.

Parameters

> **a** = Dividend
> **b** = Divisor

Returns

> Quotient in low word/r0, remainder in high word/r1.

divmod_u32u32_rem() **Inline Static**

```
static uint32_t divmod_u32u32_rem (uint32_t a, uint32_t b,
     uint32_t *    rem)
```

```
#include divider.h
```

Integer divide of two unsigned 32-bit values, with remainder.

Parameters

a = Dividend
b = Divisor
[output] rem = The remainder of dividend/divisor

Returns

Quotient result of dividend/divisor.

divmod_u32u32_rem_unsafe()

```
uint32_t divmod_u32u32_rem_unsafe (uint32_t    a, uint32_t
     b, uint32_t *rem)
```

```
#include divider.h
```

Unsafe integer divide of two unsigned 32-bit values, with remainder. Do not use in interrupts.

Parameters

a = Dividend
b = Divisor
[output] rem = The remainder of dividend/divisor

Returns

Quotient result of dividend/divisor.

divmod_u32u32_unsafe()

```
uint64_t divmod_u32u32_unsafe (uint32_t a, uint32_t b)
```

`#include divider.h`

Unsafe integer divide of two unsigned 32-bit values. Do not use in interrupts.

Parameters

a = Dividend
b = Divisor

Returns

Quotient in low word/r0, remainder in high word/r1.

divmod_u64u64()

```
uint64_t divmod_u64u64 (uint64_t a, uint64_t b)
```

`#include divider.h`

Integer divide of two signed 64-bit values.

Parameters

a = Dividend
b = Divisor

Returns

Quotient in result (r0,r1), remainder in regs (r2, r3).

divmod_u64u64_rem()

```
uint64_t divmod_u64u64_rem (uint64_t a, uint64_t b,
        uint64_t *rem)
```

`#include divider.h`

Integer divide of two unsigned 64-bit values, with remainder.

Parameters

a = Dividend
b = Divisor
[output] rem = The remainder of dividend/divisor

Returns

Quotient result of dividend/divisor.

divmod_u64u64_rem_unsafe()

```
uint64_t divmod_u64u64_rem_unsafe (uint64_t    a, uint64_t
        b, uint64_t *rem)
```

`#include divider.h`

Unsafe integer divide of two unsigned 64-bit values, with remainder. Do not use in interrupts.

Parameters

a = Dividend
b = Divisor
[output] rem = The remainder of dividend/divisor

Returns

Quotient result of dividend/divisor.

divmod_u64u64_unsafe()

`uint64_t divmod_u64u64_unsafe (uint64_t a, uint64_t b)`

`#include divider.h`

Unsafe integer divide of two signed 64-bit values. Do not use in interrupts.

Parameters

a = Dividend
b = Divisor

Returns

Quotient in result (r0,r1), remainder in regs (r2, r3).

PLATFORM

pico_platform

```
#include "pico/stdlib.h"
```

In this section, you will find a collection of macros that define specific attributes and behaviors related to memory placement, flash usage, and data manipulation. These macros allow you to fine-tune the placement of code and data in memory, optimize performance, and ensure compatibility with the Pico platform.

Additionally, the pico_platform section includes several functions that serve various purposes. These functions range from executing breakpoint instructions, ensuring memory access ordering, retrieving chip and ROM version information, managing exceptions, performing busy-wait operations, and obtaining the current core number.

By utilizing the macros and functions provided in the pico_platform section, developers can take advantage of low-level platform-specific optimizations, access system information, handle exceptions, and perform essential system-level operations. This enables fine-grained control over the Pico microcontroller and empowers developers to create efficient and reliable Pico applications tailored to their specific requirements.

MACROS

__after_data

```
#define __after_data (    group )
        __attribute__ ((section(".after_data." group)))
```

Section attribute macro for placement in RAM after the .data section. For example a 400 element uint32_t array placed after the .data section uint32_t __after_data("my_group_name") a_big_array[400]; The section attribute is .after_data.<group>

Parameters

group

A string suffix to use in the section name to distinguish groups that can be linker garbage-collected independently.

__check_type_compatible

```
#define __check_type_compatible (type_a, type_b)
```

Utility macro to assert two types are equivalent. This macro can be useful in other macros along with typeof to assert that two parameters are of equivalent type (or that a single parameter is of an expected type).

__fast_mul

```
#define __fast_mul ( a, b)
```

Multiply two integer values using the fastest method possible. Efficiently multiplies value a by possibly constant value b. If b is known to be constant and not zero or a power of 2, then a mul instruction is used rather than gcc's default which is often a slow combination of shifts and adds. If b is a power of 2 then a single shift is of course preferable and will be used.

Parameters

a   the first operand
b   the second operand

Returns

The result of a multiplied by b.

__force_inline

```
#define __force_inline
```

Attribute to force inlining of a function regardless of optimization level. For example my_function here will always be inlined:

int __force_inline my_function (int x) {

__in_flash

```
#define __in_flash (group )
```

Section attribute macro for placement in flash even in a COPY_TO_RAM binary. For example a uint32_t variable explicitly placed in flash (it will hard fault if you attempt to write it!) The section attribute is .flashdata.<group>

uint32_t __in_flash("my_group_name") foo = 23;

Parameters

group

A string suffix to use in the section name to distinguish groups that can be linker garbage-collected independently.

__isr

```
#define __isr
```

Marker for an interrupt handlerFor example an IRQ handler function called my_interrupt_handler:

void __isr my_interrupt_handler(void) {

__no_inline_not_in_flash_func

```
#define __no_inline_not_in_flash_func (func_name )
```

Indicate a function should not be stored in flash and should not be inlined. Decorates a function name, such that the function will execute from RAM, explicitly marking it as noinline to prevent it being inlined into a flash function by the compiler. The function is placed in the .time_critical.<func_name> linker section. For example a function called my_func taking an int parameter:

void __no_inline_not_in_flash_func (my_func)(int some_arg) {

__not_in_flash

```
#define    __not_in_flash (group)
```

Section attribute macro for placement not in flash (i.e in RAM) For example a 3 element uint32_t array placed in RAM (even though it is static const) The section attribute is .time_critical.<group>

static const uint32_t __not_in_flash("my_group_name") an_array[3];

Parameters

group

A string suffix to use in the section name to distinguish groups that can be linker garbage-collected independently.

__not_in_flash_func

```
#define    __not_in_flash_func (func_name )
```

Indicates a function should not be stored in flash. Decorates a function name, such that the function will execute from RAM (assuming it is not inlined into a flash function by the compiler) The function is placed in the .time_critical.<func_name> linker section. For example a function called my_func taking an int parameter:

void __not_in_flash_func (my_func)(int some_arg) {

See also__no_inline_not_in_flash_func

__scratch_x

`#define __scratch_x (group)`

Section attribute macro for placement in the SRAM bank 4 (known as "scratch X") Scratch X is commonly used for critical data and functions accessed only by one core (when only one core is accessing the RAM bank, there is no opportunity for stalls) The section attribute is .scratch_x.<group>. For example a uint32_t variable placed in "scratch X".

uint32_t __scratch_x("my_group_name") foo = 23;

Parameters

group

A string suffix to use in the section name to distinguish groups that can be linker garbage-collected independently.

__scratch_y

`#define __scratch_y (group)`

Section attribute macro for placement in the SRAM bank 5 (known as "scratch Y") Scratch Y is commonly used for critical data and functions accessed only by one core (when only one core is accessing the RAM bank, there is no opportunity for stalls) The section attribute is .scratch_y.<group>. For example a uint32_t variable placed in "scratch Y".

uint32_t __scratch_y ("my_group_name") foo = 23;

Parameters

group

A string suffix to use in the section name to distinguish groups that can be linker garbage-collected independently.

__time_critical_func

```
#define __time_critical_func (func_name)
```

Indicates a function is time/latency critical and should not run from flash. Decorates a function name, such that the function will execute from RAM (assuming it is not inlined into a flash function by the compiler) to avoid possible flash latency. Currently this macro is identical in implementation to __not_in_flash_func, however the semantics are distinct and a __time_critical_func may in the future be treated more specially to reduce the overhead when calling such function from a flash function. The function is placed in the .time_critical.<func_name> linker section. For example a function called my_func taking an int parameter:

void __time_critical(my_func)(int some_arg) {

See also__not_in_flash_func

__uninitialized_ram

```
#define __uninitialized_ram (group)
```

Section attribute macro for data that is to be left uninitialized. Data marked this way will retain its value across a reset (normally uninitialized data - in the .bss section) is initialized to zero during runtime initialization. The section attribute is .uninitialized_data.<group>. For example a uint32_t foo that will retain its value if the program is restarted by reset.

uint32_t __uninitialized_ram(foo);

Parameters

group

A string suffix to use in the section name to distinguish groups that can be linker garbage-collected independently.

host_safe_hw_ptr

```
#define host_safe_hw_ptr (x)
```

Macro for converting memory addresses to 32 bit addresses suitable for DMA. This is just a cast to uintptr_t on the RP2040, however you may want to use this when developing code that also runs in "host" mode. If the host mode is 64 bit and you are embedding data pointers in other data (e.g. DMA chaining), then there is a need in "host" mode to convert a 64 bit native pointer to a 32 bit value for storage, which can be done using this macro.

FUNCTIONS

__compiler_memory_barrier()   Static

```
static __always_inline void __compiler_memory_barrier
      (void )
```

Ensure that the compiler does not move memory access across this method call.

For example in the following code:

*some_memory_location = var_a;
__compiler_memory_barrier();
uint32_t var_b = *some_other_memory_location

The compiler will not move the load from some_other_memory_location above the memory barrier (which it otherwise might - even above the memory store!)

__get_current_exception()   Inline Static

```
static uint __get_current_exception(void)
```

Get the current exception level on this core.

Returns

> The exception number if the CPU is handling an exception, or 0 otherwise.

The Pico C API Functionary

__mul_instruction()   Static

```
static __always_inline int32_t __mul_instruction (int32_t
      a, int32_t b)
```

Multiply two integers using an assembly MUL instruction. This multiplies a by b using multiply instruction using the ARM mul instruction regardless of values (the compiler might otherwise choose to perform shifts/adds), i.e. this is a 1 cycle operation.

Parameters

a   the first operand
b   the second operand

Returns

The result of a multiplied by b.

busy_wait_at_least_cycles()   Inline Static

```
static void busy_wait_at_least_cycles (uint32_t
      minimum_cycles)
```

Helper method to busy-wait for at least the given number of cycles. This method is useful for introducing very short delays. This method busy-waits in a tight loop for the given number of system clock cycles. The total wait time is only accurate to within 2 cycles, and this method uses a loop counter rather than a hardware timer, so the method will always take longer than expected if an interrupt is handled on the calling core during the busy-wait; you can of course disable interrupts to prevent this. You can use clock_get_hz(clk_sys) to determine the number of clock cycles per second if you want to convert an actual time duration to a number of cycles.

Parameters

minimum_cycles
The minimum number of system clock cycles to delay for.

get_core_num()   Static

```
static __always_inline uint get_core_num (void)
```

Get the current core number.

Returns

The core number the call was made from.

panic()

```
void panic(const char *fmt, ... )
```

Displays a panic message and halts execution. An attempt is made to output the message to all registered STDOUT drivers after which this method executes a BKPT instruction.

Parameters

fmt

format string (printf-like)

...

printf-like arguments

panic_unsupported()

```
void panic_unsupported (void)
```

Panics with the message "Unsupported".

See also panic.

rp2040_chip_version()

```
uint8_t rp2040_chip_version (void)
```

Returns the RP2040 chip revision number.

Returns

The RP2040 chip revision number (1 for B0/B1, 2 for B2).

rp2040_rom_version()   Inline Static

```
static uint8_t rp2040_rom_version (void)
```

Returns the RP2040 rom version number.

Returns

The RP2040 rom version number (1 for RP2040-B0, 2 for RP2040-B1, 3 for RP2040-B2).

tight_loop_contents()   Static

```
static __always_inline void tight_loop_contents (void)
```

No-op function for the body of tight loops. No-op function intended to be called by any tight hardware polling loop. Using this ubiquitously makes it much easier to find tight loops, but also in the future #ifdef-ed support for lockup debugging might be added.

STDIO

pico_stdio

```
#include "pico/stdlib.h"
```

The pico_stdio section of the Pico API provides a customized stdio support mechanism that allows for flexible input and output operations using various communication interfaces. With pico_stdio, developers can seamlessly connect their Pico applications to different devices and channels, including UART (Universal Asynchronous Receiver-Transmitter), USB, semi-hosting, and more.

It is important to note that while the core functionality of pico_stdio supports UART, USB, semi-hosting, and other built-in communication interfaces, the API for adding additional input/output devices is still under development and considered unstable. However, the existing capabilities provide a solid foundation for handling standard input and output operations in a flexible and customizable manner.

Please note that as the Pico ecosystem continues to evolve, it is recommended to refer to the official Pico documentation and resources for the most up-to-date information and guidelines on utilizing the pico_stdio functionality in your projects.

getchar_timeout_us()

```
int getchar_timeout_us (uint32_t timeout_us)
```

Return a character from stdin if there is one available within a timeout.

Parameters

timeout_us

The timeout in microseconds, or 0 to not wait for a character if none available.

Returns

The character from 0-255 or PICO_ERROR_TIMEOUT if timeout occurs.

stdio_filter_driver()

```
void stdio_filter_driver (stdio_driver_t *driver)
```

Control limiting of output to a single driver.

NOTE this method should always be called on an initialized driver.

Parameters

driver

If non-null then only that driver will be used for input/output (assuming it is in the list of enabled drivers). if NULL then all enabled drivers will be used.

stdio_init_all()

```
bool stdio_init_all (void)
```

Initialize all of the present standard stdio types that are linked into the binary. Call this method once you have set up your clocks to enable the stdio support for UART, USB and semihosting based on the presence of the respective libraries in the binary.

When stdio_usb is configured, this method can be optionally made to block, waiting for a connection via the variables specified in stdio_usb_init.
(i.e. PICO_STDIO_USB_CONNECT_WAIT_TIMEOUT_MS)

Returns

True if at least one output was successfully initialized, false otherwise.

See also stdio_uart, stdio_usb, stdio_semihosting

stdio_set_chars_available_callback()

```
void stdio_set_chars_available_callback (void(*)(void *)
        fn, void *param)
```

Get notified when there are input characters available.

Parameters

fnCallback

Function to be called when characters are available. Pass NULL to cancel any existing callback.

param

Pointer to pass to the callback.

stdio_set_driver_enabled()

```
void stdio_set_driver_enabled (stdio_driver_t *driver,
        bool enabled)
```

Adds or removes a driver from the list of active drivers used for input/output.

NOTE this method should always be called on an initialized driver and is not re-entrant.

Parameters

driver	The driver.
enabled	Tue to add, false to remove.

stdio_set_translate_crlf()

```
void stdio_set_translate_crlf (stdio_driver_t *driver,
                               bool translate)
```

Control conversion of line feeds to carriage return on transmissions.

NOTE this method should always be called on an initialized driver.

Parameters

driver   The driver.

translate If true, convert line feeds to carriage return on transmissions.

SEMIHOSTING

Semihosting is a mechanism that allows embedded systems to communicate with the host computer's operating system during the development and debugging process. It provides a way to perform input/output operations, access file systems, and interact with various system services from the embedded application code.

When semihosting is enabled, certain system calls made by the embedded program are intercepted by the debugger or development environment and redirected to the host computer's operating system. This enables the embedded program to utilize the input/output capabilities and services provided by the host environment, such as reading from or writing to files, printing debug messages to the console, and accessing other system resources.

Linking this library or calling pico_enable_stdio_semihosting(TARGET ENABLED) in the CMake (which achieves the same thing) will add semihosting to the drivers used for standard output.

stdio_semihosting_init()

```
void stdio_semihosting_init (void)
```

Explicitly initialize stdout over semihosting and add it to the current set of stdout targets.

NOTE this method is automatically called by stdio_init_all() if pico_stdio_semihosting is included in the build.

UART

UART (Universal Asynchronous Receiver-Transmitter) is a widely used communication interface that allows for serial communication between electronic devices. It provides a simple and efficient means of transmitting and receiving data over two wires (typically labeled as TX for transmit and RX for receive) between a sender and a receiver.

UART is commonly used in various applications, ranging from computer interfaces (e.g., RS-232) to microcontroller-based systems. It provides a straightforward and reliable method for serial communication between devices, allowing for the exchange of data over short distances. UART interfaces are often used for tasks such as sending and receiving commands, transmitting sensor data, establishing communication with peripherals, and interfacing with external devices or modules.

The UART interface's simplicity, versatility, and wide availability make it a popular choice for many applications that require serial communication between electronic devices.

Linking this library or calling pico_enable_stdio_uart(TARGET ENABLED) in the CMake (which achieves the same thing) will add UART to the drivers used for standard input/output.

stdin_uart_init()

```
void stdin_uart_init (void )
```

Explicitly initialize stdin only (no stdout) over UART and add it to the current set of stdin drivers. This method sets up PICO_DEFAULT_UART_RX_PIN for UART input (if defined) , and configures the baud rate as PICO_DEFAULT_UART_BAUD_RATE

stdio_uart_init()

```
void stdio_uart_init (void)
```

Explicitly initialize stdin/stdout over UART and add it to the current set of stdin/stdout drivers. This method sets up PICO_DEFAULT_UART_TX_PIN for UART output (if defined), PICO_DEFAULT_UART_RX_PIN for input (if defined) and configures the baud rate as PICO_DEFAULT_UART_BAUD_RATE.

NOTE this method is automatically called by stdio_init_all() if pico_stdio_uart is included in the build.

The Pico C API Functionary

stdio_uart_init_full()

```
void stdio_uart_init_full (uart_inst_t *uart, uint
            baud_rate, int tx_pin, int rx_pin)
```

Perform custom initialization initialize stdin/stdout over UART and add it to the current set of stdin/stdout drivers.

Parameters

uart	The uart instance to use, uart0 or uart1.
baud_rate	The baud rate in Hz.
tx_pin	The UART pin to use for stdout (or -1 for no stdout).
rx_pin	The UART pin to use for stdin (or -1 for no stdin).

stdout_uart_init()

```
void stdout_uart_init (void)
```

Explicitly initialize stdout only (no stdin) over UART and add it to the current set of stdout drivers. This method sets up PICO_DEFAULT_UART_TX_PIN for UART output (if defined) , and configures the baud rate as PICO_DEFAULT_UART_BAUD_RATE.

USB

USB (Universal Serial Bus) is a widely used industry standard for connecting and communicating between electronic devices. It provides a versatile and efficient interface for data transfer, power supply, and device control.

Linking this library or calling pico_enable_stdio_usb(TARGET ENABLED) in the CMake (which achieves the same thing) will add USB CDC to the drivers used for standard input/output

Note this library is a developer convenience. It is not applicable in all cases; for one it takes full control of the USB device precluding your use of the USB in device or host mode. For this reason, this library will automatically disengage if you try to using it alongside tinyusb_device or tinyusb_host. It also takes control of a lower level IRQ and sets up a periodic background task.

This library also includes (by default) functionality to enable the RP2040 to be reset over the USB interface.

stdio_usb_connected()

```
bool stdio_usb_connected (void)
```

Check if there is an active stdio CDC connection to a host.

Returns

true if stdio is connected over CDC

stdio_usb_init()

```
bool stdio_usb_init (void)
```

Explicitly initialize USB stdio and add it to the current set of stdin drivers. PICO_STDIO_USB_CONNECT_WAIT_TIMEOUT_MS can be set to cause this method to wait for a CDC connection from the host before returning, which is useful if you don't want any initial stdout output to be discarded before the connection is established.

Returns

True if the USB CDC was initialized, false if an error occurred.

HARDWARE LEVEL

The Hardware section of the Pico C API provides developers with access to the low-level hardware functionalities of the Raspberry Pi Pico microcontroller board. This section is designed to give you direct control and interaction with the hardware components of the board, allowing you to utilize its full potential for your embedded systems projects.

By delving into the Hardware section, you will be able to manipulate and configure various aspects of the Pico's hardware, including GPIO (General-Purpose Input/Output) pins, timers, PWM (Pulse Width Modulation) channels, ADC (Analog-to-Digital Converter) inputs, and more. These hardware components are essential for interfacing with external devices, sensing the environment, generating precise timings, and controlling various aspects of your embedded applications.

The hardware level provides an abstraction layer and a set of functions that allow you to interact with these hardware peripherals in a straightforward and efficient manner. You can configure pin modes, set output values, read input values, configure and utilize timers for precise timing operations, generate PWM signals for controlling motors or LEDs, and perform analog-to-digital conversions to capture analog sensor data. However, it is recommended to have a basic understanding of microcontroller concepts, such as GPIO, timers, and analog-to-digital conversion, to make the most out of this section.

Whether you're a hobbyist, a maker, or a professional embedded systems developer, understanding and utilizing the hardware capabilities of the Pico microcontroller board can significantly enhance your projects. With direct access to the hardware, you can tailor the behavior of your applications to meet specific requirements, optimize performance, and create innovative solutions.

ADC – ANALOG TO DIGITAL CONVERSION

hardware_adc

```
#include "hardware/adc.h"
```

The purpose of an ADC is to convert analog signals, which are continuous and varying in nature, into digital signals, which are discrete and can be processed by digital systems.

In the context of embedded systems, an ADC allows you to interface with analog sensors, such as temperature sensors, light sensors, or potentiometers, and convert their analog output into a digital representation that can be understood and processed by the microcontroller or other digital circuits.

The ADC works by sampling the analog signal at specific intervals and measuring its voltage level. It divides the voltage range into discrete steps and assigns a digital value to each step. The resulting digital value represents the magnitude of the analog signal at that particular sampling point.

The RP2040 has an internal analogue-digital converter (ADC) with the following features:

- **SAR (Successive Approximation Register) ADC**
- **500 kS/s (Using an independent 48MHz clock)**
- **12 bit (8.7 ENOB)**
- **5 input mux:**
  - **4 inputs that are available on package pins shared with GPIO[29:26]**
  - **1 input is dedicated to the internal temperature sensor**
- **4 element receive sample FIFO**
- **Interrupt generation**
- **DMA interface**

Although there is only one ADC you can specify the input to it using the adc_select_input() function. In round robin mode (adc_set_round_robin()), the ADC will use that input and move to the next one after a read.

User ADC inputs are on 0-3 (GPIO 26-29), the temperature sensor is on input 4.

The FIFO, if used, can contain up to 4 entries.

adc_fifo_drain()   Inline Static

```
static void adc_fifo_drain (void)
```

Drain the ADC FIFO. Will wait for any conversion to complete then drain the FIFO, discarding any results.

adc_fifo_get()   Inline Static

```
static uint16_t adc_fifo_get (void)
```

Get ADC result from FIFO.

Returns

Pops the latest result from the ADC FIFO.

adc_fifo_get_blocking()   Inline Static

```
static uint16_t adc_fifo_get_blocking (void)
```

Wait for the ADC FIFO to have data. Blocks until data is present in the FIFO.

Returns

The latest result from the ADC FIFO once one is available.

adc_fifo_get_level()   Inline Static

```
static uint8_t adc_fifo_get_level (void)
```

Get number of entries in the ADC FIFO. The ADC FIFO is 4 entries long.

Returns

This function will return how many samples are currently present. (0 - 4)

adc_fifo_is_empty() Inline Static

```
static bool adc_fifo_is_empty (void)
```

Check FIFO empty state.

Returns

Returns true if the FIFO is empty

adc_fifo_setup() Inline Static

```
static void adc_fifo_setup (bool en, bool dreq_en, uint16_t
        dreq_thresh, bool err_in_fifo, bool byte_shift)
```

Setup the ADC FIFO. FIFO is 4 samples long, if a conversion is completed and the FIFO is full, the result is dropped.

Parameters

enEnables

Write each conversion result to the FIFO.

dreq_enEnable

DMA requests when FIFO contains data.

dreq_thresh

Threshold for DMA requests/FIFO IRQ if enabled.

err_in_fifo

If enabled, bit 15 of the FIFO contains error flag for each sample.

byte_shift

Shift FIFO contents to be one byte in size (for byte DMA) - enables DMA to byte buffers.

adc_get_selected_input()   Inline Static

```
static uint adc_get_selected_input (void)
```

Get the currently selected ADC input channel.

Returns

The currently selected input channel. 0...3 are GPIOs 26...29 respectively. Input 4 is the on board temperature sensor.

adc_gpio_init()   Inline Static

```
static void adc_gpio_init (uint gpio)
```

Initialize the gpio for use as an ADC pin. Prepare a GPIO for use with ADC by disabling all digital functions.

Parameters

gpio

The GPIO number to use. Allowable GPIO numbers are 26 to 29 inclusive.

adc_init()

```
void adc_init (void)
```

Initialize the ADC HW.

adc_irq_set_enabled()   Inline Static

```
static void adc_irq_set_enabled (bool enabled)
```

Enable/Disable ADC interrupts.

Parameters

enabled

Set to true to enable the ADC interrupts, false to disable

adc_read()   Inline Static

```
static uint16_t adc_read (void)
```

Perform a single conversion. Performs an ADC conversion, waits for the result, and then returns it.

Returns

Result of the conversion.

adc_run()   Inline Static

```
static void adc_run (bool run)
```

Enable or disable free-running sampling mode.

Parameters

run

False to disable, true to enable free running conversion mode.

adc_select_input()   Inline Static

```
static void adc_select_input (uint input)
```

ADC input select. Select an ADC input. 0...3 are GPIOs 26...29 respectively. Input 4 is the onboard temperature sensor.

Parameters

input

Input to select.

adc_set_clkdiv()   Inline Static

```
static void adc_set_clkdiv (float clkdiv)
```

Set the ADC Clock divisor. Period of samples will be (1 + div) cycles on average. Note it takes 96 cycles to perform a conversion, so any period less than that will be clamped to 96.

Parameters

clkdiv

If non-zero, conversion will be started at intervals rather than back to back.

adc_set_round_robin()   Inline Static

```
static void adc_set_round_robin (uint input_mask)
```

Round Robin sampling selector. This function sets which inputs are to be run through in round robin mode. Value between 0 and 0x1f (bit 0 to bit 4 for GPIO 26 to 29 and temperature sensor input respectively).

Parameters

input_mask

A bit pattern indicating which of the 5 inputs are to be sampled. Write a value of 0 to disable round robin sampling.

adc_set_temp_sensor_enabled() Inline Static

```
static void adc_set_temp_sensor_enabled (bool enable)
```

Enable the onboard temperature sensor.

Parameters

enable

Set true to power on the onboard temperature sensor, false to power off.

BASE

hardware_base

```
#include "hardware/base.h"
```

This defines the low level types and access functions for memory mapped hardware registers. It is included by default by all other hardware libraries.

The following typedefs provide a standardized way of accessing hardware registers by specifying the access type (read or write) and the bus size (8, 16, or 32 bits) of the register. The names of these register types are formed by combining three parts: A, B, and C.

Part A represents Memory Mapped IO registers, which are special hardware registers used for input and output operations. "io_" stands for an IO register.

Part B indicates the access type:

• "ro_" stands for read-only access, meaning you can only read the value from the register.
• "rw_" represents read-write access, allowing you to both read and write values to the register.
• "wo_" signifies write-only access, which theoretically cannot be enforced through the C API. In practice, you can write values to the register, but you cannot read its contents.

Part C denotes the bus size of the register:

• "8" indicates an 8-bit wide access, allowing you to manipulate 8 bits of data at a time.
• "16" represents a 16-bit wide access, enabling you to manipulate 16 bits of data at a time.
• "32" signifies a 32-bit wide access, enabling you to manipulate 32 bits of data at a time.

When working with these register types, you will always use a pointer. For example, if you have a register of type "io_rw_32," it means you have a pointer to a read/write register that is 32 bits wide. To write a value to this register, you can use the syntax *some_reg = value, and to read the value from the register, you can use the syntax value = *some_reg.

By using these standardized typedefs, you can easily access and manipulate hardware registers in a consistent and predictable manner, ensuring proper interaction with the underlying hardware components of the system.RP2040 hardware is also aliased to provide atomic setting, clear or flipping of a subset of the bits within a hardware register so that concurrent access by two cores is always consistent with one atomic operation being performed first, followed by the second.

See hw_set_bits(), hw_clear_bits() and hw_xor_bits() which provide for atomic access via a pointer to a 32 bit register.

Additionally given a pointer to a structure representing a piece of hardware (e.g. dma_hw_t *dma_hw for the DMA controller), you can get an alias to the entire structure such that writing any member (register) within the structure is equivalent to an atomic operation via hw_set_alias(), hw_clear_alias() or hw_xor_alias()...

For example hw_set_alias(dma_hw)->inte1 = 0x80; will set bit 7 of the INTE1 register of the DMA controller, leaving the other bits unchanged.

hw_clear_bits()   Static

```
static __force_inline void hw_clear_bits (io_rw_32 *addr,
        uint32_t mask)
```

Atomically clear the specified bits to 0 in a HW register.

Parameters

> **addr**   Address of writable register.
> **mask**   Bit-mask specifying bits to clear.

hw_set_bits()   Static

```
static __force_inline void hw_set_bits (io_rw_32 *addr,
        uint32_t mask)
```

Atomically set the specified bits to 1 in a HW register.

Parameters

> **addr**   Address of writable register.
> **mask**   Bit-mask specifying bits to set.

hw_write_masked()   Static

```
static __force_inline void hw_write_masked (io_rw_32
      *addr, uint32_t values, uint32_t write_mask)
```

Set new values for a sub-set of the bits in a HW register. Sets destination bits to values specified in values, if and only if corresponding bit in write_mask is set.

Note: this method allows safe concurrent modification of different bits of a register, but multiple concurrent access to the same bits is still unsafe.

Parameters

addr	Address of writable register.
values	Bits values.
write_mask	Mask of bits to change.

hw_xor_bits()   Static

```
static __force_inline void hw_xor_bits (io_rw_32 *addr,
      uint32_t mask)
```

Atomically flip the specified bits in a HW register.

Parameters

addr	Address of writable register.
mask	Bit-mask specifying bits to invert.

CLAIM

hardware_claim

Lightweight hardware resource management. Hardware claim provides a simple API for management of hardware resources at runtime. This API is usually called by other hardware specific claiming APIs and provides simple multi-core safe methods to manipulate compact bit-sets representing hardware resources.

This API allows any other library to cooperatively participate in a scheme by which both compile time and runtime allocation of resources can co-exist, and conflicts can be avoided or detected (depending on the use case) without the libraries having any other knowledge of each other.

Facilities are providing for claiming resources (and asserting if they are already claimed), freeing (unclaiming) resources, and finding unused resources.

hw_claim_clear()

```
void hw_claim_clear (uint8_t *bits, uint bit_index)
```

Atomically unclaim a resource. The resource ownership is indicated by the bit_index bit in an array of bits.

Parameters

bits

Pointer to an array of bits (8 bits per byte).

bit_index

Resource to unclaim (bit index into array of bits).

hw_claim_lock()

```
uint32_t hw_claim_lock (void)
```

Acquire the runtime mutual exclusion lock provided by the hardware_claim library. This method is called automatically by the other hw_claim_ methods, however it is provided as a convenience to code that might want to protect other hardware initialization code from concurrent use.

NOTE hw_claim_lock() uses a spin lock internally, so disables interrupts on the calling core, and will deadlock if the calling core already owns the lock.

Returns

A token to pass to hw_claim_unlock().

hw_claim_or_assert()

```
void hw_claim_or_assert (uint8_t *bits, uint bit_index,
          const char *message)
```

Atomically claim a resource, panicking if it is already in use. The resource ownership is indicated by the bit_index bit in an array of bits.

Parameters

bits

Pointer to an array of bits (8 bits per byte).

bit_index

Resource to claim (bit index into array of bits).

message

String to display if the bit cannot be claimed; note this may have a single printf format "%d" for the bit.

The Pico C API Functionary

hw_claim_unlock()

```
void hw_claim_unlock (uint32_t token)
```

Release the runtime mutual exclusion lock provided by the hardware_claim library.

NOTE This method MUST be called from the same core that call hw_claim_lock()

Parameters

token

The token returned by the corresponding call to hw_claim_lock().

hw_claim_unused_from_range()

```
int hw_claim_unused_from_range (uint8_t *bits, bool
        required, uint bit_lsb, uint bit_msb, const char
        *message )
```

Atomically claim one resource out of a range of resources, optionally asserting if none are free.

Parameters

bits

Pointer to an array of bits (8 bits per byte).

required

True if this method should panic if the resource is not free.

bit_lsb

The lower bound (inclusive) of the resource range to claim from.

bit_msb

The upper bound (inclusive) of the resource range to claim from.

message

Sstring to display if the bit cannot be claimed.

Returns

The bit index representing the claimed or -1 if none are available in the range, and required = false.

hw_is_claimed()   Inline

```
bool hw_is_claimed (const uint8_t *bits, uint bit_index)
```

Determine if a resource is claimed at the time of the call. The resource ownership is indicated by the bit_index bit in an array of bits.

Parameters

bits

Pointer to an array of bits (8 bits per byte).

bit_index

Resource to check (bit index into array of bits).

Returns

True if the resource is claimed.

CLOCKS

hardware_clocks

```
#include "hardware/clocks.h"
```

The Hardware Clocks section in the Pico C API provides a range of functions and features to manage and control the clocks on the Pico microcontroller. Clocks are essential in embedded systems as they dictate the timing and synchronization of various operations.

This section provides a high level interface to the clock functions and focuses on configuring and manipulating clock sources, dividers, and generators available on the Pico microcontroller. It allows you to select different clock sources, set their frequencies, and divide them as needed. By effectively utilizing these functions, you can achieve precise timing, optimize power consumption, and ensure efficient operation of your Pico-based applications.

The clocks block provides independent clocks to on-chip and external components. It takes inputs from a variety of clock sources allowing the user to trade off performance against cost, board area and power consumption. From these sources it uses multiple clock generators to provide the required clocks. This architecture allows the user flexibility to start and stop clocks independently and to vary some clock frequencies whilst maintaining others at their optimum frequencies

Please refer to the datasheet for more details on the RP2040 clocks.

The clock source depends on which clock you are attempting to configure.

CLOCKS_CLK_REF_CTRL_SRC_VALUE_ROSC_CLKSRC_PH:

The reference clock source is set to the Phase-Locked Loop (PLL) Reference Oscillator (ROSC) with a phase shift configuration.

CLOCKS_CLK_REF_CTRL_SRC_VALUE_CLKSRC_CLK_REF_AUX:

The reference clock source is set to an auxiliary clock source (CLK_REF_AUX).

CLOCKS_CLK_SYS_CTRL_SRC_VALUE_CLKSRC_CLK_SYS_AUX:

The system clock source is set to an auxiliary clock source (CLK_SYS_AUX).

CLOCKS_CLK_REF_CTRL_SRC_VALUE_XOSC_CLKSRC:

The reference clock source is set to the external crystal oscillator (XOSC).

CLOCKS_CLK_SYS_CTRL_SRC_VALUE_CLK_REF:

The system clock source is set to the reference clock.

CLOCKS_CLK_GPOUTx_CTRL_AUXSRC_VALUE_CLKSRC_PLL_SYS:

The auxiliary clock source for the general-purpose output clock (clk_gpout[x]) is set to the system PLL.

CLOCKS_CLK_GPOUTx_CTRL_AUXSRC_VALUE_CLKSRC_GPIN0:

The auxiliary clock source for the general-purpose output clock (clk_gpout[x]) is set to GPIO input pin 0 (GPIN0).

CLOCKS_CLK_GPOUTx_CTRL_AUXSRC_VALUE_CLKSRC_GPIN1:

The auxiliary clock source for the general-purpose output clock (clk_gpout[x]) is set to GPIO input pin 1 (GPIN1).

CLOCKS_CLK_GPOUTx_CTRL_AUXSRC_VALUE_CLKSRC_PLL_USB:

The auxiliary clock source for the general-purpose output clock (clk_gpout[x]) is set to the USB PLL.

CLOCKS_CLK_GPOUTx_CTRL_AUXSRC_VALUE_ROSC_CLKSRC:

The auxiliary clock source for the general-purpose output clock (clk_gpout[x]) is set to the ROSC.

CLOCKS_CLK_GPOUTx_CTRL_AUXSRC_VALUE_XOSC_CLKSRC:

The auxiliary clock source for the general-purpose output clock (clk_gpout[x]) is set to the XOSC.

CLOCKS_CLK_GPOUTx_CTRL_AUXSRC_VALUE_CLK_SYS:

The auxiliary clock source for the general-purpose output clock (clk_gpout[x]) is set to the system clock.

CLOCKS_CLK_GPOUTx_CTRL_AUXSRC_VALUE_CLK_USB:

The auxiliary clock source for the general-purpose output clock (clk_gpout[x]) is set to the USB clock.

CLOCKS_CLK_GPOUTx_CTRL_AUXSRC_VALUE_CLK_ADC:

The auxiliary clock source for the general-purpose output clock (clk_gpout[x]) is set to the ADC clock.

CLOCKS_CLK_GPOUTx_CTRL_AUXSRC_VALUE_CLK_RTC:

The auxiliary clock source for the general-purpose output clock (clk_gpout[x]) is set to the RTC clock.

CLOCKS_CLK_GPOUTx_CTRL_AUXSRC_VALUE_CLK_REF:

The auxiliary clock source for the general-purpose output clock (clk_gpout[x]) is set to the reference clock.

CLOCKS_CLK_PERI_CTRL_AUXSRC_VALUE_CLKSRC_PLL_SYS,
CLOCKS_CLK_USB_CTRL_AUXSRC_VALUE_CLKSRC_PLL_SYS,
CLOCKS_CLK_ADC_CTRL_AUXSRC_VALUE_CLKSRC_PLL_SYS:

The auxiliary clock sources for peripherals (clk_peri, clk_usb, clk_adc) respectively are set to the system PLL. "clk_peri" refers to the peripheral clock.

CLOCKS_CLK_PERI_CTRL_AUXSRC_VALUE_CLKSRC_GPIN0,
CLOCKS_CLK_USB_CTRL_AUXSRC_VALUE_CLKSRC_GPIN0,
CLOCKS_CLK_ADC_CTRL_AUXSRC_VALUE_CLKSRC_GPIN0:

The auxiliary clock sources for peripherals (clk_peri, clk_usb, clk_adc) respectively are set to GPIO input pin 0 (GPIN0).

CLOCKS_CLK_PERI_CTRL_AUXSRC_VALUE_CLKSRC_GPIN1,
CLOCKS_CLK_USB_CTRL_AUXSRC_VALUE_CLKSRC_GPIN1,
CLOCKS_CLK_ADC_CTRL_AUXSRC_VALUE_CLKSRC_GPIN1:

The auxiliary clock sources for peripherals (clk_peri, clk_usb, clk_adc) respectively are set to GPIO input pin 1 (GPIN1).

CLOCKS_CLK_PERI_CTRL_AUXSRC_VALUE_CLKSRC_PLL_USB,
CLOCKS_CLK_USB_CTRL_AUXSRC_VALUE_CLKSRC_PLL_USB,
CLOCKS_CLK_ADC_CTRL_AUXSRC_VALUE_CLKSRC_PLL_USB:

The auxiliary clock sources for peripherals (clk_peri, clk_usb, clk_adc) respectively are set to the USB PLL.

CLOCKS_CLK_PERI_CTRL_AUXSRC_VALUE_ROSC_CLKSRC_PH,
CLOCKS_CLK_USB_CTRL_AUXSRC_VALUE_ROSC_CLKSRC_PH,
CLOCKS_CLK_ADC_CTRL_AUXSRC_VALUE_ROSC_CLKSRC_PH:

The auxiliary clock sources for peripherals (clk_peri, clk_usb, clk_adc) respectively are set to the ROSC with a phase shift configuration.

CLOCKS_CLK_PERI_CTRL_AUXSRC_VALUE_XOSC_CLKSRC,
CLOCKS_CLK_USB_CTRL_AUXSRC_VALUE_XOSC_CLKSRC,
CLOCKS_CLK_ADC_CTRL_AUXSRC_VALUE_XOSC_CLKSRC:

The auxiliary clock sources for peripherals (clk_peri, clk_usb, clk_adc) respectively are set to the XOSC.

CLOCKS_CLK_RTC_CTRL_AUXSRC_VALUE_CLKSRC_PLL_SYS:

The auxiliary clock source for the RTC clock is set to the system PLL.

CLOCKS_CLK_RTC_CTRL_AUXSRC_VALUE_CLKSRC_GPIN0:

The auxiliary clock source for the RTC clock is set to GPIO input pin 0 (GPIN0).

CLOCKS_CLK_RTC_CTRL_AUXSRC_VALUE_CLKSRC_GPIN1:

The auxiliary clock source for the RTC clock is set to GPIO input pin 1 (GPIN1).

CLOCKS_CLK_RTC_CTRL_AUXSRC_VALUE_CLKSRC_PLL_USB:

The auxiliary clock source for the RTC clock is set to the USB PLL.

CLOCKS_CLK_RTC_CTRL_AUXSRC_VALUE_ROSC_CLKSRC_PH:

The auxiliary clock source for the RTC clock is set to the ROSC with a phase shift configuration.

CLOCKS_CLK_RTC_CTRL_AUXSRC_VALUE_XOSC_CLKSRC:

The auxiliary clock source for the RTC clock is set to the XOSC.

TYPEDEFS

resus_callback_t

```
typedef void(*resus_callback_t) (void)
```

Resus callback function type. User provided callback for a resus event (when clk_sys is stopped by the programmer and is restarted for them).

ENUMERATIONS

clock_index

```
enum clock_index
```

Enumeration identifying a hardware clock.

Enumerator

clk_gpout0	GPIO Muxing 0.
clk_gpout1	GPIO Muxing 1.
clk_gpout2	GPIO Muxing 2.
clk_gpout3	GPIO Muxing 3.
clk_ref	Watchdog and timers reference clock.
clk_sys	Processors, bus fabric, memory, memory mapped registers.
clk_peri	Peripheral clock for UART and SPI.
clk_usb	USB clock.
clk_adc	ADC clock.
clk_rtc	Real time clock.

FUNCTIONS

clock_configure()

```
bool clock_configure (enum clock_index clk_index,
        uint32_t src, uint32_t auxsrc, uint32_t src_freq,
        uint32_t freq)
```

Configure the specified clock. See the introduction to the clock section for details on the possible values for clock sources.

Parameters

clk_index

The clock to configure.

src

The main clock source, can be 0.

auxsrc

The auxiliary clock source, which depends on which clock is being set. Can be 0.

src_freq

Frequency of the input clock source.

freq

Requested frequency.

Returns

Always returns true.

clock_configure_gpin()

```
bool clock_configure_gpin(enum clock_index clk_index,
        uint gpio, uint32_t src_freq, uint32_t freq)
```

Configure a clock to come from a gpio input.

Parameters

clk_index

>The clock to configure.

gpio

>The GPIO pin to run the clock from. Valid GPIOs are: 20 and 22.

src_freq

>Frequency of the input clock source.

freqRequested

>Frequency.

Returns

>The value from clock_configure() function call which is always true.

clock_get_hz()

```
uint32_t clock_get_hz (enum clock_index clk_index)
```

Get the current frequency of the specified clock.

Parameters

clk_index   Clock

Returns

>Clock frequency in Hz.

clock_gpio_init() Inline Static

```
static void clock_gpio_init(uint gpio, uint src, float div)
```

Output an optionally divided clock to the specified gpio pin.

Parameters

gpio

> The GPIO pin to output the clock to. Valid GPIOs are: 21, 23, 24, 25. These GPIOs are connected to the GPOUT0-3 clock generators.

src

> The source clock. See the register field CLOCKS_CLK_GPOUT0_CTRL_AUXSRC for a full list. The list is the same for each GPOUT clock generator.

div

> The float amount to divide the source clock by. This is useful to not overwhelm the GPIO pin with a fast clock.

clock_gpio_init_int_frac()

```
void clock_gpio_init_int_frac(uint gpio, uint src,
       uint32_t div_int, uint8_t div_frac)
```

Output an optionally divided clock to the specified gpio pin.

Parameters

gpio

> The GPIO pin to output the clock to. Valid GPIOs are: 21, 23, 24, 25. These GPIOs are connected to the GPOUT0-3 clock generators.

src

> The source clock. See the register field CLOCKS_CLK_GPOUT0_CTRL_AUXSRC for a full list. The list is the same for each GPOUT clock generator.

div_int

> The integer part of the value to divide the source clock by. This is useful to not overwhelm the GPIO pin with a fast clock. this is in range of 1..2^24-1.

div_frac

> The fractional part of the value to divide the source clock by.

clock_set_reported_hz()

```
void clock_set_reported_hz (enum clock_index clk_index,
         uint hz)
```

Set the "current frequency" of the clock as reported by clock_get_hz without actually changing the clock. See also clock_get_hz()

Parameters

clk_index	Clock
hz	Frequency value to report in Hz.

clock_stop()

```
void clock_stop (enum clock_index clk_index)
```

Stop the specified clock.

Parameters

clk_index	The clock to stop.

clocks_enable_resus()

```
void clocks_enable_resus (resus_callback_t resus_callback)
```

Enable the resus function. Restarts clk_sys if it is accidentally stopped. The resuscitate function will restart the system clock if it falls below a certain speed (or stops). This could happen if the clock source the system clock is running from stops. For example if a PLL is stopped.

Parameters

resus_callback

A function pointer provided by the user to call if a resus event happens.

clocks_init()

```
void clocks_init (void )
```

Initialize the clock hardware. Must be called before any other clock function.

frequency_count_khz()

```
uint32_t frequency_count_khz (uint src)
```

Measure a clocks frequency using the Frequency counter. Uses the inbuilt frequency counter to measure the specified clocks frequency. Currently, this function is accurate to +/-1KHz. See the datasheet for more details.

Parameters

src   The source clock.

Returns

The frequency of the clock plus or minus 1KHz.

DIVIDER

hardware_divider

```
#include "hardware/divider.h"
```

Low-level hardware-divider access. The SIO (Serial Input/Output peripheral) contains an 8-cycle signed/unsigned divide/modulo circuit, per core. Calculation is started by writing a dividend and divisor to the two argument registers, DIVIDEND and DIVISOR. The divider calculates the quotient / and remainder % of this division over the next 8 cycles, and on the 9th cycle the results can be read from the two result registers DIV_QUOTIENT and DIV_REMAINDER. A 'ready' bit in register DIV_CSR can be polled to wait for the calculation to complete, or software can insert a fixed 8-cycle delay

This header provides low level macros and inline functions for accessing the hardware dividers directly, and perhaps most usefully performing asynchronous divides. These functions however do not follow the regular SDK conventions for saving/restoring the divider state, so are not generally safe to call from interrupt handlers

The pico_divider library provides a more user friendly set of APIs over the divider (and support for 64 bit divides), and of course by default regular C language integer divisions are redirected through that library, meaning you can just use C level / and % operators and gain the benefits of the fast hardware divider.

hw_divider_divmod_s32()

```
divmod_result_t hw_divider_divmod_s32 (int32_t a,
       int32_t b)
```

Do a signed HW divide and wait for result. Divide a by b, wait for calculation to complete, return result as a fixed point 32p32 value.

Parameters

a   The dividend.
b   The divisor.

Returns

Results of divide as a 32p32 fixed point value.

hw_divider_divmod_s32_start() Inline Static

```
static void hw_divider_divmod_s32_start (int32_t a,
        int32_t b)
```

Start a signed asynchronous divide. Start a divide of the specified signed parameters. You should wait for 8 cycles (__div_pause()) or wait for the ready bit to be set (hw_divider_wait_ready()) prior to reading the results.

Parameters

a	The dividend.
b	The divisor.

hw_divider_divmod_u32()

```
divmod_result_t hw_divider_divmod_u32 (uint32_t a,
        uint32_t b)
```

Do an unsigned HW divide and wait for result. Divide a by b, wait for calculation to complete, return result as a fixed point 32p32 value.

Parameters

a	The dividend.
b	The divisor.

Returns

Results of divide as a 32p32 fixed point value.

hw_divider_divmod_u32_start()   Inline Static

```
static void hw_divider_divmod_u32_start (uint32_t a,
        uint32_t b)
```

Start an unsigned asynchronous divide. Start a divide of the specified unsigned parameters. You should wait for 8 cycles (__div_pause()) or wait for the ready bit to be set (hw_divider_wait_ready()) prior to reading the results.

Parameters

a   The dividend.
b   The divisor.

hw_divider_quotient_s32()   Inline Static

static int32_t hw_divider_quotient_s32 (int32_t a, int32_t b)

Do a signed HW divide, wait for result, return quotient. Divide a by b, wait for calculation to complete, return quotient.

Parameters

a   The dividend.
b   The divisor.

Returns

Quotient results of the divide.

hw_divider_remainder_s32()   Inline Static

```
static int32_t hw_divider_remainder_s32 (int32_t a,
        int32_t b)
```

Do a signed HW divide, wait for result, return remainder. Divide a by b, wait for calculation to complete, return remainder.

Parameters

a   The dividend.

b   The divisor.

Returns

Remainder results of the divide.

hw_divider_restore_state()

```
void hw_divider_restore_state (hw_divider_state_t *src)
```

Load a saved hardware divider state into the current core's hardware divider. Copy the passed hardware divider state into the hardware divider.

Parameters

src   The location to load the divider state from.

hw_divider_result_nowait()   Inline Static

```
static divmod_result_t hw_divider_result_nowait (void )
```

Return result of HW divide, nowait.

NOTE This is UNSAFE in that the calculation may not have been completed.

Returns

Current result. Most significant 32 bits are the remainder, lower 32 bits are the quotient.

hw_divider_result_wait()   Inline Static

```
static divmod_result_t hw_divider_result_wait (void )
```

Return result of last asynchronous HW divide. This function waits for the result to be ready by calling hw_divider_wait_ready().

Returns

Current result. Most significant 32 bits are the remainder, lower 32 bits are the quotient.

hw_divider_s32_quotient_inlined()   Inline Static

```
static int32_t hw_divider_s32_quotient_inlined (int32_t a,
        int32_t b)
```

Do a hardware signed HW divide, wait for result, return quotient. Divide a by b, wait for calculation to complete, return quotient.

Parameters

a   The dividend.
b   The divisor.

Returns

Quotient result of the divide.

hw_divider_s32_quotient_wait()   Inline Static

```
static int32_t hw_divider_s32_quotient_wait (void )
```

Return result of last asynchronous HW divide, signed quotient only. This function waits for the result to be ready by calling hw_divider_wait_ready().

Returns

Current signed quotient result.

hw_divider_s32_remainder_inlined()   Inline Static

```
static int32_t hw_divider_s32_remainder_inlined (int32_t
    a, int32_t b)
```

Do a hardware signed HW divide, wait for result, return remainder. Divide a by b, wait for calculation to complete, return remainder.

Parameters

a   The dividend.

b   The divisor.

Returns

Remainder result of the divide.

hw_divider_s32_remainder_wait()   Inline Static

```
static int32_t hw_divider_s32_remainder_wait (void )
```

Return result of last asynchronous HW divide, signed remainder only. This function waits for the result to be ready by calling hw_divider_wait_ready().

Returns

Current remainder results.

hw_divider_save_state()

```
void hw_divider_save_state (hw_divider_state_t *dest)
```

Save the calling cores hardware divider state. Copy the current core's hardware divider state into the provided structure. This method waits for the divider results to be stable, then copies them to memory. They can be restored via hw_divider_restore_state()

Parameters

dest   The location to store the divider state.

hw_divider_u32_quotient()   Inline Static

```
static uint32_t hw_divider_u32_quotient (uint32_t a,
        uint32_t b)
```

Do an unsigned HW divide, wait for result, return quotient. Divide a by b, wait for calculation to complete, return quotient.

Parameters

a   The dividend.

b   The divisor.

Returns

Quotient results of the divide.

hw_divider_u32_quotient_inlined()   Inline Static

```
static uint32_t hw_divider_u32_quotient_inlined (uint32_t
        a, uint32_t b)
```

Do a hardware unsigned HW divide, wait for result, return quotient. Divide a by b, wait for calculation to complete, return quotient.

Parameters

a   The dividend.

b   The divisor.

Returns

Quotient result of the divide.

hw_divider_u32_quotient_wait()   Inline Static

```
static uint32_t hw_divider_u32_quotient_wait (void )
```

Return result of last asynchronous HW divide, unsigned quotient only. This function waits for the result to be ready by calling hw_divider_wait_ready().

Returns

Current unsigned quotient result.

hw_divider_u32_remainder()   Inline Static

```
static uint32_t hw_divider_u32_remainder (uint32_t a,
        uint32_t b)
```

Do an unsigned HW divide, wait for result, return remainder. Divide a by b, wait for calculation to complete, return remainder.

Parameters

a   The dividend.
b   The divisor.

Returns

Remainder results of the divide.

hw_divider_u32_remainder_inlined()   Inline Static

static uint32_t hw_divider_u32_remainder_inlined (uint32_t a, uint32_t b)

Do a hardware unsigned HW divide, wait for result, return remainder. Divide a by b, wait for calculation to complete, return remainder.

Parameters

a   The dividend.
b   The divisor.

Returns

Remainder result of the divide.

hw_divider_u32_remainder_wait()   Inline Static

```
static uint32_t hw_divider_u32_remainder_wait (void )
```

Return result of last asynchronous HW divide, unsigned remainder only. This function waits for the result to be ready by calling hw_divider_wait_ready().

Returns

Current unsigned remainder result.

hw_divider_wait_ready()   Inline Static

```
static void hw_divider_wait_ready (void )
```

Wait for a divide to complete. Wait for a divide to complete.

to_quotient_s32()   Inline Static

```
static int32_t to_quotient_s32 (divmod_result_t r)
```

Efficient extraction of signed quotient from 32p32 fixed point.

Parameters

    r   32p32 fixed point value.

Returns

Unsigned quotient.

to_quotient_u32()   Inline Static

```
static uint32_t to_quotient_u32 (divmod_result_t r)
```

Efficient extraction of unsigned quotient from 32p32 fixed point.

Parameters

r   32p32 fixed point value.

Returns

Unsigned quotient.

to_remainder_s32()

```
static int32_t to_remainder_s32 (divmod_result_t r)
```

Efficient extraction of signed remainder from 32p32 fixed point. *NOTE On arm this is just a 32 bit register move or a nop.*

Parameters

r   32p32 fixed point value.

Returns

Signed remainder.

to_remainder_u32()   Inline Static

```
static uint32_t to_remainder_u32 (divmod_result_t r)
```

Efficient extraction of unsigned remainder from 32p32 fixed point. *NOTE On arm this is just a 32 bit register move or a nop.*

Parameters

r   32p32 fixed point value.

Returns

Unsigned remainder.

DMA - Direct Memory Access

hardware_dma

```
#include "hardware/dma.h"
```

The RP2040 microcontroller's Direct Memory Access (DMA) master efficiently handles bulk data transfers on behalf of the processor, allowing the processor to focus on other tasks or enter low-power sleep states. The DMA offers significantly higher data throughput compared to the RP2040 processors.

With the ability to perform simultaneous read and write accesses of up to 32 bits in size per clock cycle, the DMA provides impressive data transfer capabilities. It features 12 independent channels, each responsible for supervising a sequence of bus transfers in various scenarios, including memory to peripheral, peripheral to memory, and memory to memory transfers.

To utilize a DMA channel, it needs to be properly configured. This API section provides convenient helper functions to set up the required configuration structures, simplifying the process of initializing and managing DMA channels.

ENUMERATIONS

dma_channel_transfer_size

```
enum dma_channel_transfer_size
```

Enumeration of available DMA channel transfer sizes. Names indicate the number of bits.

DMA_SIZE_8	Byte transfer (8 bits).
DMA_SIZE_16	Half word transfer (16 bits).
DMA_SIZE_32	Word transfer (32 bits).

STRUCTURES

dma_channel_config

```
struct dma_channel_config
```

uint32_t ctrl

The ctrl value contains the bit setting for various channel configurations. See the RP2040 datasheet for the breakdown of this control registers settings.

FUNCTIONS

channel_config_get_ctrl_value()   Inline Static

```
static uint32_t channel_config_get_ctrl_value (const
        dma_channel_config *config)
```

Get the raw configuration register from a channel configuration.

Parameters

config   Pointer to a config structure.

Returns

Register content.

channel_config_set_bswap()   Inline Static

```
static void channel_config_set_bswap (dma_channel_config *c,
        bool bswap)
```

Set DMA byte swapping config in a channel configuration object. No effect for byte data, for halfword data, the two bytes of each halfword are swapped. For word data, the four bytes of each word are swapped to reverse their order.

Parameters

c   Pointer to channel configuration object.
bswap   True to enable byte swapping.

The Pico C API Functionary

channel_config_set_chain_to()   Inline Static

```
static void channel_config_set_chain_to (dma_channel_config
            *c, uint chain_to)
```

Set DMA channel chain_to channel in a channel configuration object. When this channel completes, it will trigger the channel indicated by chain_to. Disable by setting chain_to to itself (the same channel)

Parameters

c	Pointer to channel configuration object.
chain_to	Channel to trigger when this channel completes.

channel_config_set_dreq()   Inline Static

```
static void channel_config_set_dreq (dma_channel_config *c,
            uint dreq)
```

Select a transfer request signal in a channel configuration object. The channel uses the transfer request signal to pace its data transfer rate. Sources for TREQ signals are internal (TIMERS) or external (DREQ, a Data Request from the system).

```
0x0 to 0x3a -> select DREQ n as TREQ
0x3b -> Select Timer 0 as TREQ
0x3c -> Select Timer 1 as TREQ
0x3d -> Select Timer 2 as TREQ (Optional)
0x3e -> Select Timer 3 as TREQ (Optional)
0x3f -> Permanent request, for unpaced transfers.
```

Parameters

c	Pointer to channel configuration data.
dreq	Source (see description).

channel_config_set_enable() Inline Static

```
static void channel_config_set_enable (dma_channel_config
              *c, bool enable)
```

Enable/Disable the DMA channel in a channel configuration object. When false, the channel will ignore triggers, stop issuing transfers, and pause the current transfer sequence (i.e. BUSY will remain high if already high)

Parameters

c

> Pointer to channel configuration object

enable

> True to enable the DMA channel. When enabled, the channel will respond to triggering events, and start transferring data.

channel_config_set_high_priority() Inline Static

```
static void channel_config_set_high_priority
          (dma_channel_config *c, bool high_priority)
```

Set the channel priority in a channel configuration object. When true, gives a channel preferential treatment in issue scheduling: in each scheduling round, all high priority channels are considered first, and then only a single low priority channel, before returning to the high priority channels.

This only affects the order in which the DMA schedules channels. The DMA's bus priority is not changed. If the DMA is not saturated then a low priority channel will see no loss of throughput.

Parameters

c

> Pointer to channel configuration object.

high_priority

> True to enable high priority.

channel_config_set_irq_quiet()   Inline Static

```
static void channel_config_set_irq_quiet (dma_channel_config
          *c, bool irq_quiet)
```

Set IRQ quiet mode in a channel configuration object. In QUIET mode, the channel does not generate IRQs at the end of every transfer block. Instead, an IRQ is raised when NULL is written to a trigger register, indicating the end of a control block chain.

Parameters

c   Pointer to channel configuration object.
irq_quiet   True to enable quiet mode, false to disable.

channel_config_set_read_increment()   Inline Static

```
static void channel_config_set_read_increment
          (dma_channel_config *c, bool incr)
```

Set DMA channel read increment in a channel configuration object.

Parameters

c

Pointer to channel configuration object.

incr

True to enable read address increments, if false, each read will be from the same address Usually disabled for peripheral to memory transfers.

channel_config_set_ring()   Inline Static

```
static void channel_config_set_ring (dma_channel_config *c,
        bool write, uint size_bits)
```

Set address wrapping parameters in a channel configuration object. Size of address wrap region. If 0, don't wrap. For values n > 0, only the lower n bits of the address will change. This wraps the address on a (1 << n) byte boundary, facilitating access to naturally-aligned ring buffers. Ring sizes between 2 and 32768 bytes are possible (size_bits from 1 - 15). 0x0 -> No wrapping.

Parameters

c

Pointer to channel configuration object.

write

True to apply to write addresses, false to apply to read addresses.

size_bits

0 to disable wrapping. Otherwise the size in bits of the changing part of the address. Effectively wraps the address on a (1 << size_bits) byte boundary.

                                                                  Inline Static

channel_config_set_sniff_enable()

```
static void channel_config_set_sniff_enable
        (dma_channel_config *c, bool sniff_enable)
```

Enable access to channel by sniff hardware in a channel configuration object. Sniff HW must be enabled and have this channel selected.

Parameters

c

Pointer to channel configuration object

sniff_enable

True to enable the Sniff HW access to this DMA channel.

channel_config_set_transfer_data_size()   Inline Static

```
static void channel_config_set_transfer_data_size
        (dma_channel_config *c,
         enum dma_channel_transfer_size size)
```

Set the size of each DMA bus transfer in a channel configuration object. Set the size of each bus transfer (byte/halfword/word). The read and write addresses advance by the specific amount (1/2/4 bytes) with each transfer.

Parameters

c

Pointer to channel configuration object.

size

See enum for possible values.

channel_config_set_write_increment()   Inline Static

```
static void channel_config_set_write_increment
        (dma_channel_config *c, bool incr)
```

Set DMA channel write increment in a channel configuration object.

Parameters

c

Pointer to channel configuration object.

incr

True to enable write address increments, if false, each write will be to the same address Usually disabled for memory to peripheral transfers

dma_channel_get_default_config()   Inline Static

```
static dma_channel_config dma_channel_get_default_config
             (uint channel)
```

Get the default channel configuration for a given channel.

Setting	Default Value
Read Increment	true
Write Increment	false
DReq	DREQ_FORCE
Chain to	self
Data size	DMA_SIZE_32
Ring	write=false, size=0 (i.e. off)
Byte Swap	false
Quiet IRQs	false
High Priority	false
Channel Enable	true
Sniff Enable	false

Parameters

channel   DMA channel.

Returns

The default configuration which can then be modified.

dma_get_channel_config()   Inline Static

```
static dma_channel_config dma_get_channel_config (uint
             channel)
```

Get the current configuration for the specified channel.

Parameters

channel   DMA channel.

Returns

The current configuration as read from the HW register (not cached).

The Pico C API Functionary

dma_channel_abort()   Inline Static

```
static void dma_channel_abort (uint channel)
```

Stop a DMA transfer. Function will only return once the DMA has stopped.

Note that due to errata RP2040-E13, aborting a channel which has transfers in-flight (i.e. an individual read has taken place but the corresponding write has not), the ABORT status bit will clear prematurely, and subsequently the in-flight transfers will trigger a completion interrupt once they complete.

The effect of this is that you may see a spurious completion interrupt on the channel as a result of calling this method.

The calling code should be sure to ignore a completion IRQ as a result of this method. This may not require any additional work, as aborting a channel which may be about to complete, when you have a completion IRQ handler registered, is inherently race-prone, and so code is likely needed to disambiguate the two occurrences.

Parameters

> **channel**   DMA channel.

dma_channel_acknowledge_irq0()   Inline Static

```
static void dma_channel_acknowledge_irq0 (uint channel)
```

Acknowledge a channel IRQ, resetting it as the cause of DMA_IRQ_0.

Parameters

> **channel**   DMA channel.

dma_channel_acknowledge_irq1()   Inline Static

```
static void dma_channel_acknowledge_irq1 (uint channel)
```

Acknowledge a channel IRQ, resetting it as the cause of DMA_IRQ_1.

Parameters

> **channel**   DMA channel.

dma_channel_claim()

```
void dma_channel_claim (uint channel)
```

Mark a dma channel as used. Method for cooperative claiming of hardware. Will cause a panic if the channel is already claimed. Use of this method by libraries detects accidental configurations that would fail in unpredictable ways.

Parameters

channel	DMA channel.

dma_channel_configure()   **Inline Static**

```
static void dma_channel_configure (uint channel, const
        dma_channel_config *config, volatile void
        *write_addr, const volatile void *read_addr, uint
        transfer_count, bool trigger)
```

Configure all DMA parameters and optionally start transfer.

Parameters

channel	DMA channel.
config	Pointer to DMA config structure.
write_addr	Initial write address.
read_addr	Initial read address.
transfer_count	Number of transfers to perform.
trigger	True to start the transfer immediately.

dma_channel_get_irq0_status()   Inline Static

```
static bool dma_channel_get_irq0_status (uint channel)
```

Determine if a particular channel is a cause of DMA_IRQ_0.

Parameters

channel   DMA channel.

Returns

True if the channel is a cause of DMA_IRQ_0, false otherwise.

dma_channel_get_irq1_status()   Inline Static

```
static bool dma_channel_get_irq1_status (uint channel)
```

Determine if a particular channel is a cause of DMA_IRQ_1.

Parameters

channel   DMA channel.

Returns

True if the channel is a cause of DMA_IRQ_1, false otherwise.

dma_channel_is_busy()   Inline Static

```
static bool dma_channel_is_busy (uint channel)
```

Check if DMA channel is busy.

Parameters

channel   DMA channel.

Returns

True if the channel is currently busy.

dma_channel_is_claimed()

```
bool dma_channel_is_claimed (uint channel)
```

Determine if a dma channel is claimed. See also dma_channel_claim dma_channel_claim_mask.

Parameters

channel   DMA channel.

Returns

True if the channel is claimed, false otherwise

dma_channel_set_config()   Inline Static

```
static void dma_channel_set_config (uint channel, const
        dma_channel_config *config, bool trigger)
```

Set a channel configuration.

Parameters

channel   DMA channel.
config   Pointer to a config structure with required configuration.
trigger   True to trigger the transfer immediately.

dma_channel_set_irq0_enabled()   Inline Static

```
static void dma_channel_set_irq0_enabled (uint channel,
        bool enabled)
```

Enable single DMA channel's interrupt via DMA_IRQ_0.

Parameters

channel
    DMA channel.
enabled
    True to enable interrupt 0 on specified channel, false to disable.

dma_channel_set_irq1_enabled()   Inline Static

```
static void dma_channel_set_irq1_enabled (uint channel,
        bool enabled)
```

Enable single DMA channel's interrupt via DMA_IRQ_1.

Parameters

channel

> DMA channel.

enabled

> True to enable interrupt 1 on specified channel, false to disable.

dma_channel_set_read_addr()   Inline Static

```
static void dma_channel_set_read_addr (uint channel, const
        volatile void *read_addr, bool trigger)
```

Set the DMA initial read address.

channel

> DMA channel.

read_addr

> Initial read address of transfer.

trigger

> True to start the transfer immediately.

dma_channel_set_trans_count()   Inline Static

```
static void dma_channel_set_trans_count (uint channel,
        uint32_t trans_count, bool trigger)
```

Set the number of bus transfers the channel will do.

channel

> DMA channel.

trans_count

> The number of transfers (not NOT bytes, see
> channel_config_set_transfer_data_size).

trigger

> True to start the transfer immediately

dma_channel_set_write_addr()   Inline Static

```
static void dma_channel_set_write_addr (uint channel,
        volatile void *write_addr, bool trigger)
```

Set the DMA initial write address.

channel

> DMA channel.

write_addr

> Initial write address of transfer.

trigger

> True to start the transfer immediately.

dma_channel_start()   Inline Static

```
static void dma_channel_start (uint channel)
```

Start a single DMA channel.

channel

> DMA channel.

The Pico C API Functionary

dma_channel_transfer_from_buffer_now()   Inline Static

```
static void dma_channel_transfer_from_buffer_now (
        uint channel, const volatile void *read_addr,
        uint32_t transfer_count)
```

Start a DMA transfer from a buffer immediately.

Parameters

channel

DMA channel.

read_addr

Sets the initial read address.

transfer_count

Number of transfers to make. Not bytes, but the number of transfers of channel_config_set_transfer_data_size() to be sent.

dma_channel_transfer_to_buffer_now()   Inline Static

```
static void dma_channel_transfer_to_buffer_now (
        uint channel, volatile void *rite_addr, uint32_t
        transfer_count)
```

Start a DMA transfer to a buffer immediately.

Parameters

channel

DMA channel.

write_addr

Sets the initial write address.

transfer_count

Number of transfers to make. Not bytes, but the number of transfers of channel_config_set_transfer_data_size() to be sent.

dma_channel_unclaim()

```
void dma_channel_unclaim (uint channel)
```

Mark a dma channel as no longer used.

Parameters

channel

> The dma channel to release.

dma_channel_wait_for_finish_blocking()   Inline Static

```
static void dma_channel_wait_for_finish_blocking (
        uint channel)
```

Wait for a DMA channel transfer to complete.

Parameters

channel

> DMA channel.

dma_claim_mask()

```
void dma_claim_mask (uint32_t channel_mask)
```

Mark multiple dma channels as used. Method for cooperative claiming of hardware. Will cause a panic if any of the channels are already claimed. Use of this method by libraries detects accidental configurations that would fail in unpredictable ways.

Parameters

channel_mask

> Bitfield of all required channels to claim (bit 0 == channel 0, bit 1 == channel 1 etc)

dma_claim_unused_channel()

```
int dma_claim_unused_channel (bool required)
```

Claim a free dma channel.

Parameters

required

If true the function will panic if none are available.

Returns

The dma channel number or -1 if required was false, and none were free.

dma_claim_unused_timer()

```
int dma_claim_unused_timer (bool required)
```

Claim a free dma timer.

Parameters

required

If true the function will panic if none are available.

Returns

The dma timer number or -1 if required was false, and none were free.

dma_get_timer_dreq()   Inline Static

```
static uint dma_get_timer_dreq (uint timer_num)
```

Return the DREQ number for a given DMA timer.

Parameters

timer_num

DMA timer number 0-3

dma_irqn_acknowledge_channel()   Inline Static

```
static void dma_irqn_acknowledge_channel (uint irq_index,
        uint channel)
```

Acknowledge a channel IRQ, resetting it as the cause of DMA_IRQ_N.

Parameters

irq_index

The IRQ index; either 0 or 1 for DMA_IRQ_0 or DMA_IRQ_1.

channel

DMA channel

dma_irqn_get_channel_status()   Inline Static

```
static bool dma_irqn_get_channel_status (uint irq_index,
        uint channel)
```

Determine if a particular channel is a cause of DMA_IRQ_N.

Parameters

irq_index

The IRQ index; either 0 or 1 for DMA_IRQ_0 or DMA_IRQ_1.

channel

DMA channel

Returns

True if the channel is a cause of the DMA_IRQ_N, false otherwise.

dma_irqn_set_channel_enabled()   Inline Static

```
static void dma_irqn_set_channel_enabled( uint irq_index,
       uint channel, bool enabled)
```

Enable single DMA channel interrupt on either DMA_IRQ_0 or DMA_IRQ_1.

Parameters

irq_index

> The IRQ index; either 0 or 1 for DMA_IRQ_0 or DMA_IRQ_1.

channel

> DMA channel.

enabled

> True to enable interrupt via irq_index for specified channel, false to disable.

dma_irqn_set_channel_mask_enabled()   Inline Static

```
static void dma_irqn_set_channel_mask_enabled
       (uint irq_index, uint32_t channel_mask,
       bool enabled)
```

Enable multiple DMA channels' interrupt via either DMA_IRQ_0 or DMA_IRQ_1.

Parameters

irq_index

> The IRQ index; either 0 or 1 for DMA_IRQ_0 or DMA_IRQ_1

channel_mask

> Bitmask of all the channels to enable/disable. Channel 0 = bit 0, channel 1 = bit 1 etc.

enabled

> True to enable all the interrupts specified in the mask, false to disable all the interrupts specified in the mask.

dma_set_irq0_channel_mask_enabled()   Inline Static

```
static void dma_set_irq0_channel_mask_enabled
        (uint32_t channel_mask, bool enabled)
```

Enable multiple DMA channels' interrupts via DMA_IRQ_0.

Parameters

channel_mask

> Bitmask of all the channels to enable/disable. Channel 0 = bit 0, channel 1 = bit 1 etc.

enabled

> True to enable all the interrupts specified in the mask, false to disable all the interrupts specified in the mask.

dma_set_irq1_channel_mask_enabled()   Inline Static

```
static void dma_set_irq1_channel_mask_enabled
        (uint32_t channel_mask, bool enabled)
```

Enable multiple DMA channels' interrupts via DMA_IRQ_1.

Parameters

channel_mask

> Bitmask of all the channels to enable/disable. Channel 0 = bit 0, channel 1 = bit 1 etc.

enabled

> True to enable all the interrupts specified in the mask, false to disable all the interrupts specified in the mask.

dma_sniffer_disable()   Inline Static

```
static void dma_sniffer_disable(void )
```

Disable the DMA sniffer.

The Pico C API Functionary

dma_sniffer_enable()

```
static void dma_sniffer_enable(uint channel, uint mode,
          bool force_channel_enable)
```

Enable the DMA sniffing targeting the specified channel. The mode can be one of the following:

- **0x0** Calculate a CRC-32 (IEEE802.3 polynomial).
- **0x1** Calculate a CRC-32 (IEEE802.3 polynomial) with bit reversed data.
- **0x2** Calculate a CRC-16-CCITT.
- **0x3** Calculate a CRC-16-CCITT with bit reversed data.
- **0xe** XOR reduction over all data. == 1 if the total 1 population count is odd.
- **0xf** Calculate a simple 32-bit checksum (addition with a 32 bit accumulator).

Parameters

channel

DMA channel.

mode

See description.

force_channel_enable

Set true to also turn on sniffing in the channel configuration (this is usually what you want, but sometimes you might have a chain DMA with only certain segments of the chain sniffed, in which case you might pass false).

dma_sniffer_get_data_accumulator()   Inline Static

```
static uint32_t dma_sniffer_get_data_accumulator(void )
```

Get the sniffer's data accumulator value.

Returns

Read value calculated by the hardware from sniffing the DMA stream.

dma_sniffer_set_byte_swap_enabled()   Inline Static

```
static void dma_sniffer_set_byte_swap_enabled(bool swap)
```

Enable the Sniffer byte swap function. Locally perform a byte reverse on the sniffed data, before feeding into checksum.

Note that the sniff hardware is downstream of the DMA channel byteswap performed in the read master: if channel_config_set_bswap() and dma_sniffer_set_byte_swap_enabled() are both enabled, their effects cancel from the sniffer's point of view.

Parameters

swap

Set true to enable byte swapping.

dma_sniffer_set_data_accumulator()   Inline Static

```
static void dma_sniffer_set_data_accumulator
          (uint32_t seed_value)
```

Set the sniffer's data accumulator with initial value. Generally, CRC algorithms are used with the data accumulator initially seeded with 0xFFFF or 0xFFFFFFFF (for crc16 and crc32 algorithms).

Parameters

seed_value

Value to set data accumulator.

dma_sniffer_set_output_invert_enabled()   Inline Static

```
static void dma_sniffer_set_output_invert_enabled
          (bool invert)
```

Enable the Sniffer output invert function. If enabled, the sniff data result appears bit-inverted when read. This does not affect the way the checksum is calculated.

Parameters

invert   Set true to enable output bit inversion.

dma_sniffer_set_output_reverse_enabled()   Inline Static

```
static void dma_sniffer_set_output_reverse_enabled
          (bool reverse)
```

Enable the Sniffer output bit reversal function. If enabled, the sniff data result appears bit-reversed when read. This does not affect the way the checksum is calculated.

Parameters

reverse

Set true to enable output bit reversal.

dma_start_channel_mask()   Inline Static

static void dma_start_channel_mask(uint32_t chan_mask)

Start one or more channels simultaneously.

Parameters

chan_mask

Bitmask of all the channels requiring starting. Channel 0 = bit 0, channel 1 = bit 1 etc.

dma_timer_claim()

```
void dma_timer_claim(uint timer)
```

Mark a dma timer as used. Method for cooperative claiming of hardware. Will cause a panic if the timer is already claimed. Use of this method by libraries detects accidental configurations that would fail in unpredictable ways.

Parameters

timer

The dma timer.

dma_timer_is_claimed()

```
bool dma_timer_is_claimed(uint timer)
```

Determine if a dma timer is claimed. See also dma_timer_claim.

Parameters

timer
> The dma timer.

Returns

> True if the timer is claimed, false otherwise.

dma_timer_set_fraction()   Inline Static

```
static void dma_timer_set_fraction(uint timer, uint16_t
        numerator, uint16_t denominator)
```

Set the divider for the given DMA timer. The timer will run at the system_clock_freq *numerator / denominator, so this is the speed that data elements will be transferred at via a DMA channel using this timer as a DREQ.

Parameters

timer
> The dma timer.

numerator
> The fraction's numerator.

denominator
> The fraction's denominator.

dma_timer_unclaim()

```
void dma_timer_unclaim(uint timer)
```

Mark a dma timer as no longer used. Method for cooperative claiming of hardware.

Parameters

timer

The dma timer to release.

dma_unclaim_mask()

```
void dma_unclaim_mask(uint32_t channel_mask)
```

Mark multiple dma channels as no longer used.

Parameters

channel_mask

Bitfield of all channels to unclaim (bit 0 == channel 0, bit 1 == channel 1 etc).

HARDWARE EXCEPTIONS

hardware_exception

```
#include "hardware/exception.h"
```

Methods for setting processor exception handlers. Exceptions are identified by a exception_number which is a number from -15 to -1; these are the numbers relative to the index of the first IRQ vector in the vector table. (i.e. vector table index is exception_num plus 16) There is one set of exception handlers per core, so the exception handlers for each core as set by these methods are independent.

NOTE: That all exception APIs affect the executing core only (i.e. the core calling the function).

TYPEDEFS

exception_handler_t

```
typedef void(*exception_handler_t) (void)
```

Exception handler function type. All exception handlers should be of this type, and follow normal ARM EABI register saving conventions.

ENUMERATIONS

exception_number

```
enum exception_number
```

Exception number definitions. Note for consistency with irq numbers, these numbers are defined to be negative. The VTABLE index is the number here plus 16.

Name	Value	Exception
NMI_EXCEPTION	-14	Non Maskable Interrupt
HARDFAULT_EXCEPTION	-13	HardFault
SVCALL_EXCEPTION	-5	SV Call
PENDSV_EXCEPTION	-2	Pend SV
SYSTICK_EXCEPTION	-1	System Tick

FUNCTIONS

exception_get_vtable_handler()

```
exception_handler_t exception_get_vtable_handler
          (enum exception_number num)
```

Get the current exception handler for the specified exception from the currently installed vector table of the execution core.

Parameters

num

Exception number.

Returns

The address stored in the VTABLE for the given exception number.

exception_restore_handler()

```
void exception_restore_handler (enum exception_number num,
        exception_handler_t original_handler)
```

Restore the original exception handler for an exception on this core. This method may be used to restore the exception handler for an exception on this core to the state prior to the call to exception_set_exclusive_handler(), so that exception_set_exclusive_handler() may be called again in the future. See also exception_set_exclusive_handler()

Parameters

num

Exception number exception_number.

original_handler

The original handler returned from exception_set_exclusive_handler.

exception_set_exclusive_handler()

```
exception_handler_t exception_set_exclusive_handler
            (enum exception_number num,
             exception_handler_t handler)
```

Set the exception handler for an exception on the executing core. This method will assert if an exception handler has been set for this exception number on this core via this method, without an intervening restore via exception_restore_handler. See also exception_number.

NOTE: this method may not be used to override an exception handler that was specified at link time by providing a strong replacement for the weakly defined stub exception handlers. It will assert in this case too.

Parameters

num

> Exception number.

handler

> The handler to set.

FLASH

hardware_flash

```
#include "hardware/flash.h"
```

Low level flash programming and erase API. Note these functions are unsafe if you are using both cores, and the other is executing from flash concurrently with the operation. In this case, you must perform your own synchronization to make sure that no XIP accesses take place during flash programming. One option is to use the lockout functions.

Likewise they are unsafe if you have interrupt handlers or an interrupt vector table in flash, so you must disable interrupts before calling.

If PICO_NO_FLASH=1 is not defined (i.e. if the program is built to run from flash) then these functions will make a static copy of the second stage bootloader in SRAM, and use this to reenter execute-in-place mode after programming or erasing flash, so that they can safely be called from flash-resident code.

flash_do_cmd()

```
void flash_do_cmd (const uint8_t *txbuf, uint8_t *rxbuf,
     size_t count)
```

Execute bidirectional flash command. This is a low-level function to execute a serial command on a flash device attached to the QSPI interface. Bytes are simultaneously transmitted and received from txbuf and to rxbuf. Therefore, both buffers must be the same length, count, which is the length of the overall transaction. This is useful for reading metadata from the flash chip, such as device ID or SFDP parameters.

The XIP cache is flushed following each command, in case flash state has been modified. Like other hardware_flash functions, the flash is not accessible for execute-in-place transfers whilst the command is in progress, so entering a flash-resident interrupt handler or executing flash code on the second core concurrently will be fatal. To avoid these pitfalls it is recommended that this function only be used to extract flash metadata during startup, before the main application begins to run: see the implementation of pico_get_unique_id() for an example of this.

Parameters

txbuf   Pointer to a byte buffer which will be transmitted to the flash.

rxbuf

        Pointer to a byte buffer where data received from the flash will be written. txbuf and rxbuf may be the same buffer.

count   Length in bytes of txbuf and of rxbuf.

flash_get_unique_id()

```
void flash_get_unique_id (uint8_t *id_out)
```

Get flash unique 64 bit identifier. Use a standard 4Bh RUID instruction to retrieve the 64 bit unique identifier from a flash device attached to the QSPI interface. Since there is a 1:1 association between the MCU and this flash, this also serves as a unique identifier for the board.

Parameters

id_out

        Pointer to an 8-byte buffer to which the ID will be written.

The Pico C API Functionary

flash_range_erase()

```
void flash_range_erase (uint32_t flash_offs, size_t count)
```

Erase areas of flash.

Parameters

flash_offs

Offset into flash, in bytes, to start the erase. Must be aligned to a 4096-byte flash sector.

count

Number of bytes to be erased. Must be a multiple of 4096 bytes (one sector).

flash_range_program()

```
void flash_range_program (uint32_t flash_offs, const uint8_t
        *data, size_t count)
```

Program flash.

Parameters

flash_offs

Flash address of the first byte to be programmed. Must be aligned to a 256-byte flash page.

data

Pointer to the data to program into flash.

count

Number of bytes to program. Must be a multiple of 256 bytes (one page).

GPIO

hardware_gpio

```
#include "hardware/gpio.h"
```

The General Purpose Input/Output (GPIO) API in the Pico SDK provides access to the versatile GPIO pins available on the RP2040 microcontroller. With a total of 36 GPIO pins divided into two banks, the QSPI bank and the User bank. These banks provide a range of options for connecting and controlling external devices in your application.

The QSPI bank consists of specific GPIO pins, including QSPI_SS, QSPI_SCLK, and QSPI_SD0 to QSPI_SD3. These pins are primarily designed for connecting and executing code from an external flash device using the Quad Serial Peripheral Interface (QSPI) protocol. The QSPI bank is particularly useful when you need to store and execute code from an external flash memory, offloading the program memory requirement from the microcontroller itself. By dedicating these pins to QSPI functionality, you can ensure reliable and efficient communication with external flash devices.

On the other hand, the User bank comprises GPIO0 to GPIO29, offering a significant number of pins for general-purpose use. These pins are available for the programmer to utilize according to the specific requirements of their application. They can be used for various tasks such as digital input, output, or control signals for interfacing with external components, sensors, actuators, or other peripheral devices.

All GPIO pins support digital input and output functionality, allowing for basic interaction with external circuits. However, GPIO26 to GPIO29 offer an additional capability as inputs to the chip's Analogue to Digital Converter (ADC), enabling analog signal measurement.

The function assigned to each GPIO pin is determined by calling the *gpio_set_function* function. It's important to note that not all functions are available on every pin, so the selection of functions should be made carefully based on the specific capabilities of each pin. Furthermore, it's crucial to avoid assigning the same peripheral input (e.g., UART0 RX) to multiple GPIOs simultaneously. If multiple GPIOs are connected to the same peripheral input, the peripheral will interpret it as a logical OR of those GPIO inputs.

For a comprehensive understanding of GPIO function selection and pin capabilities, it's recommended to refer to the RP2040 datasheet. The GPIO API in the Pico SDK offers a flexible and powerful interface for controlling and utilizing the GPIO pins to suit a variety of application requirements.

Function Select Table (*See gpio_set_function*)

GPIO	F1	F2	F3	F4	F5	F6	F7	F8	F9
0	SPI0 RX	UART0 TX	I2C0 SDA	PWM0A	SIO	PIO0	PIO1		USB OVCUR DET
1	SPI0 CSn	UART0 RX	I2C0 SCL	PWM0B	SIO	PIO0	PIO1		USB VBUS DET
2	SPI0 SCK	UART0 CTS	I2C1 SDA	PWM1A	SIO	PIO0	PIO1		USB VBUS EN
3	SPI0 TX	UART0 RTS	I2C1 SCL	PWM1B	SIO	PIO0	PIO1		USB OVCUR DET
4	SPI0 RX	UART1 TX	I2C0 SDA	PWM2A	SIO	PIO0	PIO1		USB VBUS DET
5	SPI0 CSn	UART1 RX	I2C0 SCL	PWM2B	SIO	PIO0	PIO1		USB VBUS EN
6	SPI0 SCK	UART1 CTS	I2C1 SDA	PWM3A	SIO	PIO0	PIO1		USB OVCUR DET
7	SPI0 TX	UART1 RTS	I2C1 SCL	PWM3B	SIO	PIO0	PIO1		USB VBUS DET
8	SPI1 RX	UART1 TX	I2C0 SDA	PWM4A	SIO	PIO0	PIO1		USB VBUS EN
9	SPI1 CSn	UART1 RX	I2C0 SCL	PWM4B	SIO	PIO0	PIO1		USB OVCUR DET
10	SPI1 SCK	UART1 CTS	I2C1 SDA	PWM5A	SIO	PIO0	PIO1		USB VBUS DET
11	SPI1 TX	UART1 RTS	I2C1 SCL	PWM5B	SIO	PIO0	PIO1		USB VBUS EN
12	SPI1 RX	UART0 TX	I2C0 SDA	PWM6A	SIO	PIO0	PIO1		USB OVCUR DET
13	SPI1 CSn	UART0 RX	I2C0 SCL	PWM6B	SIO	PIO0	PIO1		USB VBUS DET
14	SPI1 SCK	UART0 CTS	I2C1 SDA	PWM7A	SIO	PIO0	PIO1		USB VBUS EN
15	SPI1 TX	UART0 RTS	I2C1 SCL	PWM7B	SIO	PIO0	PIO1		USB OVCUR DET
16	SPI0 RX	UART0 TX	I2C0 SDA	PWM0A	SIO	PIO0	PIO1		USB VBUS DET
17	SPI0 CSn	UART0 RX	I2C0 SCL	PWM0B	SIO	PIO0	PIO1		USB VBUS EN
18	SPI0 SCK	UART0 CTS	I2C1 SDA	PWM1A	SIO	PIO0	PIO1		USB OVCUR DET
19	SPI0 TX	UART0 RTS	I2C1 SCL	PWM1B	SIO	PIO0	PIO1		USB VBUS DET
20	SPI0 RX	UART1 TX	I2C0 SDA	PWM2A	SIO	PIO0	PIO1	CLOCK GPIN0	USB VBUS EN
21	SPI0 CSn	UART1 RX	I2C0 SCL	PWM2B	SIO	PIO0	PIO1	CLOCK GPOUT0	USB OVCUR DET
22	SPI0 SCK	UART1 CTS	I2C1 SDA	PWM3A	SIO	PIO0	PIO1	CLOCK GPIN1	USB VBUS DET
23	SPI0 TX	UART1 RTS	I2C1 SCL	PWM3B	SIO	PIO0	PIO1	CLOCK GPOUT1	USB VBUS EN
24	SPI1 RX	UART1 TX	I2C0 SDA	PWM4A	SIO	PIO0	PIO1	CLOCK GPOUT2	USB OVCUR DET
25	SPI1 CSn	UART1 RX	I2C0 SCL	PWM4B	SIO	PIO0	PIO1	CLOCK GPOUT3	USB VBUS DET
26	SPI1 SCK	UART1 CTS	I2C1 SDA	PWM5A	SIO	PIO0	PIO1		USB VBUS EN
27	SPI1 TX	UART1 RTS	I2C1 SCL	PWM5B	SIO	PIO0	PIO1		USB OVCUR DET
28	SPI1 RX	UART0 TX	I2C0 SDA	PWM6A	SIO	PIO0	PIO1		USB VBUS DET
29	SPI1 CSn	UART0 RX	I2C0 SCL	PWM6B	SIO	PIO0	PIO1		USB VBUS EN

DEFINITIONS

GPIO_IN	= 0
GPIO_OUT	= 1

TYPEDEFS

gpio_irq_callback_t

```
typedef void(*gpio_irq_callback_t) (uint gpio,
        uint32_t event_mask)
```

Callback function type for GPIO events. See also gpio_set_irq_enabled_with_callback()
gpio_set_irq_callback().

Parameters

gpio

Which GPIO caused this interrupt.

event_mask

Which events caused this interrupt. See gpio_irq_level for details.

ENUMERATIONS

gpio_drive_strength

```
enum gpio_drive_strength
```

Drive strength levels for GPIO outputs. See also gpio_set_drive_strength.

GPIO_DRIVE_STRENGTH_2MA	Sets a 2 mA nominal drive strength.
GPIO_DRIVE_STRENGTH_4MA	Sets a 4 mA nominal drive strength.
GPIO_DRIVE_STRENGTH_8MA	Sets a 8 mA nominal drive strength.
GPIO_DRIVE_STRENGTH_12MA	Sets a 12 mA nominal drive strength.

gpio_function

```
enum gpio_function
```

Each GPIO can have one function selected at a time. Likewise, each peripheral input (e.g. UART0 RX) should only be selected on one GPIO at a time. If the same peripheral input is connected to multiple GPIOs, the peripheral sees the logical OR of these GPIO inputs. Please refer to the datasheet for more information on GPIO function selection.

GPIO function definitions for use with function select.

GPIO_FUNC_XIP	= 0
GPIO_FUNC_SPI	= 1
GPIO_FUNC_UART	= 2
GPIO_FUNC_I2C	= 3
GPIO_FUNC_PWM	= 4
GPIO_FUNC_SIO	= 5
GPIO_FUNC_PIO0	= 6
GPIO_FUNC_PIO1	= 7
GPIO_FUNC_GPCK	= 8
GPIO_FUNC_USB	= 9
GPIO_FUNC_NULL	= 0x1f

gpio_irq_level

```
enum gpio_irq_level
```

GPIO Interrupt level definitions (GPIO events). An interrupt can be generated for every GPIO pin in 4 scenarios: Level High: the GPIO pin is a logical 1. Level Low: the GPIO pin is a logical 0. Edge High: the GPIO has transitioned from a logical 0 to a logical 1. Edge Low: the GPIO has transitioned from a logical 1 to a logical 0.

The level interrupts are not latched. This means that if the pin is a logical 1 and the level high interrupt is active, it will become inactive as soon as the pin changes to a logical 0. The edge interrupts are stored in the INTR register and can be cleared by writing to the INTR register.

GPIO_IRQ_LEVEL_LOW	= 0x1u
GPIO_IRQ_LEVEL_HIGH	= 0x2u
GPIO_IRQ_EDGE_FALL	= 0x4u
GPIO_IRQ_EDGE_RISE	= 0x8u

gpio_override   **Undocumented**

`enum gpio_override`

GPIO_OVERRIDE_NORMAL	= 0	Peripheral signal selected via \ref gpio_set_function.
GPIO_OVERRIDE_INVERT	= 1	Invert peripheral signal selected via \ref gpio_set_function.
GPIO_OVERRIDE_LOW	= 2	Drive low/disable output.
GPIO_OVERRIDE_HIGH	= 3	Drive high/enable output.

gpio_slew_rate

`enum gpio_slew_rate`

Slew rate limiting levels for GPIO outputs. Slew rate limiting increases the minimum rise/fall time when a GPIO output is lightly loaded, which can help to reduce electromagnetic emissions. See also gpio_set_slew_rate.

Enumerator

GPIO_SLEW_RATE_SLOW	= 0	Slew rate limiting enabled.
GPIO_SLEW_RATE_FAST	= 1	Slew rate limiting disabled.

FUNCTIONS

gpio_acknowledge_irq()

```
void gpio_acknowledge_irq (uint gpio, uint32_t event_mask)
```

Acknowledge a GPIO interrupt for the specified events on the calling core. This may be called with a mask of any of valid bits specified in gpio_irq_level, however it has no effect on level sensitive interrupts which remain pending while the GPIO is at the specified level. When handling level sensitive interrupts, you should generally disable the interrupt (see gpio_set_irq_enabled) and then set it up again later once the GPIO level has changed (or to catch the opposite level).

NOTE For callbacks set with gpio_set_irq_enabled_with_callback, or gpio_set_irq_callback, this function is called automatically.

Parameters

gpio

GPIO number.

event_mask

Bitmask of events to clear. See gpio_irq_level for details.

gpio_add_raw_irq_handler()   Inline Static

```
static void gpio_add_raw_irq_handler (uint gpio,
       irq_handler_t handler)
```

Adds a raw GPIO IRQ handler for a specific GPIO on the current core. In addition to the default mechanism of a single GPIO IRQ event callback per core (see gpio_set_irq_callback), it is possible to add explicit GPIO IRQ handlers which are called independent of the default event callback. This method adds such a callback, and disables the "default" callback for the specified GPIO. A raw handler should check for whichever GPIOs and events it handles, and acknowledge them itself. *NOTE Multiple raw handlers should not be added for the same GPIO, and this method will assert if you attempt to.*

Parameters

gpio

> The GPIO number that will no longer be passed to the default callback for this core.

handler

> The handler to add to the list of GPIO IRQ handlers for this core.

gpio_add_raw_irq_handler_masked()

```
void gpio_add_raw_irq_handler_masked (uint gpio_mask,
       irq_handler_t handler)
```

Adds a raw GPIO IRQ handler for the specified GPIOs on the current core. In addition to the default mechanism of a single GPIO IRQ event callback per core (see gpio_set_irq_callback), it is possible to add explicit GPIO IRQ handlers which are called independent of the default event callback. This method adds such a callback, and disables the "default" callback for the specified GPIOs. A raw handler should check for whichever GPIOs and events it handles, and acknowledge them itself. *NOTE Multiple raw handlers should not be added for the same GPIOs, and this method will assert if you attempt to.*

Parameters

gpio_maska

> bit mask of the GPIO numbers that will no longer be passed to the default callback for this core.

handler

> The handler to add to the list of GPIO IRQ handlers for this core.

gpio_add_raw_irq_handler_with_order_priority()   Inline Static

```
static void gpio_add_raw_irq_handler_with_order_priority
        (uint gpio, irq_handler_t handler,
        uint8_t order_priority)
```

Adds a raw GPIO IRQ handler for a specific GPIO on the current core. In addition to the default mechanism of a single GPIO IRQ event callback per core (see gpio_set_irq_callback), it is possible to add explicit GPIO IRQ handlers which are called independent of the default callback. The order relative to the default callback can be controlled via the order_priority parameter(the default callback has the priority GPIO_IRQ_CALLBACK_ORDER_PRIORITY which defaults to the lowest priority with the intention of it running last). This method adds such a callback, and disables the "default" callback for the specified GPIO. A raw handler should check for whichever GPIOs and events it handles, and acknowledge them itself.

NOTE Multiple raw handlers should not be added for the same GPIO, and this method will assert if you attempt to.

Parameters

gpio

The GPIO number that will no longer be passed to the default callback for this core.

handler

The handler to add to the list of GPIO IRQ handlers for this core.

order_priority

The priority order to determine the relative position of the handler in the list of GPIO IRQ handlers for this core.

gpio_add_raw_irq_handler_with_order_priority_masked()

```
void gpio_add_raw_irq_handler_with_order_priority_masked
        (uint gpio_mask, irq_handler_t handler,
         uint8_t order_priority)
```

Adds a raw GPIO IRQ handler for the specified GPIOs on the current core. In addition to the default mechanism of a single GPIO IRQ event callback per core (see gpio_set_irq_callback), it is possible to add explicit GPIO IRQ handlers which are called independent of the default callback. The order relative to the default callback can be controlled via the order_priority parameter (the default callback has the priority GPIO_IRQ_CALLBACK_ORDER_PRIORITY which defaults to the lowest priority with the intention of it running last).

This method adds such an explicit GPIO IRQ handler, and disables the "default" callback for the specified GPIOs. A raw handler should check for whichever GPIOs and events it handles, and acknowledge them itself.

NOTE Multiple raw handlers should not be added for the same GPIOs, and this method will assert if you attempt to.

Parameters

gpio_mask

A bit mask of the GPIO numbers that will no longer be passed to the default callback for this core.

handler

The handler to add to the list of GPIO IRQ handlers for this core

order_priority

The priority order to determine the relative position of the handler in the list of GPIO IRQ handlers for this core.

gpio_clr_mask()   **Inline Static**

```
static void gpio_clr_mask (uint32_t mask)
```

Drive low every GPIO appearing in mask.

Parameters

mask   Bitmask of GPIO values to clear, as bits 0-29.

gpio_deinit()

```
void gpio_deinit (uint gpio)
```

Resets a GPIO back to the NULL function, i.e. disables it.

Parameters

gpio   GPIO number.

gpio_disable_pulls()   **Inline Static**

```
static void gpio_disable_pulls (uint gpio)
```

Disable the internal pull-up and pull-down resistors on a GPIO pin.

Parameters

gpio   GPIO number.

gpio_get()   **Inline Static**

```
static bool gpio_get (uint gpio)
```

Get state of a single specified GPIO.

Parameters

gpio   GPIO number

Returns

Current state of the GPIO. 0 for low, non-zero for high.

gpio_get_all()   Inline Static

```
static uint32_t gpio_get_all(void)
```

Get raw value of all GPIOs.

Returns

Bitmask of raw GPIO values, as bits 0-29.

gpio_get_dir()   Inline Static

```
static uint gpio_get_dir(uint gpio)
```

Get a specific GPIO direction.

Parameters

gpio   GPIO number.

Returns

1 for out, 0 for in.

gpio_get_drive_strength()

```
enum gpio_drive_strength gpio_get_drive_strength
        uint gpio)
```

Determine current slew rate for a specified GPIO. See also gpio_set_drive_strength.

Parameters

gpio   GPIO number.

Returns

Current drive strength of that GPIO.

gpio_get_function()

```
enum gpio_function gpio_get_function (uint gpio)
```

Determine current GPIO function.

Parameters

gpio   GPIO number.

Returns

Which GPIO function is currently selected from list gpio_function.

gpio_get_irq_event_mask()   Inline Static

```
static uint32_t gpio_get_irq_event_mask (uint gpio)
```

Return the current interrupt status (pending events) for the given GPIO. See alsogpio_acknowledge_irq.

Parameters

gpio   GPIO number.

Returns

Bitmask of events that are currently pending for the GPIO. See gpio_irq_level for details.

gpio_get_out_level()   Inline Static

```
static bool gpio_get_out_level (uint gpio)
```

Determine whether a GPIO is currently driven high or low. This function returns the high/low output level most recently assigned to a GPIO via gpio_put() or similar. This is the value that is presented outward to the IO muxing, not the input level back from the pad (which can be read using gpio_get()).

To avoid races, this function must not be used for read-modify-write sequences when driving GPIOs – instead functions like gpio_put() should be used to atomically update GPIOs. This accessor is intended for debug use only.

Parameters

gpio   GPIO number.

Returns

True if the GPIO output level is high, false if low.

gpio_get_slew_rate()

```
enum gpio_slew_rate gpio_get_slew_rate (uint gpio)
```

Determine current slew rate for a specified GPIO. See also gpio_set_slew_rate.

Parameters

gpio   GPIO number.

Returns

Current slew rate of that GPIO.

gpio_init()

```
void gpio_init (uint gpio)
```

Initialize a GPIO for (enabled I/O and set func to GPIO_FUNC_SIO). Clear the output enable (i.e. set to input). Clear any output value.

Parameters

gpio   GPIO number.

gpio_init_mask()

```
void gpio_init_mask (uint gpio_mask)
```

Initialize multiple GPIOs (enabled I/O and set func to GPIO_FUNC_SIO). Clear the output enable (i.e. set to input). Clear any output value.

Parameters

gpio_mask   Mask with 1 bit per GPIO number to initialize.

gpio_is_dir_out()   Inline Static

```
static bool gpio_is_dir_out(uint gpio)
```

Check if a specific GPIO direction is OUT.

Parameters

gpio   GPIO number.

Returns

True if the direction for the pin is OUT.

gpio_is_input_hysteresis_enabled()

```
bool gpio_is_input_hysteresis_enabled (uint gpio)
```

Determine whether input hysteresis is enabled on a specified GPIO. See also gpio_set_input_hysteresis_enabled.

Parameters

gpio   GPIO number.

gpio_is_pulled_down()   Inline Static

```
static bool gpio_is_pulled_down(uint gpio)
```

Determine if the specified GPIO is pulled down.

Parameters

gpio   GPIO number.

Returns

       True if the GPIO is pulled down.

gpio_is_pulled_up()   Inline Static

```
static bool gpio_is_pulled_up (uint gpio)
```

Determine if the specified GPIO is pulled up.

Parameters

gpio   GPIO number.

Returns

       True if the GPIO is pulled up.

gpio_pull_down()   Inline Static

```
static void gpio_pull_down(uint gpio)
```

Set specified GPIO to be pulled down.

Parameters

gpio   GPIO number.

gpio_pull_up()   Inline Static

```
static void gpio_pull_up(uint gpio)
```

Set specified GPIO to be pulled up.

Parameters

gpio   GPIO number.

gpio_put()   Inline Static

```
static void gpio_put (uint gpio, bool value)
```

Drive a single GPIO high/low.

Parameters

gpio   GPIO number.
value

If false clear the GPIO, otherwise set it.

gpio_put_all()   Inline Static

```
static void gpio_put_all (uint32_t value)
```

Drive all pins simultaneously.

Parameters

value

Bitmask of GPIO values to change, as bits 0-29.

gpio_put_masked()   Inline Static

```
static void gpio_put_masked (uint32_t mask,
        uint32_t value)
```

Drive GPIO high/low depending on parameters. For each 1 bit in mask, drive that pin to the value given by corresponding bit in value, leaving other pins unchanged. Since this uses the TOGL alias, it is concurrency-safe with e.g. an IRQ bashing different pins from the same core.

Parameters

mask

Bitmask of GPIO values to change, as bits 0-29.

value

Value to set.

gpio_remove_raw_irq_handler()

```
static void gpio_remove_raw_irq_handler (uint gpio,
        irq_handler_t handler)
```

Removes a raw GPIO IRQ handler for the specified GPIO on the current core. In addition to the default mechanism of a single GPIO IRQ event callback per core (see gpio_set_irq_callback), it is possible to add explicit GPIO IRQ handlers which are called independent of the default event callback.

This method removes such a callback, and enables the "default" callback for the specified GPIO.

Parameters

gpio

The GPIO number that will now be passed to the default callback for this core.

handler

The handler to remove from the list of GPIO IRQ handlers for this core.

gpio_remove_raw_irq_handler_masked()

```
void gpio_remove_raw_irq_handler_masked (uint gpio_mask,
        irq_handler_t handler)
```

Removes a raw GPIO IRQ handler for the specified GPIOs on the current core. In addition to the default mechanism of a single GPIO IRQ event callback per core (see gpio_set_irq_callback), it is possible to add explicit GPIO IRQ handlers which are called independent of the default event callback.

This method removes such a callback, and enables the "default" callback for the specified GPIOs.

Parameters

gpio_mask

A bit mask of the GPIO numbers that will now be passed to the default callback for this core.

handler

The handler to remove from the list of GPIO IRQ handlers for this core.

gpio_set_dir()   **Inline Static**

```
static void gpio_set_dir (uint gpio, bool out)
```

Set a single GPIO direction.

Parameters

gpio

GPIO number.

out

True for out, false for in.

gpio_set_dir_all_bits()   Inline Static

```
static void gpio_set_dir_all_bits (uint32_t values)
```

Set direction of all pins simultaneously.

Parameters

values

Individual settings for each gpio; for GPIO N, bit N is 1 for out, 0 for in.

gpio_set_dir_in_masked()   Inline Static

```
static void gpio_set_dir_in_masked(uint32_t mask)
```

Set a number of GPIOs to input.

Parameters

mask

Bitmask of GPIO to set to input, as bits 0-29.

gpio_set_dir_masked()

```
static void gpio_set_dir_masked (uint32_t mask,
        uint32_t value)
```

Set multiple GPIO directions. For each 1 bit in "mask", switch that pin to the direction given by corresponding bit in "value", leaving other pins unchanged. E.g. gpio_set_dir_masked(0x3, 0x2); -> set pin 0 to input, pin 1 to output, simultaneously.

Parameters

mask

Bitmask of GPIO to set to input, as bits 0-29.

value

Values to set.

gpio_set_dir_out_masked()   Inline Static

```
static void gpio_set_dir_out_masked (uint32_t mask)
```

Set a number of GPIOs to output. Switch all GPIOs in "mask" to output.

Parameters

mask

Bitmask of GPIO to set to output, as bits 0-29.

gpio_set_dormant_irq_enabled()

```
void gpio_set_dormant_irq_enabled (uint gpio, uint32_t
          event_mask, bool enabled)
```

Enable dormant wake up interrupt for specified GPIO and events. This configures IRQs to restart the XOSC or ROSC when they are disabled in dormant mode.

Parameters

gpio

GPIO number.

event_mask

Which events will cause an interrupt. See gpio_irq_level for details.

enabled

Enable/disable flag.

gpio_set_drive_strength()

```
void gpio_set_drive_strength (uint gpio,
          enum gpio_drive_strength drive)
```

Set drive strength for a specified GPIO. See also gpio_get_drive_strength.

Parameters

gpio   GPIO number.

drive   GPIO output drive strength.

gpio_set_function()

```
void gpio_set_function (uint gpio, enum gpio_function fn)
```

Select GPIO function.

Parameters

gpio

GPIO number.

fn

Which GPIO function select to use from list gpio_function.

gpio_set_inover()

```
void gpio_set_inover (uint gpio, uint value)
```

Select GPIO input override.

Parameters

gpio

GPIO number.

value

See gpio_override.

gpio_set_input_enabled()

```
void gpio_set_input_enabled (uint gpio, bool enabled)
```

Enable GPIO input.

Parameters

gpio

GPIO number.

enabled

True to enable input on specified GPIO.

gpio_set_input_hysteresis_enabled()

void gpio_set_input_hysteresis_enabled (uint gpio, bool enabled)

Enable/disable GPIO input hysteresis (Schmitt trigger). Enable or disable the Schmitt trigger hysteresis on a given GPIO. This is enabled on all GPIOs by default. Disabling input hysteresis can lead to inconsistent readings when the input signal has very long rise or fall times, but slightly reduces the GPIO's input delay.
See also gpio_is_input_hysteresis_enabled.

Parameters

gpio
> GPIO number.

enabled
> True to enable input hysteresis on specified GPIO.

gpio_set_irq_callback()

void gpio_set_irq_callback (gpio_irq_callback_t callback)

Set the generic callback used for GPIO IRQ events for the current core. This function sets the callback used for all GPIO IRQs on the current core that are not explicitly hooked via gpio_add_raw_irq_handler or other gpio_add_raw_irq_handler_ functions.

This function is called with the GPIO number and event mask for each of the (not explicitly hooked) GPIOs that have events enabled and that are pending (see gpio_get_irq_event_mask).

NOTE The IO IRQs are independent per-processor. This function affects the processor that calls the function.

Parameters

callback
> Default user function to call on GPIO irq. Note only one of these can be set per processor.

gpio_set_irq_enabled()

```
void gpio_set_irq_enabled (uint gpio, uint32_t event_mask,
        bool enabled)
```

Enable or disable specific interrupt events for specified GPIO. This function sets which GPIO events cause a GPIO interrupt on the calling core. See gpio_set_irq_callback, gpio_set_irq_enabled_with_callback and gpio_add_raw_irq_handler to set up a GPIO interrupt handler to handle the events.

NOTE The IO IRQs are independent per-processor. This configures the interrupt events for the processor that calls the function.

Events is a bitmask of the following gpio_irq_level values which are specified in gpio_irq_level:

GPIO_IRQ_LEVEL_LOW	Continuously while level is low 1.
GPIO_IRQ_LEVEL_HIGH	Continuously while level is high 2.
GPIO_IRQ_EDGE_FALL	On each transition from high to low 3.
GPIO_IRQ_EDGE_RISE	On each transition from low to high 4.

Parameters

gpio

   GPIO number.

event_mask

   Which events will cause an interrupt.

enabled

   Enable or disable flag.

gpio_set_irq_enabled_with_callback()

```
void gpio_set_irq_enabled_with_callback (uint gpio,
        uint32_t event_mask, bool enabled,
        gpio_irq_callback_t callback)
```

Convenience function which performs multiple GPIO IRQ related initializations. This method is a slightly eclectic mix of initialization, that: Updates whether the specified events for the specified GPIO causes an interrupt on the calling core based on the enable flag. Sets the callback handler for the calling core to callback (or clears the handler if the callback is NULL). Enables GPIO IRQs on the current core if enabled is true.

This method is commonly used to perform a one time setup, and following that any additional IRQs/events are enabled via gpio_set_irq_enabled. All GPIOs/events added in this way on the same core share the same callback; for multiple independent handlers for different GPIOs you should use gpio_add_raw_irq_handler and related functions.

This method is equivalent to:

gpio_set_irq_enabled(gpio, event_mask, enabled);
gpio_set_irq_callback(callback);
if (enabled) irq_set_enabled(IO_IRQ_BANK0, true);

NOTE The IO IRQs are independent per-processor. This method affects only the processor that calls the function.

Parameters

gpio

GPIO number.

event_mask

Which events will cause an interrupt. See gpio_irq_level for details.

enabled

Enable or disable flag.

callback

User function to call on GPIO irq. if NULL, the callback is removed.

gpio_set_irqover()

`void gpio set irqover (uint gpio, uint value)`

Set GPIO IRQ override. Optionally invert a GPIO IRQ signal, or drive it high or low.

Parameters

gpio

GPIO number.

value

See gpio_override.

gpio_set_mask()   **Inline Static**

`static void gpio set mask(uint32 t mask)`

Drive high every GPIO appearing in mask.

Parameters

mask

Bitmask of GPIO values to set, as bits 0-29.

gpio_set_oeover()

`void gpio set oeover (uint gpio, uint value)`

Select GPIO output enable override.

Parameters

gpio

GPIO number.

value

See gpio_override.

gpio_set_outover()

void gpio_set_outover (uint gpio, uint value)

Set GPIO output override.

Parameters

gpio

GPIO number.

value

See gpio_override.

gpio_set_pulls()

```
void gpio_set_pulls (uint gpio, bool up, bool down)
```

Select up and down pulls on specific GPIO. Setting both pulls enables a "bus keep" function, i.e. a weak pull to whatever is current high/low state of GPIO.

Parameters

gpio

GPIO number.

up

If true set a pull up on the GPIO.

down

If true set a pull down on the GPIO.

gpio_set_slew_rate()

void gpio_set_slew_rate (uint gpio, enum gpio_slew_rate slew)

Set slew rate for a specified GPIO. See also gpio_get_slew_rate.

Parameters

gpio

GPIO number.

slew

GPIO output slew rate.

gpio_xor_mask()   Inline Static

```
static void gpio_xor_mask (uint32_t mask)
```

Toggle every GPIO appearing in mask.

Parameters

mask

Bitmask of GPIO values to toggle, as bits 0-29.

I₂C

hardware_i2c

```
#include "hardware/i2c.h"
```

The I2C bus is a two-wire serial interface, consisting of a serial data line SDA and a serial clock SCL. These wires carry information between the devices connected to the bus. Each device is recognized by a unique 7-bit address and can operate as either a "transmitter" or "receiver", depending on the function of the device. Devices can also be considered as masters or slaves when performing data transfers. A master is a device that initiates a data transfer on the bus and generates the clock signals to permit that transfer. The first byte in the data transfer always contains the 7-bit address and a read/write bit in the LSB position. This API takes care of toggling the read/write bit. After this, any device addressed is considered a slave.

This API allows the controller to be set up as a master or a slave using the i2c_set_slave_mode function. The external pins of each controller are connected to GPIO pins as defined in the GPIO muxing table in the datasheet. The muxing options give some IO flexibility, but each controller external pin should be connected to only one GPIO. Note that the controller does NOT support High speed mode or Ultra-fast speed mode, the fastest operation being fast mode plus at up to 1000Kb/s.

See the datasheet for more information on the I2C controller and its usage.

i2c0_inst   extern

```
i2c_inst_t i2c0_inst
```

The I2C identifiers for use in I2C functions.

e.g. i2c_init(i2c0, 48000)

i2c_deinit()

```
void i2c_deinit(i2c_inst_t *i2c)
```

Disable the I2C HW block. Disable the I2C again if it is no longer used. Must be reinitialised before being used again.

Parameters

i2c

Either i2c0 or i2c1.

i2c_get_dreq()   Inline Static

```
static uint i2c_get_dreq(i2c_inst_t *i2c, bool is_tx)
```

Return the DREQ to use for pacing transfers to/from a particular I2C instance.

Parameters

i2c

Either i2c0 or i2c1.

is_tx

True for sending data to the I2C instance, false for receiving data from the I2C instance.

i2c_get_read_available()   Inline Static

```
static size_t i2c_get_read_available(i2c_inst_t *i2c)
```

Determine number of bytes received.

Parameters

i2c

Either i2c0 or i2c1.

Returns

0 if no data available, if return is nonzero at least that many bytes can be read without blocking.

i2c_get_write_available()   Inline Static

```
static size_t i2c_get_write_available(i2c_inst_t *i2c)
```

Determine non-blocking write space available.

Parameters

i2c

Either i2c0 or i2c1.

Returns

0 if no space is available in the I2C to write more data. If return is nonzero, at least that many bytes can be written without blocking.

i2c_hw_index()   Inline Static

```
static uint i2c_hw_index(i2c_inst_t *i2c)
```

Convert I2C instance to hardware instance number.

Parameters

i2c

Either i2c0 or i2c1.

Returns

Number of I2C, 0 or 1.

i2c_init()

```
uint i2c_init(i2c_inst_t *i2c, uint baudrate)
```

Initialize the I2C HW block. Put the I2C hardware into a known state, and enable it. Must be called before other functions. By default, the I2C is configured to operate as a master. The I2C bus frequency is set as close as possible to requested, and the actual rate set is returned

Parameters

i2c

Either i2c0 or i2c1.

baudrate

Baudrate in Hz (e.g. 100kHz is 100000)

Returns

Actual set baudrate.

i2c_read_blocking()

```
int i2c_read_blocking (i2c_inst_t *i2c, uint8_t addr,
        uint8_t *dst, size_t len, bool nostop)
```

Attempt to read specified number of bytes from address, blocking. A blocking function will not return until it has a valid answer.

Parameters

i2c

Either i2c0 or i2c1.

addr

7-bit address of device to read from.

dst

Pointer to buffer to receive data.

len

Length of data in bytes to receive.

nostop

If true, master retains control of the bus at the end of the transfer (no Stop is issued), and the next transfer will begin with a Restart rather than a Start.

Returns

Number of bytes read, or PICO_ERROR_GENERIC if address not acknowledged or no device present.

i2c_read_blocking_until()

```
int i2c_read_blocking_until (i2c_inst_t *i2c,
     uint8_t addr, uint8_t *dst, size_t len, bool
     nostop, absolute_time_t until)
```

Attempt to read specified number of bytes from address, blocking until the specified absolute time is reached. A blocking function will not return until it has a valid answer.

Parameters

i2c

Either i2c0 or i2c1.

addr

7-bit address of device to read from.

dst

Pointer to buffer to receive data.

len

Length of data in bytes to receive.

nostop

If true, master retains control of the bus at the end of the transfer (no Stop is issued), and the next transfer will begin with a Restart rather than a Start.

until

The absolute time that the block will wait until the entire transaction is complete.

Returns

Number of bytes read, or PICO_ERROR_GENERIC if address not acknowledged, no device present, or PICO_ERROR_TIMEOUT if a timeout occurred.

i2c_read_byte_raw()   Inline Static

```
static uint8_t i2c_read_byte_raw(i2c_inst_t *i2c)
```

Pop a byte from I2C Rx FIFO. This function is non-blocking and assumes the Rx FIFO isn't empty.

Parameters

i2c

Either i2c0 or i2c1.

Returns

uint8_t Byte value.

i2c_read_raw_blocking()   Inline Static

```
static void i2c_read_raw_blocking (i2c_inst_t *i2c,
        uint8_t *dst, size_t len)
```

Read direct from RX FIFO. Reads directly from the I2C RX FIFO which is mainly useful for slave-mode operation.

Parameters

i2c

Either i2c0 or i2c1.

dst

Buffer to accept data

len

Number of bytes to read

i2c_read_timeout_us() Inline Static

```
static int i2c_read_timeout_us (i2c_inst_t *i2c,
        uint8_t addr, uint8_t *dst, size_t len,
        bool nostop, uint timeout_us)
```

Attempt to read specified number of bytes from address, with timeout.

Parameters

i2c

> Either i2c0 or i2c1.

addr

> 7-bit address of device to read from.

dst

> Pointer to buffer to receive data.

len

> Length of data in bytes to receive.

nostop

> If true, master retains control of the bus at the end of the transfer (no Stop is issued), and the next transfer will begin with a Restart rather than a Start.

timeout_us

> The time that the function will wait for the entire transaction to complete

Returns

> Number of bytes read, or PICO_ERROR_GENERIC if address not acknowledged, no device present, or PICO_ERROR_TIMEOUT if a timeout occurred.

i2c_set_baudrate()

uint i2c_set_baudrate(i2c_inst_t *i2c, uint baudrate)

Set I2C baudrate. Set I2C bus frequency as close as possible to requested, and return actual rate set. Baudrate may not be as exactly requested due to clocking limitations.

Parameters

i2c

Either i2c0 or i2c1.

baudrate

Baudrate in Hz (e.g. 100kHz is 100000)

Returns

Actual set baudrate.

i2c_set_slave_mode()

```
void i2c_set_slave_mode (i2c_inst_t *i2c, bool slave,
        uint8_t addr)
```

Set I2C port to slave mode.

Parameters

i2c

Either i2c0 or i2c1.

slave

True to use slave mode, false to use master mode.

addr

If slave is true, set the slave address to this value.

i2c_write_blocking()

```
int i2c_write_blocking (i2c_inst_t *i2c, uint8_t addr,
         const uint8_t *src, size_t len, bool nostop)
```

Attempt to write specified number of bytes to address, blocking. A blocking function will not return until it has a valid answer.

Parameters

i2c

Either i2c0 or i2c1.

addr

7-bit address of device to write to.

src

Pointer to data to send.

len

Length of data in bytes to send.

nostop

If true, master retains control of the bus at the end of the transfer (no Stop is issued), and the next transfer will begin with a Restart rather than a Start.

Returns

Number of bytes written, or PICO_ERROR_GENERIC if address not acknowledged, no device present.

i2c_write_blocking_until()

```
int i2c_write_blocking_until(i2c_inst_t *i2c,
    uint8_t addr, const uint8_t *src, size_t len,
    bool nostop, absolute_time_t until)
```

Attempt to write specified number of bytes to address, blocking until the specified absolute time is reached. This blocking function will not return until it has a valid answer or the until time.

Parameters

i2c

Either i2c0 or i2c1.

addr

7-bit address of device to write to.

src

Pointer to data to send.

len

Length of data in bytes to send.

nostop

If true, master retains control of the bus at the end of the transfer (no Stop is issued), and the next transfer will begin with a Restart rather than a Start.

until

The absolute time that the block will wait until the entire transaction is complete. Note, an individual timeout of this value divided by the length of data is applied for each byte transfer, so if the first or subsequent bytes fails to transfer within that sub timeout, the function will return with an error.

Returns

Number of bytes written, or PICO_ERROR_GENERIC if address not acknowledged, no device present, or PICO_ERROR_TIMEOUT if a timeout occurred.

i2c_write_byte_raw()   Inline Static

```
static void i2c_write_byte_raw (i2c_inst_t *i2c,
        uint8_t value)
```

Push a byte into I2C Tx FIFO. This function is non-blocking and assumes the Tx FIFO isn't full.

Parameters

i2c

Either i2c0 or i2c1.

value

Byte value.

i2c_write_raw_blocking()   Inline Static

```
static void i2c_write_raw_blocking (i2c_inst_t *i2c, const
        uint8_t *src, size_t len)
```

Write direct to TX FIFO. Writes directly to the I2C TX FIFO which is mainly useful for slave-mode operation. A blocking function will not return until it has a valid answer.

Parameters

i2c

Either i2c0 or i2c1.

src

Data to send.

len

Number of bytes to send.

i2c_write_timeout_us()   Inline Static

```
static int i2c_write_timeout_us (i2c_inst_t *i2c,
        uint8_t addr, const uint8_t *src, size_t len,
        bool nostop, uint timeout_us)
```

Attempt to write specified number of bytes to address, with timeout.

Parameters

i2c

Either i2c0 or i2c1.

addr

7-bit address of device to write to.

src

Pointer to data to send.

len

Length of data in bytes to send.

nostop

If true, master retains control of the bus at the end of the transfer (no Stop is issued), and the next transfer will begin with a Restart rather than a Start.

timeout_us

The time that the function will wait for the entire transaction to complete. Note, an individual timeout of this value divided by the length of data is applied for each byte transfer, so if the first or subsequent bytes fails to transfer within that sub timeout, the function will return with an error.

Returns

Number of bytes written, or PICO_ERROR_GENERIC if address not acknowledged, no device present, or PICO_ERROR_TIMEOUT if a timeout occurred.

INTERPOLATOR

hardware_interp

```
#include "hardware/interp.h"
```

Each core is equipped with two interpolators (INTERP0 and INTERP1) which can be used to accelerate tasks by combining certain pre-configured simple operations into a single processor cycle. Intended for cases where the pre-configured operation is repeated a large number of times, this results in code which uses both fewer CPU cycles and fewer CPU registers in the time critical sections of the code.

The interpolators are used heavily to accelerate audio operations within the SDK, but their flexible configuration makes it possible to optimize many other tasks such as quantization and dithering, table lookup address generation, affine texture mapping, decompression and linear feedback.

Please refer to the RP2040 datasheet for more information on the HW interpolators and how they work.

---

interp_add_accumulater()   Inline Static

```
static void interp_add_accumulater (interp_hw_t *interp,
       uint lane, uint32_t val)
```

Add to accumulator. Atomically add the specified value to the accumulator on the specified lane.

Parameters

interp

Interpolator instance, interp0 or interp1.

lane

The lane number, 0 or 1.

val

Value to add.

Returns

The content of the FULL register.

---

interp_claim_lane()

```
void interp_claim_lane (interp_hw_t *interp, uint lane)
```

Claim the interpolator lane specified. Use this function to claim exclusive access to the specified interpolator lane. This function will panic if the lane is already claimed.

Parameters

interp

Interpolator on which to claim a lane. interp0 or interp1.

lane

The lane number, 0 or 1.

interp_claim_lane_mask()

```
void interp_claim_lane_mask (interp_hw_t *interp,
        uint lane_mask)
```

Claim the interpolator lanes specified in the mask.

Parameters

interp

Interpolator on which to claim lanes. interp0 or interp1.

lane_mask

Bit pattern of lanes to claim (only bits 0 and 1 are valid).

interp_config_set_add_raw()   **Inline Static**

```
static void interp_config_set_add_raw (interp_config *c,
        bool add_raw)
```

Set raw add option. When enabled, mask + shift is bypassed for LANE0 result. This does not affect the FULL result.

Parameters

c	Pointer to interpolation config.
add_raw	If true, enable raw add option.

interp_config_set_blend()   Inline Static

```
static void interp_config_set_blend (interp_config *c,
        bool blend)
```

This function is used to set the blend mode for the interpolator. The blend mode determines how the interpolation results are calculated. Here's a description of each aspect:

If enabled, the LANE1 result is computed as a linear interpolation between BASE0 and BASE1. The interpolation is controlled by the 8 least significant bits (LSBs) of the lane 1 shift and mask value, which represents a fractional number between 0 and 255/256ths.

The LANE0 result does not include BASE0 in the calculation. It only consists of the 8 LSBs of the lane 1 shift+mask value.

The FULL result does not include the lane 1 shift+mask value in the calculation. It is the sum of BASE2 and the lane 0 shift+mask.

The LANE1 SIGNED flag determines whether the interpolation is performed with signed or unsigned values. It controls whether the interpolation takes into account the signedness of the data being interpolated.

Parameters

c

Pointer to interpolation config.

blend

Set true to enable blend mode.

interp_config_set_clamp()

```
static void interp_config_set_clamp (interp_config *c,
        bool clamp)
```

Set interpolator clamp mode (Interpolator 1 only).

Only present on INTERP1 on each core. If CLAMP mode is enabled:

LANE0 result is a shifted and masked ACCUM0, clamped by a lower bound of BASE0 and an upper bound of BASE1.

Signedness of these comparisons is determined by LANE0_CTRL_SIGNED.

Parameters

c

Pointer to interpolation config.

clamp

Set true to enable clamp mode.

interp_config_set_cross_input()   Inline Static

```
static void interp_config_set_cross_input
        (interp_config *c, bool cross_input)
```

Enable cross input. Allows feeding of the accumulator content from the other lane back in to this lanes shift+mask hardware. This will take effect even if the interp_config_set_add_raw option is set as the cross input mux is before the shift+mask bypass.

Parameters

c

Pointer to interpolation config.

cross_input

If true, enable the cross input.

interp_config_set_cross_result()   Inline Static

```
static void interp_config_set_cross_result
        (interp_config *c, bool cross_result)
```

Enable cross results. Allows feeding of the other lane's result into this lane's accumulator on a POP operation.

Parameters

c

Pointer to interpolation config.

cross_result

If true, enables the cross result.

interp_config_set_force_bits() Inline Static

```
static void interp_config_set_force_bits (interp_config *c,
        uint bits)
```

Set interpolator Force bits. ORed into bits 29:28 of the lane result presented to the processor on the bus. No effect on the internal 32-bit datapath. Handy for using a lane to generate sequence of pointers into flash or SRAM.

Parameters

c

Pointer to interpolation config.

bits

Sets the force bits to that specified. Range 0-3 (two bits).

interp_config_set_mask() Inline Static

```
static void interp_config_set_mask (interp_config *c,
        uint mask_lsb, uint mask_msb)
```

Set the interpolator mask range. Sets the range of bits (least to most) that are allowed to pass through the interpolator.

Parameters

c

Pointer to interpolation config.

mask_lsb

The least significant bit allowed to pass.

mask_msb

The most significant bit allowed to pass.

interp_config_set_shift()   Inline Static

```
static void interp_config_set_shift(interp_config *c,
        uint shift)
```

Set the interpolator shift value. Sets the number of bits the accumulator is shifted before masking, on each iteration.

Parameters

c

Pointer to interpolation config.

shift

Number of bits

interp_config_set_signed()

```
static void interp_config_set_signed(interp_config *c,
        bool _signed)
```

Set sign extension. Enables signed mode, where the shifted and masked accumulator value is sign-extended to 32 bits before adding to BASE1, and LANE1 PEEK/POP results appear extended to 32 bits when read by processor.

Parameters

c

Pointer to interpolation config.

_signed

If true, enables sign extension.

interp_default_config()   Inline Static

```
static interp_config interp_default_config(void)
```

Get a default configuration.

Returns

A default interpolation configuration.

interp_set_config()   Inline Static

```
static void interp_set_config (interp_hw_t *interp,
        uint lane, interp_config *config)
```

Send configuration to a lane. If an invalid configuration is specified (ie a lane specific item is set on wrong lane), depending on setup this function can panic.

Parameters

interp

Interpolator instance, interp0 or interp1.

lane

The lane to set.

config

Pointer to interpolation config.

interp_get_accumulator()

```
static uint32_t interp_get_accumulator
        (interp_hw_t *interp, uint lane)
```

Gets the content of the interpolator accumulator register by lane.

Parameters

interp

Interpolator instance, interp0 or interp1.

lane

The lane number, 0 or 1.

Returns

The current content of the register.

interp_get_base()   Inline Static

```
static uint32_t interp_get_base (interp_hw_t *interp,
        uint lane)
```

Gets the content of interpolator base register by lane.

Parameters

interp

Interpolator instance, interp0 or interp1.

lane

The lane number, 0 or 1 or 2.

Returns

The current content of the lane base register.

interp_get_raw()   Inline Static

```
static uint32_t interp_get_raw(interp_hw_t *interp,
        uint lane)
```

Get raw lane value. Returns the raw shift and mask value from the specified lane, BASE0 is NOT added.

Parameters

interp

Interpolator instance, interp0 or interp1.

lane

The lane number, 0 or 1.

Returns

The raw shift/mask value.

interp_lane_is_claimed()

```
bool interp_lane_is_claimed(interp_hw_t *interp,
        uint lane)
```

Determine if an interpolator lane is claimed. See also interp_claim_lane and interp_claim_lane_mask.

Parameters

interp

Interpolator whose lane to check.

lane

The lane number, 0 or 1.

Returns

True if claimed, false otherwise.

interp_peek_full_result()   Inline Static

```
static uint32_t interp_peek_full_result
        (interp_hw_t *interp)
```

Read lane result.

Parameters

interp

Interpolator instance, interp0 or interp1.

Returns

The content of the FULL register.

interp_peek_lane_result()   **Inline Static**

```
static uint32_t interp_peek_lane_result
        (interp_hw_t *interp, uint lane)
```

Read lane result.

Parameters

interp

Interpolator instance, interp0 or interp1.

lane

The lane number, 0 or 1.

Returns

The content of the lane result register.

interp_pop_full_result()   **Inline Static**

```
static uint32_t interp_pop_full_result
        (interp_hw_t *interp)
```

Read lane result, and write lane results to both accumulators to update the interpolator.

Parameters

interp

Interpolator instance, interp0 or interp1.

Returns

The content of the FULL register.

interp_pop_lane_result()   Inline Static

```
static uint32_t interp_pop_lane_result(interp_hw_t
        *interp, uint lane)
```

Read lane result, and write lane results to both accumulators to update the interpolator.

Parameters

interp	Interpolator instance, interp0 or interp1.
lane	The lane number, 0 or 1.

Returns

The content of the lane result register.

interp_restore()

```
void interp_restore(interp_hw_t *interp,
        interp_hw_save_t *saver)
```

Restore an interpolator state.

Parameters

interp	Interpolator instance, interp0 or interp1.
saver	Pointer to save structure to reapply to the specified interpolator.

interp_save()

```
void interp_save (interp_hw_t *interp,
        interp_hw_save_t *saver)
```

Save the specified interpolator state. Can be used to save state if you need an interpolator for another purpose, state can then be recovered afterwards and continue from that point.

Parameters

interp	Interpolator instance, interp0 or interp1.
saver	Pointer to the save structure to fill in.

interp_set_accumulator() Inline Static

```
static void interp_set_accumulator(interp_hw_t *interp,
        uint lane, uint32_t val)
```

Sets the interpolator accumulator register by lane.

Parameters

interp	Interpolator instance, interp0 or interp1.
lane	The lane number, 0 or 1.
val	The value to apply to the register.

interp_set_base() Inline Static

```
static void interp_set_base(interp_hw_t *interp,
        uint lane, uint32_t val)
```

Sets the interpolator base register by lane.

Parameters

interp	Interpolator instance, interp0 or interp1.
lane	The lane number, 0 or 1 or 2.
val	The value to apply to the register.

interp_set_base_both() Inline Static

```
static void interp_set_base_both (interp_hw_t *interp,
        uint32_t val)
```

Sets the interpolator base registers simultaneously. The lower 16 bits go to BASE0, upper bits to BASE1 simultaneously. Each half is sign-extended to 32 bits if that lane's SIGNED flag is set.

Parameters

interp	Interpolator instance, interp0 or interp1.
val	The value to apply to the register.

interp_set_force_bits()   Inline Static

```
static void interp_set_force_bits (interp_hw_t *interp,
        uint lane, uint bits)
```

Directly set the force bits on a specified lane. These bits are ORed into bits 29:28 of the lane result presented to the processor on the bus. There is no effect on the internal 32-bit datapath. Useful for using a lane to generate sequence of pointers into flash or SRAM, saving a subsequent OR or add operation.

Parameters

interp	Interpolator instance, interp0 or interp1.
lane	The lane to set.
bits	The bits to set (bits 0 and 1, value range 0-3).

interp_unclaim_lane()

```
void interp_unclaim_lane (interp_hw_t *interp, uint lane)
```

Release a previously claimed interpolator lane.

Parameters

interp	Interpolator on which to release a lane. interp0 or interp1.
lane	The lane number, 0 or 1.

interp_unclaim_lane_mask()

```
void interp_unclaim_lane_mask (interp_hw_t *interp,
        uint lane_mask)
```

Release previously claimed interpolator lanes.See also interp_claim_lane_mask.

Parameters

interp	Interpolator on which to release lanes. interp0 or interp1.
lane_mask	Bit pattern of lanes to unclaim (only bits 0 and 1 are valid).

IRQ – INTERUPT REQUEST

hardware_irq

```
#include "hardware/irq.h"
```

Hardware interrupt handling. The RP2040 uses the standard ARM nested vectored interrupt controller (NVIC). Interrupts are identified by a number from 0 to 31.

On the RP2040, only the lower 26 IRQ signals are connected on the NVIC; IRQs 26 to 31 are tied to zero (never firing). There is one NVIC per core, and each core's NVIC has the same hardware interrupt lines routed to it, with the exception of the IO interrupts where there is one IO interrupt per bank, per core. These are completely independent, so, for example, processor 0 can be interrupted by GPIO 0 in bank 0, and processor 1 by GPIO 1 in the same bank. *NOTE That all IRQ APIs affect the executing core only (i.e. the core calling the function).*

You should not enable the same (shared) IRQ number on both cores, as this will lead to race conditions or starvation of one of the cores. Additionally, don't forget that disabling interrupts on one core does not disable interrupts on the other core.

There are three different ways to set handlers for an IRQ:

1. Calling irq_add_shared_handler() at runtime to add a handler for a multiplexed interrupt (e.g. GPIO bank) on the current core. Each handler, should check and clear the relevant hardware interrupt source

2. Calling irq_set_exclusive_handler() at runtime to install a single handler for the interrupt on the current core

3. Defining the interrupt handler explicitly in your application (e.g. by defining void isr_dma_0 will make that function the handler for the DMA_IRQ_0 on core 0, and you will not be able to change it using the above APIs at runtime). Using this method can cause link conflicts at runtime, and offers no runtime performance benefit (i.e, it should not generally be used).

NOTE If an IRQ is enabled and fires with no handler installed, a breakpoint will be hit and the IRQ number will be in register r0.

INTERRUPT NUMBERS

Interrupts are numbered as follows, a set of defines is available (intctrl.h) with these names to avoid using the numbers directly.

IRQ	Interrupt Source	IRQ	Interrupt Source
0	TIMER_IRQ_0	13	IO_IRQ_BANK0
1	TIMER_IRQ_1	14	IO_IRQ_QSPI
2	TIMER_IRQ_2	15	SIO_IRQ_PROC0
3	TIMER_IRQ_3	16	SIO_IRQ_PROC1
4	PWM_IRQ_WRAP	17	CLOCKS_IRQ
5	USBCTRL_IRQ	18	SPI0_IRQ
6	XIP_IRQ	19	SPI1_IRQ
7	PIO0_IRQ_0	20	UART0_IRQ
8	PIO0_IRQ_1	21	UART1_IRQ
9	PIO1_IRQ_0	22	ADC0_IRQ_FIFO
10	PIO1_IRQ_1	23	I2C0_IRQ
11	DMA_IRQ_0	24	I2C1_IRQ
12	DMA_IRQ_1	25	RTC_IRQ

TYPEDEFS

irq_handler_t

```
typedef void(*irq_handler_t) (void)
```

Interrupt handler function type. All interrupts handlers should be of this type, and follow normal ARM EABI register saving conventions.

FUNCTIONS

irq_add_shared_handler()

```
void irq_add_shared_handler (uint num,
          irq_handler_t handler, uint8_t order_priority)
```

Add a shared interrupt handler for an interrupt on the executing core. Use this method to add a handler on an irq number shared between multiple distinct hardware sources (e.g. GPIO, DMA or PIO IRQs). Handlers added by this method will all be called in sequence from highest order_priority to lowest. The irq_set_exclusive_handler() method should be used instead if you know there will or should only ever be one handler for the interrupt.

This method will assert if there is an exclusive interrupt handler set for this irq number on this core, or if the (total across all IRQs on both cores) maximum (configurable via PICO_MAX_SHARED_IRQ_HANDLERS) number of shared handlers would be exceeded.

NOTE The order_priority uses higher values for higher priorities which is the opposite of the CPU interrupt priorities passed to irq_set_priority() which use lower values for higher priorities.

See also irq_set_exclusive_handler()

Parameters

num

Interrupt number Interrupt Numbers.

handler

The handler to set. See irq_handler_t.

order_priority

The order priority controls the order that handlers for the same IRQ number on the core are called. The shared irq handlers for an interrupt are all called when an IRQ fires, however the order of the calls is based on the order_priority (higher priorities are called first, identical priorities are called in undefined order). A good rule of thumb is to use PICO_SHARED_IRQ_HANDLER_DEFAULT_ORDER_PRIORITY if you don't much care, as it is in the middle of the priority range by default.

irq_clear()   Inline Static

```
static void irq_clear(uint int_num)
```

Clear a specific interrupt on the executing core. This method is only useful for "software" IRQs that are not connected to hardware (i.e. IRQs 26-31) as the the NVIC always reflects the current state of the IRQ state of the hardware for hardware IRQs, and clearing of the IRQ state of the hardware is performed via the hardware's registers instead.

Parameters

    int_num   Interrupt number.

irq_get_exclusive_handler()

```
irq_handler_t irq_get_exclusive_handler(uint num)
```

Get the exclusive interrupt handler for an interrupt on the executing core. This method will return an exclusive IRQ handler set on this core by irq_set_exclusive_handler if there is one. See also irq_set_exclusive_handler().

Parameters

    num   Interrupt number.

Returns

        The handler if an exclusive handler is set for the IRQ, NULL if no handler is set or shared/shareable handlers are installed.

irq_get_priority()

```
uint irq_get_priority(uint num)
```

Get specified interrupt's priority. Numerically-lower values indicate a higher priority. Hardware priorities range from 0 (highest priority) to 255 (lowest priority) though only the top 2 bits are significant on ARM Cortex-M0+. To make it easier to specify higher or lower priorities than the default, all IRQ priorities are initialized to PICO_DEFAULT_IRQ_PRIORITY by the SDK runtime at startup. PICO_DEFAULT_IRQ_PRIORITY defaults to 0x80

Parameters

num

Interrupt number.

Returns

The IRQ priority.

irq_get_vtable_handler()

```
irq_handler_t irq_get_vtable_handler(uint num)
```

Get the current IRQ handler for the specified IRQ from the currently installed hardware vector table (VTOR) of the execution core.

Parameters

num

Interrupt number.

Returns

The address stored in the VTABLE for the given irq number.

irq_has_shared_handler()

```
bool irq_has_shared_handler(uint num)
```

Determine if the current handler for the given number is shared.

Parameters

num

Interrupt number.

Returns

Tue if the specified IRQ has a shared handler.

irq_is_enabled()

```
bool irq_is_enabled(uint num)
```

Determine if a specific interrupt is enabled on the executing core.

Parameters

num

Interrupt number.

Returns

True if the interrupt is enabled.

irq_remove_handler()

```
void irq_remove_handler(uint num, irq_handler_t handler)
```

Remove a specific interrupt handler for the given irq number on the executing core. This method may be used to remove an irq set via either irq_set_exclusive_handler() or irq_add_shared_handler(), and will assert if the handler is not currently installed for the given IRQ number. See also irq_set_exclusive_handler() irq_add_shared_handler().

NOTE This method may only be called from user (non IRQ code) or from within the handler itself (i.e. an IRQ handler may remove itself as part of handling the IRQ). Attempts to call from another IRQ will cause an assertion.

Parameters

num

Interrupt number.

handler

The handler to removed.

irq_set_enabled()

```
void irq_set_enabled(uint num, bool enabled)
```

Enable or disable a specific interrupt on the executing core.

Parameters

num

Interrupt number.

enabled

True to enable the interrupt, false to disable

irq_set_exclusive_handler()

```
void irq_set_exclusive_handler(uint num,
       irq_handler_t handler)
```

Set an exclusive interrupt handler for an interrupt on the executing core. Use this method to set a handler for single IRQ source interrupts, or when your code, use case or performance requirements dictate that there should no other handlers for the interrupt. This method will assert if there is already any sort of interrupt handler installed for the specified irq number. See also irq_add_shared_handler().

Parameters

num

Interrupt number.

handler

The handler to set. See irq_handler_t.

irq_set_mask_enabled()

```
void irq_set_mask_enabled(uint32_t mask, bool enabled)
```

Enable/disable multiple interrupts on the executing core.

Parameters

mask

32-bit mask with one bits set for the interrupts to enable/disable Interrupt Numbers.

enabled

True to enable the interrupts, false to disable them.

irq_set_pending()

```
void irq_set_pending(uint num)
```

Force an interrupt to be pending on the executing core. This should generally not be used for IRQs connected to hardware.

Parameters

num   Interrupt number.

irq_set_priority()

```
void irq_set_priority(uint num, uint8_t hardware_priority)
```

Set specified interrupt's priority.

Parameters

num   Interrupt number.

hardware_priority

Priority to set. Numerically-lower values indicate a higher priority. Hardware priorities range from 0 (highest priority) to 255 (lowest priority) though only the top 2 bits are significant on ARM Cortex-M0+. To make it easier to specify higher or lower priorities than the default, all IRQ priorities are initialized to PICO_DEFAULT_IRQ_PRIORITY by the SDK runtime at startup. PICO_DEFAULT_IRQ_PRIORITY defaults to 0x80.

user_irq_claim()

```
void user_irq_claim(uint irq_num)
```

Claim ownership of a user IRQ on the calling core. User IRQs are numbered 26-31 and are not connected to any hardware, but can be triggered by irq_set_pending. This method explicitly claims ownership of a user IRQ, so other code can know it is being used.

NOTE User IRQs are a core local feature; they cannot be used to communicate between cores. Therefore all functions dealing with Uer IRQs affect only the calling core.

Parameters

irq_num

The user IRQ to claim.

user_irq_claim_unused()

```
int user_irq_claim_unused(bool required)
```

Claim ownership of a free user IRQ on the calling core. User IRQs are numbered 26-31 and are not connected to any hardware, but can be triggered by irq_set_pending. This method explicitly claims ownership of an unused user IRQ if there is one, so other code can know it is being used.

NOTE User IRQs are a core local feature; they cannot be used to communicate between cores. Therfore all functions dealing with Uer IRQs affect only the calling core.

Parameters

required

If true the function will panic if none are available.

Returns

The user IRQ number or -1 if required was false, and none were free.

user_irq_unclaim()

```
void user_irq_unclaim(uint irq_num)
```

Mark a user IRQ as no longer used on the calling core. User IRQs are numbered 26-31 and are not connected to any hardware, but can be triggered by irq_set_pending. This method explicitly releases ownership of a user IRQ, so other code can know it is free to use.

NOTE User IRQs are a core local feature; they cannot be used to communicate between cores. Therfore all functions dealing with Uer IRQs affect only the calling core.

NOTE it is customary to have disabled the irq and removed the handler prior to calling this method.

Parameters

irq_num

The irq irq_num to unclaim.

PIO – PROGRAMMABLE IO

hardware_pio

```
#include "hardware/pio.h"
```

Programmable I/O (PIO) API. A programmable input/output block (PIO) is a versatile hardware interface which can support a number of different IO standards. There are two PIO blocks in the RP2040.

Each PIO is programmable in the same sense as a processor: the four state machines independently execute short, sequential programs, to manipulate GPIOs and transfer data. Unlike a general purpose processor, PIO state machines are highly specialized for IO, with a focus on determinism, precise timing, and close integration with fixed-function hardware. Each state machine is equipped with:

- **Two** 32-bit shift registers – either direction, any shift count.
- **Two** 32-bit scratch registers.
- **4×32** bit bus FIFO in each direction (TX/RX), re-configurable as 8×32 in a single direction.
- **Fractional** clock divider (16 integer, 8 fractional bits).
- **Flexible** GPIO mapping.
- **DMA** interface, sustained throughput up to 1 word per clock from system DMA.
- **IRQ** flag set/clear/status.

Full details of the PIO can be found in the RP2040 datasheet.

MACROS

pio0

```
#define pio0    pio0_hw
```

Identifier for the first (PIO 0) hardware PIO instance (for use in PIO functions). e.g. pio_gpio_init(pio0, 5).

pio1

```
#define pio1    pio1_hw
```

Identifier for the second (PIO 1) hardware PIO instance (for use in PIO functions). e.g. pio_gpio_init(pio1, 5).

TYPEDEFS

typedef pio_hw_t

```
typedef pio_hw_t *PIO;
```

By defining PIO as pio_hw_t *, it becomes a more convenient and readable way to declare variables or parameters that point to PIO hardware objects.

STRUCTURES

struct pio_sm_config

This data structure is used to configure the state machine (SM) of the Programmable I/O (PIO) peripheral. It contains several fields that define various settings for the state machine.

uint32_t clkdiv;

This field sets the clock divider for the state machine. It determines the frequency of the state machine's clock signal relative to the system clock. The value stored in this field specifies the integer and fractional parts of the clock divider.

uint32_t execctrl;

This field configures the execution control of the state machine. It controls the flow of instructions and execution behavior of the state machine. It includes settings such as whether to enable the state machine, how to handle instructions and branches, and the delay between instructions.

uint32_t shiftctrl;

This field determines the behavior of the shift registers in the state machine. It specifies the shift direction (input or output), the shift format (left or right), and the shift count. The shift registers are used to input or output data to or from the state machine.

uint32_t pinctrl;

This field configures the input and output pin behavior of the state machine. It controls the mapping of state machine pins to physical GPIO pins and specifies the pin mode (input, output, or function select). It also includes settings for pull-up and pull-down resistors and pin slew rate.

ENUMERATIONS

pio_fifo_join

```
enum  pio_fifo_join
```

FIFO join states.

PIO_FIFO_JOIN_NONE	= 0
PIO_FIFO_JOIN_TX	= 1
PIO_FIFO_JOIN_RX	= 2

pio_interrupt_source

```
enum  pio_interrupt_source
```

PIO interrupt source numbers for pio related IRQs.

pis_interrupt0	= PIO_INTR_SM0_LSB
pis_interrupt1	= PIO_INTR_SM1_LSB
pis_interrupt2	= PIO_INTR_SM2_LSB
pis_interrupt3	= PIO_INTR_SM3_LSB
pis_sm0_tx_fifo_not_full	= PIO_INTR_SM0_TXNFULL_LSB
pis_sm1_tx_fifo_not_full	= PIO_INTR_SM1_TXNFULL_LSB
pis_sm2_tx_fifo_not_full	= PIO_INTR_SM2_TXNFULL_LSB
pis_sm3_tx_fifo_not_full	= PIO_INTR_SM3_TXNFULL_LSB
pis_sm0_rx_fifo_not_empty	= PIO_INTR_SM0_RXNEMPTY_LSB
pis_sm1_rx_fifo_not_empty	= PIO_INTR_SM1_RXNEMPTY_LSB
pis_sm2_rx_fifo_not_empty	= PIO_INTR_SM2_RXNEMPTY_LSB
pis_sm3_rx_fifo_not_empty	= PIO_INTR_SM3_RXNEMPTY_LSB

pio_mov_status_type

```
enum  pio_mov_status_type
```

MOV status types.

STATUS_TX_LESSTHAN	= 0
STATUS_RX_LESSTHAN	= 1

pio_src_dest

`enum pio_src_dest`

Enumeration of values to pass for source/destination args for instruction encoding functions.

NOTE Not all values are suitable for all functions. Validity is only checked in debug mode when PARAM_ASSERTIONS_ENABLED_PIO_INSTRUCTIONS is 1.

pio_pins	= 0u
pio_x	= 1u
pio_y	= 2u
pio_null	= 3u | 0x20u | 0x80u
pio_pindirs	= 4u | 0x08u | 0x40u | 0x80u
pio_exec_mov	= 4u | 0x08u | 0x10u | 0x20u | 0x40u
pio_status	= 5u | 0x08u | 0x10u | 0x20u | 0x80u
pio_pc	= 5u | 0x08u | 0x20u | 0x40u
pio_isr	= 6u | 0x20u
pio_osr	= 7u | 0x10u | 0x20u
pio_exec_out	= 7u | 0x08u | 0x20u | 0x40u | 0x80u

FUNCTIONS

pio_add_program()

```
uint pio_add_program(PIO pio,
        const pio_program_t *program)
```

Attempt to load the program, panicking if not possible. See also pio_can_add_program() if you need to check whether the program can be loaded.

Parameters

pio	The PIO instance; either pio0 or pio1.
program	The program definition.

Returns

the instruction memory offset the program is loaded at

pio_add_program_at_offset()

```
void pio_add_program_at_offset(PIO pio,
        const pio_program_t *program, uint offset)
```

Attempt to load the program at the specified instruction memory offset, panicking if not possible. See also pio_can_add_program_at_offset() if you need to check whether the program can be loaded.

Parameters

pio

The PIO instance; either pio0 or pio1.

program

The program definition.

offset

The instruction memory offset wanted for the start of the program.

pio_can_add_program()

```
bool pio_can_add_program(PIO pio,
        const pio_program_t *program)
```

Determine whether the given program can (at the time of the call) be loaded onto the PIO instance.

Parameters

pio

The PIO instance; either pio0 or pio1.

program

The program definition.

Returns

True if the program can be loaded; false if there is not suitable space in the instruction memory.

pio_can_add_program_at_offset()

```
bool pio_can_add_program_at_offset(PIO pio,
        const pio_program_t *program, uint offset)
```

Determine whether the given program can (at the time of the call) be loaded onto the PIO instance starting at a particular location.

Parameters

pio

The PIO instance; either pio0 or pio1.

program

The program definition.

offset

The instruction memory offset wanted for the start of the program.

Returns

True if the program can be loaded at that location; false if there is not space in the instruction memory.

pio_claim_sm_mask()

```
void pio_claim_sm_mask(PIO pio, uint sm_mask)
```

Mark multiple state machines as used. Method for cooperative claiming of hardware. Will cause a panic if any of the state machines are already claimed. Use of this method by libraries detects accidental configurations that would fail in unpredictable ways.

Parameters

pio

The PIO instance; either pio0 or pio1.

sm_mask

Mask of state machine indexes.

pio_claim_unused_sm()

```
int pio_claim_unused_sm(PIO pio, bool required)
```

Claim a free state machine on a PIO instance.

Parameters

pio

The PIO instance; either pio0 or pio1.

required

If true the function will panic if none are available.

Returns

The state machine index or -1 if required was false, and none were free.

pio_clear_instruction_memory()

```
void pio_clear_instruction_memory(PIO pio)
```

Clears all of a PIO instance's instruction memory.

Parameters

pio

The PIO instance; either pio0 or pio1.

pio_clkdiv_restart_sm_mask()   Inline Static

```
static void pio_clkdiv_restart_sm_mask(PIO pio,
        uint32_t mask)
```

Restart multiple state machines' clock dividers from a phase of 0. Each state machine's clock divider is a free-running piece of hardware, that generates a pattern of clock enable pulses for the state machine, based only on the configured integer/fractional divisor. The pattern of running/halted cycles slows the state machine's execution to some controlled rate.

This function simultaneously clears the integer and fractional phase accumulators of multiple state machines' clock dividers. If these state machines all have the same integer and fractional divisors configured, their clock dividers will run in precise deterministic lockstep from this point.

With their execution clocks synchronized in this way, it is then safe to e.g. have multiple state machines performing a 'wait irq' on the same flag, and all clear it on the same cycle.

Also note that this function can be called whilst state machines are running (e.g. if you have just changed the clock divisors of some state machines and wish to synchronize them), and that disabling a state machine does not halt its clock divider: that is, if multiple state machines have their clocks synchronized, you can safely disable and reenable one of the state machines without losing synchronization.

Parameters

pio

The PIO instance; either pio0 or pio1.

mask

Bit mask of state machine indexes to modify the enabled state of.

The Pico C API Functionary

pio_enable_sm_mask_in_sync()   Inline Static

```
static void pio_enable_sm_mask_in_sync(PIO pio, uint32_t
      mask)
```

Enable multiple PIO state machines synchronizing their clock dividers. This is equivalent to calling both pio_set_sm_mask_enabled() and pio_clkdiv_restart_sm_mask() on the same clock cycle. All state machines specified by 'mask' are started simultaneously and, assuming they have the same clock divisors, their divided clocks will stay precisely synchronized.

Parameters

pio

The PIO instance; either pio0 or pio1.

mask

Bit mask of state machine indexes to modify the enabled state of.

pio_encode_delay()   Inline Static

```
static uint pio_encode_delay(uint cycles)
```

Encode just the delay slot bits of an instruction.

NOTE This function does not return a valid instruction encoding; instead it returns an encoding of the delay slot suitable for ORing with the result of an encoding function for an actual instruction. Care should be taken when combining the results of this function with the results of pio_encode_sideset and pio_encode_sideset_opt as they share the same bits within the instruction encoding.

Parameters

cycles

The number of cycles 0-31 (or less if side set is being used).

Returns

The delay slot bits to be ORed with an instruction encoding.

pio_encode_in()   Inline Static

```
static uint pio_encode_in(enum pio_src_dest src,
        uint count)
```

Encode an IN instruction. This is the equivalent of IN <src>, <count>

See also pio_encode_delay, pio_encode_sideset, pio_encode_sideset_opt.

Parameters

src

> The source to take data from.

count

> The number of bits 1-32.

Returns

> The instruction encoding with 0 delay and no side set value.

pio_encode_irq_clear()   Inline Static

```
static uint pio_encode_irq_clear(bool relative, uint irq)
```

Encode a IRQ CLEAR instruction.

This is the equivalent of IRQ CLEAR <irq> <relative>

See also pio_encode_delay, pio_encode_sideset, pio_encode_sideset_opt.

Parameters

relative

> True for a IRQ CLEAR <irq> REL, false for regular IRQ CLEAR <irq>.

irq

> The irq number 0-7.

Returns

> The instruction encoding with 0 delay and no side set value.

pio_encode_irq_set()   Inline Static

```
static uint pio_encode_irq_set(bool relative, uint irq)
```

Encode a IRQ SET instruction.

This is the equivalent of IRQ SET <irq> <relative>

See also pio_encode_delay, pio_encode_sideset, pio_encode_sideset_opt.

Parameters

relative

True for a IRQ SET <irq> REL, false for regular IRQ SET <irq>

irq

The irq number 0-7.

Returns

The instruction encoding with 0 delay and no side set value.

pio_encode_irq_wait()   Inline Static

```
static uint pio_encode_irq_wait(bool relative, uint irq)
```

Encode a IRQ WAIT instruction.

This is the equivalent of IRQ WAIT <irq> <relative>

See also pio_encode_delay, pio_encode_sideset, pio_encode_sideset_opt.

Parameters

relative

True for a IRQ SET <irq> REL, false for regular IRQ SET <irq>

irq

The irq number 0-7.

Returns

The instruction encoding with 0 delay and no side set value.

pio_encode_jmp() **Inline Static**

```
static uint pio_encode_jmp(uint addr)
```

Encode an unconditional JMP instruction.

This is the equivalent of JMP <addr>

See also pio_encode_delay, pio_encode_sideset, pio_encode_sideset_opt.

Parameters

addr

> The target address 0-31 (an absolute address within the PIO instruction memory).

Returns

> The instruction encoding with 0 delay and no side set value.

pio_encode_jmp_not_osre() **Inline Static**

```
static uint pio_encode_jmp_not_osre(uint addr)
```

Encode a conditional JMP if output shift register not empty instruction.

This is the equivalent of JMP !OSRE <addr>

See also pio_encode_delay, pio_encode_sideset, pio_encode_sideset_opt.

Parameters

addr

> The target address 0-31 (an absolute address within the PIO instruction memory).

Returns

> The instruction encoding with 0 delay and no side set value.

pio_encode_jmp_not_x()   Inline Static

```
static uint pio_encode_jmp_not_x(uint addr)
```

Encode a conditional JMP if scratch X zero instruction.

This is the equivalent of JMP !X <addr>

See also pio_encode_delay, pio_encode_sideset, pio_encode_sideset_opt.

Parameters

addr

> The target address 0-31 (an absolute address within the PIO instruction memory).

Returns

> The instruction encoding with 0 delay and no side set value.

pio_encode_jmp_not_y()   Inline Static

```
static uint pio_encode_jmp_not_y(uint addr)
```

Encode a conditional JMP if scratch Y zero instruction.

This is the equivalent of JMP !Y <addr>

See also pio_encode_delay, pio_encode_sideset, pio_encode_sideset_opt.

Parameters

addr

> The target address 0-31 (an absolute address within the PIO instruction memory).

Returns

> The instruction encoding with 0 delay and no side set value.

pio_encode_jmp_pin()   Inline Static

```
static uint pio_encode_jmp_pin(uint addr)
```

Encode a conditional JMP if input pin high instruction.

This is the equivalent of JMP PIN <addr>

See also pio_encode_delay, pio_encode_sideset, pio_encode_sideset_opt.

Parameters

addr

> The target address 0-31 (an absolute address within the PIO instruction memory).

Returns

> The instruction encoding with 0 delay and no side set value.

pio_encode_jmp_x_dec()   Inline Static

```
static uint pio_encode_jmp_x_dec(uint addr)
```

Encode a conditional JMP if scratch X non-zero (and post-decrement X) instruction.

This is the equivalent of JMP X-- <addr>

See also pio_encode_delay, pio_encode_sideset, pio_encode_sideset_opt.

Parameters

addr

> The target address 0-31 (an absolute address within the PIO instruction memory).

Returns

> The instruction encoding with 0 delay and no side set value.

pio_encode_jmp_x_ne_y()   Inline Static

```
static uint pio_encode_jmp_x_ne_y(uint addr)
```

Encode a conditional JMP if scratch X not equal scratch Y instruction.

This is the equivalent of JMP X!=Y <addr>

See also pio_encode_delay, pio_encode_sideset, pio_encode_sideset_opt.

Parameters

addr

> The target address 0-31 (an absolute address within the PIO instruction memory).

Returns

> The instruction encoding with 0 delay and no side set value.

pio_encode_jmp_y_dec()   Inline Static

```
static uint pio_encode_jmp_y_dec(uint addr)
```

Encode a conditional JMP if scratch Y non-zero (and post-decrement Y) instruction.

This is the equivalent of JMP Y-- <addr>

See also pio_encode_delay, pio_encode_sideset, pio_encode_sideset_opt.

Parameters

addr

> The target address 0-31 (an absolute address within the PIO instruction memory).

Returns

> The instruction encoding with 0 delay and no side set value.

pio_encode_mov()   Inline Static

```
static uint pio_encode_mov(enum pio_src_dest dest,
          enum pio_src_dest src)
```

Encode a MOV instruction.

This is the equivalent of MOV <dest>, <src>

See also pio_encode_delay, pio_encode_sideset, pio_encode_sideset_opt.

Parameters

dest

> The destination to write data to.

src

> The source to take data from.

Returns

> The instruction encoding with 0 delay and no side set value.

pio_encode_mov_not()   Inline Static

```
static uint pio_encode_mov_not(enum pio_src_dest dest,
          enum pio_src_dest src)
```

Encode a MOV instruction with bit invert.

This is the equivalent of MOV <dest>, ~<src>

See also pio_encode_delay, pio_encode_sideset, pio_encode_sideset_opt.

Parameters

dest	The destination to write inverted data to.
src	The source to take data from.

Returns

> The instruction encoding with 0 delay and no side set value.

pio_encode_mov_reverse()   Inline Static

```
static uint pio_encode_mov_reverse(enum pio_src_dest dest,
            enum pio_src_dest src)
```

Encode a MOV instruction with bit reverse.

This is the equivalent of MOV <dest>, ::<src>

See also pio_encode_delay, pio_encode_sideset, pio_encode_sideset_opt.

Parameters

dest

The destination to write bit reversed data to.

src

The source to take data from.

Returns

The instruction encoding with 0 delay and no side set value.

pio_encode_nop()   Inline Static

```
static uint pio_encode_nop(void )
```

Encode a NOP instruction.

This is the equivalent of NOP which is itself encoded as MOV y, y

See also pio_encode_delay, pio_encode_sideset, pio_encode_sideset_opt.

Returns

The instruction encoding with 0 delay and no side set value.

pio_encode_out()   Inline Static

```
static uint pio_encode_out(enum pio_src_dest dest,
        uint count)
```

Encode an OUT instruction.

This is the equivalent of OUT <src>, <count>

See also pio_encode_delay, pio_encode_sideset, pio_encode_sideset_opt.

Parameters

dest
> The destination to write data to.

count
> The number of bits 1-32.

Returns

> The instruction encoding with 0 delay and no side set value.

pio_encode_pull()   Inline Static

```
static uint pio_encode_pull(bool if_empty, bool block)
```

Encode a PULL instruction.

This is the equivalent of PULL <if_empty>, <block>

See also pio_encode_delay, pio_encode_sideset, pio_encode_sideset_opt.

Parameters

if_empty
> True for PULL IF_EMPTY ..., false for PULL ...

block
> True for PULL ... BLOCK, false for PULL ...

Returns

> The instruction encoding with 0 delay and no side set value.

pio_encode_push() Inline Static

```
static uint pio_encode_push(bool if_full, bool block)
```

Encode a PUSH instruction.

This is the equivalent of PUSH <if_full>, <block>

See also pio_encode_delay, pio_encode_sideset, pio_encode_sideset_opt.

Parameters

if_full

True for PUSH IF_FULL ..., false for PUSH ...

block

True for PUSH ... BLOCK, false for PUSH ...

Returns

The instruction encoding with 0 delay and no side set value

pio_encode_set() Inline Static

```
static uint pio_encode_set(enum pio_src_dest dest,
        uint value)
```

Encode a SET instruction.

This is the equivalent of SET <dest>, <value>

See also pio_encode_delay, pio_encode_sideset, pio_encode_sideset_opt.

Parameters

dest

The destination to apply the value to.

value

The value 0-31.

Returns

The instruction encoding with 0 delay and no side set value.

pio_encode_sideset()   Inline Static

```
static uint pio_encode_sideset(uint sideset_bit_count,
        uint value)
```

Encode just the side set bits of an instruction (in non optional side set mode)

NOTE This function does not return a valid instruction encoding; instead it returns an encoding of the side set bits suitable for ORing with the result of an encoding function for an actual instruction. Care should be taken when combining the results of this function with the results of pio_encode_delay as they share the same bits within the instruction encoding.

Parameters

sideset_bit_count

Number of side set bits as would be specified via .sideset in pioasm.

value

The value to sideset on the pins.

Returns

The side set bits to be ORed with an instruction encoding.

pio_encode_sideset_opt()   Inline Static

```
static uint pio_encode_sideset_opt(uint sideset_bit_count,
        uint value)
```

Encode just the side set bits of an instruction (in optional -opt side set mode).

NOTE This function does not return a valid instruction encoding; instead it returns an encoding of the side set bits suitable for ORing with the result of an encoding function for an actual instruction. Care should be taken when combining the results of this function with the results of pio_encode_delay as they share the same bits within the instruction encoding.

Parameters

sideset_bit_count

Number of side set bits as would be specified via .sideset <n> opt in pioasm.

value

The value to sideset on the pins.

Returns

The side set bits to be ORed with an instruction encoding.

pio_encode_wait_gpio()   Inline Static

```
static uint pio_encode_wait_gpio(bool polarity, uint gpio)
```

Encode a WAIT for GPIO pin instruction.

This is the equivalent of WAIT <polarity> GPIO <gpio>

See also pio_encode_delay, pio_encode_sideset, pio_encode_sideset_opt.

Parameters

polarity   True for WAIT 1, false for WAIT 0.

gpio   The real GPIO number 0-31.

Returns

The instruction encoding with 0 delay and no side set value.

pio_encode_wait_irq()   **Inline Static**

```
static uint pio_encode_wait_irq(bool polarity,
       bool relative, uint irq)
```

Encode a WAIT for IRQ instruction.

This is the equivalent of WAIT <polarity> IRQ <irq> <relative>

See also pio_encode_delay, pio_encode_sideset, pio_encode_sideset_opt.

Parameters

polarity

True for WAIT 1, false for WAIT 0.

relative

True for a WAIT IRQ <irq> REL, false for regular WAIT IRQ <irq>.

irq

The irq number 0-7.

Returns

The instruction encoding with 0 delay and no side set value

pio_encode_wait_pin()   **Inline Static**

```
static uint pio_encode_wait_pin(bool polarity, uint pin)
```

Encode a WAIT for pin instruction.

This is the equivalent of WAIT <polarity> PIN <pin>

See also pio_encode_delay, pio_encode_sideset, pio_encode_sideset_opt.

Parameters

polarity   True for WAIT 1, false for WAIT 0.

pin   The pin number 0-31 relative to the executing SM's input pin mapping.

Returns

The instruction encoding with 0 delay and no side set value.

pio_get_dreq()   Inline Static

```
static uint pio_get_dreq(PIO pio, uint sm, bool is_tx)
```

Return the DREQ to use for pacing transfers to/from a particular state machine FIFO.

Parameters

pio

> The PIO instance; either pio0 or pio1.

sm

> State machine index (0..3).

is_tx

> true for sending data to the state machine, false for receiving data from the state machine.

pio_get_index()   Inline Static

```
static uint pio_get_index(PIO pio)
```

Return the instance number of a PIO instance.

Parameters

pio

> The PIO instance; either pio0 or pio1.

Returns

> The PIO instance number (either 0 or 1).

pio_gpio_init()   Inline Static

```
static void pio_gpio_init(PIO pio, uint pin)
```

Setup the function select for a GPIO to use output from the given PIO instance. PIO appears as an alternate function in the GPIO muxing, just like an SPI or UART. This function configures that multiplexing to connect a given PIO instance to a GPIO. Note that this is not necessary for a state machine to be able to read the input value from a GPIO, but only for it to set the output value or output enable.

Parameters

pio

> The PIO instance; either pio0 or pio1.

pin

> The GPIO pin whose function select to set.

pio_interrupt_clear()   Inline Static

```
static void pio_interrupt_clear(PIO pio,
        uint pio_interrupt_num)
```

Clear a particular PIO interrupt.

Parameters

pio

> The PIO instance; either pio0 or pio1.

pio_interrupt_num

> The PIO interrupt number 0-7.

pio_interrupt_get() Inline Static

```
static bool pio_interrupt_get(PIO pio,
        uint pio_interrupt_num)
```

Determine if a particular PIO interrupt is set.

Parameters

pio

The PIO instance; either pio0 or pio1.

pio_interrupt_num

The PIO interrupt number 0-7.

Returns

True if corresponding PIO interrupt is currently set.

pio_remove_program()

```
void pio_remove_program(PIO pio,
        const pio_program_t *program, uint loaded_offset)
```

Remove a program from a PIO instance's instruction memory.

Parameters

pio

The PIO instance; either pio0 or pio1.

program

The program definition.

loaded_offset

The loaded offset returned when the program was added.

pio_restart_sm_mask()   Inline Static

```
static void pio_restart_sm_mask(PIO pio, uint32_t mask)
```

Restart multiple state machine with a known state. This method clears the ISR, shift counters, clock divider counter pin write flags, delay counter, latched EXEC instruction, and IRQ wait condition.

Parameters

pio

The PIO instance; either pio0 or pio1.

mask

Bit mask of state machine indexes to modify the enabled state of.

pio_set_irq0_source_enabled()   Inline Static

```
static void pio_set_irq0_source_enabled(PIO pio,
          enum pio_interrupt_source source, bool enabled)
```

Enable/Disable a single source on a PIO's IRQ 0.

Parameters

pio

The PIO instance; either pio0 or pio1.

source

The source number (see pio_interrupt_source).

enabled

True to enable IRQ 0 for the source, false to disable.

pio_set_irq0_source_mask_enabled()   Inline Static

```
static void pio_set_irq0_source_mask_enabled(PIO pio,
        uint32_t source_mask, bool enabled)
```

Enable/Disable multiple sources on a PIO's IRQ 0.

Parameters

pio

The PIO instance; either pio0 or pio1.

source_mask

Mask of bits, one for each source number (see pio_interrupt_source) to affect.

enabled

True to enable all the sources specified in the mask on IRQ 0, false to disable all the sources specified in the mask on IRQ 0.

pio_set_irq1_source_enabled()   Inline Static

```
static void pio_set_irq1_source_enabled(PIO pio,
        enum pio_interrupt_source source, bool enabled)
```

Enable/Disable a single source on a PIO's IRQ 1.

Parameters

pio

The PIO instance; either pio0 or pio1.

source

The source number (see pio_interrupt_source).

enabled

True to enable IRQ 0 for the source, false to disable.

pio_set_irq1_source_mask_enabled()   Inline Static

static void pio_set_irq1_source_mask_enabled(PIO pio, uint32_t source_mask, bool enabled)

Enable/Disable multiple sources on a PIO's IRQ 1.

Parameters

pio

The PIO instance; either pio0 or pio1.

source_mask

Mask of bits, one for each source number (see pio_interrupt_source) to affect

enabled

True to enable all the sources specified in the mask on IRQ 1, false to disable all the source specified in the mask on IRQ 1.

pio_set_irqn_source_enabled()   Inline Static

```
static void pio_set_irqn_source_enabled(PIO pio,
        uint irq_index, enum pio_interrupt_source source,
        bool enabled)
```

Enable/Disable a single source on a PIO's specified (0/1) IRQ index.

Parameters

pio

The PIO instance; either pio0 or pio1.

irq_index

The IRQ index; either 0 or 1.

source

The source number (see pio_interrupt_source).

enabled

True to enable the source on the specified IRQ, false to disable.

pio_set_irqn_source_mask_enabled()   Inline Static

```
static void pio_set_irqn_source_mask_enabled(PIO pio,
          uint irq_index, uint32_t source_mask, bool enabled)
```

Enable/Disable multiple sources on a PIO's specified (0/1) IRQ index.

Parameters

pio

> The PIO instance; either pio0 or pio1.

irq_index

> The IRQ index; either 0 or 1.

source_mask

> Mask of bits, one for each source number (see pio_interrupt_source) to affect.

enabled

> True to enable all the sources specified in the mask on the specified IRQ, false to disable all the sources specified in the mask on the specified IRQ.

pio_set_sm_mask_enabled()   Inline Static

```
static void pio_set_sm_mask_enabled(PIO pio,
          uint32_t mask, bool enabled)
```

Enable or disable multiple PIO state machines. See also pio_enable_sm_mask_in_sync() if you wish to enable multiple state machines and ensure their clock dividers are in sync.

Note that this method just sets the enabled state of the state machine; if now enabled they continue exactly from where they left off.

Parameters

pio

> The PIO instance; either pio0 or pio1.

mask

> Bit mask of state machine indexes to modify the enabled state of.

enable

> True to enable the state machines; false to disable.

pio_sm_claim()

```
void pio_sm_claim(PIO pio, uint sm)
```

Mark a state machine as used. Method for cooperative claiming of hardware. Will cause a panic if the state machine is already claimed. Use of this method by libraries detects accidental configurations that would fail in unpredictable ways.

Parameters

pio

> The PIO instance; either pio0 or pio1.

sm

> State machine index (0..3).

pio_sm_clear_fifos()   **Inline Static**

```
static void pio_sm_clear_fifos(PIO pio, uint sm)
```

Clear a state machine's TX and RX FIFOs.

Parameters

pio

> The PIO instance; either pio0 or pio1.

sm

> State machine index (0..3).

pio_sm_clkdiv_restart()   Inline Static

```
static void pio_sm_clkdiv_restart(PIO pio, uint sm)
```

Restart a state machine's clock divider from a phase of 0. Each state machine's clock divider is a free-running piece of hardware, that generates a pattern of clock enable pulses for the state machine, based only on the configured integer/fractional divisor. The pattern of running/halted cycles slows the state machine's execution to some controlled rate.

This function clears the divider's integer and fractional phase accumulators so that it restarts this pattern from the beginning. It is called automatically by pio_sm_init() but can also be called at a later time, when you enable the state machine, to ensure precisely consistent timing each time you load and run a given PIO program.

More commonly this hardware mechanism is used to synchronize the execution clocks of multiple state machines – see pio_clkdiv_restart_sm_mask().

Parameters

pio

> The PIO instance; either pio0 or pio1.

sm

> State machine index (0..3).

pio_sm_drain_tx_fifo()

```
void pio_sm_drain_tx_fifo(PIO pio, uint sm)
```

Empty out a state machine's TX FIFO. This method executes pull instructions on the state machine until the TX FIFO is empty. This disturbs the contents of the OSR, so see also pio_sm_clear_fifos() which clears both FIFOs but leaves the state machine's internal state undisturbed. See also pio_sm_clear_fifos().

Parameters

pio

> The PIO instance; either pio0 or pio1.

sm

> State machine index (0..3).

pio_sm_exec()   Inline Static

```
static void pio_sm_exec(PIO pio, uint sm, uint instr)
```

Immediately execute an instruction on a state machine. This instruction is executed instead of the next instruction in the normal control flow on the state machine. Subsequent calls to this method replace the previous executed instruction if it is still running.

See also pio_sm_is_exec_stalled() to see if an executed instruction is still running (i.e. it is stalled on some condition).

Parameters

pio

   The PIO instance; either pio0 or pio1.

sm

   State machine index (0..3).

instr

   The encoded PIO instruction.

pio_sm_exec_wait_blocking()   Inline Static

```
static void pio_sm_exec_wait_blocking(PIO pio, uint sm,
         uint instr)
```

Immediately execute an instruction on a state machine and wait for it to complete. This instruction is executed instead of the next instruction in the normal control flow on the state machine. Subsequent calls to this method replace the previous executed instruction if it is still running.

See also pio_sm_is_exec_stalled() to see if an executed instruction is still running (i.e. it is stalled on some condition).

Parameters

pio

   The PIO instance; either pio0 or pio1.

sm

   State machine index (0..3).

instr

   The encoded PIO instruction.

pio_sm_get()   Inline Static

```
static uint32_t pio_sm_get(PIO pio, uint sm)
```

Read a word of data from a state machine's RX FIFO. This is a raw FIFO access that does not check for emptiness. If the FIFO is empty, the hardware ignores the attempt to read from the FIFO (the FIFO remains in an empty state following the read) and the sticky RXUNDER flag for this FIFO is set in FDEBUG to indicate that the system tried to read from this FIFO when empty. The data returned by this function is undefined when the FIFO is empty. See also pio_sm_get_blocking().

Parameters

pio

    The PIO instance; either pio0 or pio1.

sm

    State machine index (0..3).

pio_sm_get_blocking()   Inline Static

```
static uint32_t pio_sm_get_blocking(PIO pio, uint sm)
```

Read a word of data from a state machine's RX FIFO, blocking if the FIFO is empty.

Parameters

pio

    The PIO instance; either pio0 or pio1.

sm

    State machine index (0..3).

pio_sm_get_pc() Inline Static

```
static uint8_t pio_sm_get_pc(PIO pio, uint sm)
```

Return the current program counter for a state machine.

Parameters

pio

The PIO instance; either pio0 or pio1.

sm

State machine index (0..3).

Returns

Tthe program counter.

pio_sm_get_rx_fifo_level() Inline Static

```
static uint pio_sm_get_rx_fifo_level(PIO pio, uint sm)
```

Return the number of elements currently in a state machine's RX FIFO.

Parameters

pio

The PIO instance; either pio0 or pio1.

sm

State machine index (0..3).

Returns

The number of elements in the RX FIFO.

pio_sm_get_tx_fifo_level() Inline Static

```
static uint pio_sm_get_tx_fifo_level(PIO pio, uint sm)
```

Return the number of elements currently in a state machine's TX FIFO.

Parameters

pio

The PIO instance; either pio0 or pio1.

sm

State machine index (0..3).

Returns

The number of elements in the TX FIFO.

pio_sm_init()

```
void pio_sm_init(PIO pio, uint sm, uint initial_pc,
        const pio_sm_config *config)
```

Resets the state machine to a consistent state, and configures it. This method:

- **Disables** the state machine (if running)
- **Clears** the FIFOs
- **Applies** the configuration specified by 'config'
- **Resets** any internal state e.g. shift counters
- **Jumps** to the initial program location given by 'initial_pc'

The state machine is left disabled on return from this call.

Parameters

pio	The PIO instance; either pio0 or pio1.
sm	State machine index (0..3).
initial_pc	The initial program memory offset to run from.
config	The configuration to apply (or NULL to apply defaults).

pio_sm_is_claimed()

```
bool pio_sm_is_claimed(PIO pio, uint sm)
```

Determine if a PIO state machine is claimed. See also pio_sm_claim pio_claim_sm_mask.

Parameters

pio

The PIO instance; either pio0 or pio1.

sm

State machine index (0..3).

Returns

True if claimed, false otherwise.

pio_sm_is_exec_stalled()   **Inline Static**

```
static bool pio_sm_is_exec_stalled(PIO pio, uint sm)
```

Determine if an instruction set by pio_sm_exec() is stalled executing.

Parameters

pio

The PIO instance; either pio0 or pio1.

sm

State machine index (0..3).

Returns

True if the executed instruction is still running (stalled).

pio_sm_is_rx_fifo_empty() Inline Static

```
static bool pio_sm_is_rx_fifo_empty(PIO pio, uint sm)
```

Determine if a state machine's RX FIFO is empty.

Parameters

pio	The PIO instance; either pio0 or pio1.
sm	State machine index (0..3).

Returns

True if the RX FIFO is empty.

pio_sm_is_rx_fifo_full() Inline Static

static bool pio_sm_is_rx_fifo_full(PIO pio, uint sm)

Determine if a state machine's RX FIFO is full.

Parameters

pio	The PIO instance; either pio0 or pio1.
sm	State machine index (0..3).

Returns

True if the RX FIFO is full.

pio_sm_is_tx_fifo_empty() Inline Static

```
static bool pio_sm_is_tx_fifo_empty(PIO pio, uint sm)
```

Determine if a state machine's TX FIFO is empty.

Parameters

pio	The PIO instance; either pio0 or pio1.
sm	State machine index (0..3).

Returns

True if the TX FIFO is empty.

pio_sm_is_tx_fifo_full() Inline Static

```
static bool pio_sm_is_tx_fifo_full(PIO pio, uint sm)
```

Determine if a state machine's TX FIFO is full.

Parameters

pio	The PIO instance; either pio0 or pio1.
sm	State machine index (0..3).

Returns

True if the TX FIFO is full.

pio_sm_put() Inline Static

```
static void pio_sm_put(PIO pio, uint sm, uint32_t data)
```

Write a word of data to a state machine's TX FIFO.This is a raw FIFO access that does not check for fullness. If the FIFO is full, the FIFO contents and state are not affected by the write attempt. Hardware sets the TXOVER sticky flag for this FIFO in FDEBUG, to indicate that the system attempted to write to a full FIFO. See also pio_sm_put_blocking().

Parameters

pio	The PIO instance; either pio0 or pio1.
sm	State machine index (0..3).
data	The 32 bit data value.

pio_sm_put_blocking() Inline Static

```
static void pio_sm_put_blocking(PIO pio, uint sm,
        uint32_t data)
```

Write a word of data to a state machine's TX FIFO, blocking if the FIFO is full.

Parameters

pio	The PIO instance; either pio0 or pio1.
sm	State machine index (0..3).
data	The 32 bit data value.

pio_sm_restart() Inline Static

```
static void pio_sm_restart(PIO pio, uint sm)
```

Restart a state machine with a known state. This method clears the ISR, shift counters, clock divider counter pin write flags, delay counter, latched EXEC instruction, and IRQ wait condition.

Parameters

pio	The PIO instance; either pio0 or pio1.
sm	State machine index (0..3).

pio_sm_set_clkdiv()

```
static void pio_sm_set_clkdiv(PIO pio, uint sm, float div)
```

Set the current clock divider for a state machine.

Parameters

pio	The PIO instance; either pio0 or pio1.
sm	State machine index (0..3).
div	The floating point clock divider.

pio_sm_set_clkdiv_int_frac()   Inline Static

```
static void pio_sm_set_clkdiv_int_frac(PIO pio, uint sm,
        uint16_t div_int, uint8_t div_frac)
```

Set the current clock divider for a state machine using a 16:8 fraction.

Parameters

pio	The PIO instance; either pio0 or pio1.
sm	State machine index (0..3).
div_int	The integer part of the clock divider.
div_frac	The fractional part of the clock divider in 1/256s.

pio_sm_set_config()   Inline Static

```
static void pio_sm_set_config(PIO pio, uint sm,
        const pio_sm_config *config)
```

Apply a state machine configuration to a state machine.

Parameters

pio	The PIO instance; either pio0 or pio1.
sm	State machine index (0..3).
config	The configuration to apply.

pio_sm_set_consecutive_pindirs()

```
void pio_sm_set_consecutive_pindirs(PIO pio, uint sm,
        uint pin_base, uint pin_count, bool is_out)
```

Use a state machine to set the same pin direction for multiple consecutive pins for the PIO instance. This method repeatedly reconfigure the target state machine's pin configuration and executes 'set' instructions to set the pin direction on consecutive pins, before restoring the state machine's pin configuration to what it was.

This method is provided as a convenience to set initial pin directions, and should not be used against a state machine that is enabled.

Parameters

pio	The PIO instance; either pio0 or pio1.
sm	State machine index (0..3).
pin_base	The first pin to set a direction for.
pin_count	The count of consecutive pins to set the direction for.
is_out	The direction to set; true = out, false = in.

pio_sm_set_enabled()   Inline Static

```
static void pio_sm_set_enabled(PIO pio, uint sm,
        bool enabled)
```

Enable or disable a PIO state machine.

Parameters

pio	The PIO instance; either pio0 or pio1.
sm	State machine index (0..3).
enabled	True to enable the state machine; false to disable.

pio_sm_set_in_pins()   Inline Static

```
static void pio_sm_set_in_pins(PIO pio, uint sm,
        uint in_base)
```

Set the current 'in' pins for a state machine. Can overlap with the 'out', 'set' and 'sideset' pins.

Parameters

pio	The PIO instance; either pio0 or pio1.
sm	State machine index (0..3).
in_base	0-31 First pin to use as input.

pio_sm_set_out_pins()   Inline Static

```
static void pio_sm_set_out_pins(PIO pio, uint sm, uint
        out_base, uint out_count)
```

Set the current 'out' pins for a state machine. Can overlap with the 'in', 'set' and 'sideset' pins.

Parameters

pio	The PIO instance; either pio0 or pio1.
sm	State machine index (0..3).
out_base	0-31 First pin to set as output.
out_count	0-32 Number of pins to set.

pio_sm_set_pindirs_with_mask()

```
void pio_sm_set_pindirs_with_mask(PIO pio, uint sm,
       uint32_t pin_dirs, uint32_t pin_mask)
```

Use a state machine to set the pin directions for multiple pins for the PIO instance. This method repeatedly reconfigures the target state machine's pin configuration and executes 'set' instructions to set pin directions on up to 32 pins, before restoring the state machine's pin configuration to what it was. This method is provided as a convenience to set initial pin directions, and should not be used against a state machine that is enabled.

Parameters

pio

The PIO instance; either pio0 or pio1.

sm

State machine index (0..3).

pin_dirs

The pin directions to set - 1 = out, 0 = in (if the corresponding bit in pin_mask is set).

pin_mask

A bit for each pin to indicate whether the corresponding pin_value for that pin should be applied.

pio_sm_set_pins()

```
void pio_sm_set_pins(PIO pio, uint sm,
       uint32_t pin_values)
```

Use a state machine to set a value on all pins for the PIO instance. This method repeatedly reconfigures the target state machine's pin configuration and executes 'set' instructions to set values on all 32 pins, before restoring the state machine's pin configuration to what it was. This method is provided as a convenience to set initial pin states, and should not be used against a state machine that is enabled.

Parameters

pio	The PIO instance; either pio0 or pio1.
sm	State machine index (0..3).
pin_values	The pin values to set.

pio_sm_set_pins_with_mask()

```
void pio_sm_set_pins_with_mask(PIO pio, uint sm,
        uint32_t pin_values, uint32_t pin_mask)
```

Use a state machine to set a value on multiple pins for the PIO instance. This method repeatedly reconfigures the target state machine's pin configuration and executes 'set' instructions to set values on up to 32 pins, before restoring the state machine's pin configuration to what it was. This method is provided as a convenience to set initial pin states, and should not be used against a state machine that is enabled.

Parameters

pio

The PIO instance; either pio0 or pio1.

sm

State machine index (0..3).

pin_values

The pin values to set (if the corresponding bit in pin_mask is set).

pin_mask

A bit for each pin to indicate whether the corresponding pin_value for that pin should be applied.

pio_sm_set_set_pins()   Inline Static

```
static void pio_sm_set_set_pins(PIO pio, uint sm, uint
        set_base, uint set_count)
```

Set the current 'set' pins for a state machine. Can overlap with the 'in', 'out' and 'sideset' pins.

Parameters

pio	The PIO instance; either pio0 or pio1.
sm	State machine index (0..3).
set_base	0-31 First pin to set as.
set_count	0-5 Number of pins to set.

pio_sm_set_sideset_pins()   Inline Static

```
static void pio_sm_set_sideset_pins(PIO pio, int sm, uint
        sideset_base)
```

Set the current 'sideset' pins for a state machine. Can overlap with the 'in', 'out' and 'set' pins.

Parameters

pio	The PIO instance; either pio0 or pio1.
sm	State machine index (0..3).
sideset_base	0-31 base pin for 'side set'.

pio_sm_set_wrap()   Inline Static

```
static void pio_sm_set_wrap(PIO pio, uint sm,
        uint wrap_target, uint wrap)
```

Set the current wrap configuration for a state machine.

Parameters

pio

> The PIO instance; either pio0 or pio1.

sm

> State machine index (0..3).

wrap_target

> The instruction memory address to wrap to.

wrap

> The instruction memory address after which to set the program counter to wrap_target if the instruction does not itself update the program_counter.

pio_sm_unclaim()

```
void pio_sm_unclaim(PIO pio, uint sm)
```

Mark a state machine as no longer used. Method for cooperative claiming of hardware.

Parameters

pio	The PIO instance; either pio0 or pio1.
sm	State machine index (0..3).

pio_get_default_sm_config()   **Inline Static**

```
static pio_sm_config pio_get_default_sm_config(void )
```

Get the default state machine configuration.

Setting	Default
Out Pins	32 starting at 0
Set Pins	0 starting at 0
In Pins (base)	0
Side Set Pins (base)	0
Side Set	disabled
Wrap	wrap=31, wrap_to=0
In Shift	shift_direction=right, autopush=false, push_threshold=32
Out Shift	shift_direction=right, autopull=false, pull_threshold=32
Jmp	Pin0
Out Special	sticky=false, has_enable_pin=false, enable_pin_index=0
Mov Status	status_sel=STATUS_TX_LESSTHAN, n=0

Returns

The default state machine configuration which can then be modified.

sm_config_set_clkdiv()   Inline Static

```
static void sm_config_set_clkdiv(pio_sm_config *c,
       float div)
```

Set the state machine clock divider (from a floating point value) in a state machine configuration. The clock divider slows the state machine's execution by masking the system clock on some cycles, in a repeating pattern, so that the state machine does not advance. Effectively this produces a slower clock for the state machine to run from, which can be used to generate e.g. a particular UART baud rate. See the datasheet for further detail.

Parameters

c

Pointer to the configuration structure to modify.

div

The fractional divisor to be set. 1 for full speed. An integer clock divisor of n will cause the state machine to run 1 cycle in every n. Note that for small n, the jitter introduced by a fractional divider (e.g. 2.5) may be unacceptable although it will depend on the use case.

sm_config_set_clkdiv_int_frac()   Inline Static

```
static void sm_config_set_clkdiv_int_frac(pio_sm_config *c,
       uint16_t div_int, uint8_t div_frac)
```

Set the state machine clock divider (from integer and fractional parts - 16:8) in a state machine configuration. The clock divider can slow the state machine's execution to some rate below the system clock frequency, by enabling the state machine on some cycles but not on others, in a regular pattern. This can be used to generate e.g. a given UART baud rate. See the datasheet for further detail. See also sm_config_set_clkdiv().

Parameters

c	Pointer to the configuration structure to modify.
div_int	Integer part of the divisor.
div_frac	Fractional part in 1/256ths.

sm_config_set_fifo_join() Inline Static

```
static void sm_config_set_fifo_join(pio_sm_config *c,
        enum pio_fifo_join join)
```

Setup the FIFO joining in a state machine configuration. See also enum pio_fifo_join.

Parameters

c	Pointer to the configuration structure to modify.
join	Specifies the join type.

sm_config_set_in_pins() Inline Static

```
static void sm_config_set_in_pins(pio_sm_config *c,
        uint in_base)
```

Set the 'in' pins in a state machine configuration. Can overlap with the 'out', 'set' and 'sideset' pins.

Parameters

c	Pointer to the configuration structure to modify.
in_base	0-31 First pin to use as input.

sm_config_set_in_shift() Inline Static

```
static void sm_config_set_in_shift(pio_sm_config *c,
        bool shift_right, bool autopush,
        uint push_threshold)
```

Setup 'in' shifting parameters in a state machine configuration.

Parameters

c	Pointer to the configuration structure to modify.
shift_right	True to shift ISR to right, false to shift ISR to left.
autopush	Whether autopush is enabled.
push_threshold	Threshold in bits to shift in before auto/conditional re-pushing of the ISR.

sm_config_set_jmp_pin()   Inline Static

```
static void sm_config_set_jmp_pin(pio_sm_config *c,
        uint pin)
```

Set the 'jmp' pin in a state machine configuration.

Parameters

c   Pointer to the configuration structure to modify.

pin   The raw GPIO pin number to use as the source for a jmp pin
                instruction.

sm_config_set_mov_status()   Inline Static

```
static void sm_config_set_mov_status(pio_sm_config *c,
        enum pio_mov_status_type status_sel, uint status_n)
```

Set source for 'mov status' in a state machine configuration. See also enum
pio_mov_status_type.

Parameters

c   Pointer to the configuration structure to modify.

status_sel   The status operation selector.

status_n   Parameter for the mov status operation (currently a bit count).

sm_config_set_out_pins()   Inline Static

```
static void sm_config_set_out_pins(pio_sm_config *c,
        uint out_base, uint out_count)
```

Set the 'out' pins in a state machine configuration. Can overlap with the 'in', 'set' and
'sideset' pins.

Parameters

c   Pointer to the configuration structure to modify.

out_base   0-31 First pin to set as output.

out_count   0-32 Number of pins to set.

sm_config_set_out_shift()

```
static void sm_config_set_out_shift(pio_sm_config *c,
        bool shift_right, bool autopull, uint
        pull_threshold)
```

Setup 'out' shifting parameters in a state machine configuration.

Parameters

c	Pointer to the configuration structure to modify.
shift_right	True to shift OSR to right, false to shift OSR to left.
autopull	Whether autopull is enabled.
pull_threshold	Threshold in bits to shift out before auto/conditional re-pulling of the OSR.

sm_config_set_out_special()

```
static void sm_config_set_out_special(pio_sm_config *c, bool
        sticky, bool has_enable_pin, uint enable_pin_index)
```

Set special 'out' operations in a state machine configuration.

Parameters

c

Pointer to the configuration structure to modify.

sticky

To enable 'sticky' output (i.e. re-asserting most recent OUT/SET pin values on subsequent cycles).

has_enable_pin

True to enable auxiliary OUT enable pin.

enable_pin_index

Pin index for auxiliary OUT enable.

sm_config_set_set_pins()   Inline Static

```
static void sm_config_set_set_pins(pio_sm_config *c,
        int set_base, uint set_count)
```

Set the 'set' pins in a state machine configuration. Can overlap with the 'in', 'out' and 'sideset' pins.

Parameters

c	Pointer to the configuration structure to modify.
set_base	0-31 First pin to set as.
set_count	0-5 Number of pins to set.

sm_config_set_sideset()   Inline Static

```
static void sm_config_set_sideset(pio_sm_config *c,
        uint bit_count, bool optional, bool pindirs)
```

Set the 'sideset' options in a state machine configuration.

Parameters

c

Pointer to the configuration structure to modify.

bit_count

Number of bits to steal from delay field in the instruction for use of side set (max 5)

optional

True if the topmost side set bit is used as a flag for whether to apply side set on that instruction

pindirs

True if the side set affects pin directions rather than values

sm_config_set_sideset_pins() Inline Static

```
static void sm_config_set_sideset_pins(pio_sm_config *c,
        uint sideset_base)
```

Set the 'sideset' pins in a state machine configuration. Can overlap with the 'in', 'out' and 'set' pins.

Parameters

c

> Pointer to the configuration structure to modify.

sideset_base

> 0-31 base pin for 'side set'.

sm_config_set_wrap() Inline Static

```
static void sm_config_set_wrap(pio_sm_config *c, uint
        wrap_target, uint wrap)
```

Set the wrap addresses in a state machine configuration.

Parameters

c

> Pointer to the configuration structure to modify.

wrap_target

> The instruction memory address to wrap to.

wrap

> The instruction memory address after which to set the program counter to wrap_target if the instruction does not itself update the program_counter.

PLL – Phase Lock Loop

hardware_pll

```
#include "hardware/pll.h"
```

The hardware Phase-Locked Loop (PLL) control APIs are essential components of the Pico API SDK, providing convenient access to the two PLLs available in the RP2040 microcontroller. These PLLs, namely pll_sys and pll_usb, offer precise clock generation capabilities for specific purposes.

The pll_sys is utilized to generate a system clock with a frequency of up to 133MHz. This clock serves as a fundamental timing reference for various system operations, ensuring efficient execution and synchronization of tasks within the RP2040 microcontroller.

On the other hand, the pll_usb is dedicated to generating a 48MHz USB reference clock. This clock plays a crucial role in supporting USB functionality and ensuring reliable data communication between the RP2040 microcontroller and external USB devices.

To fully understand the intricacies of PLL configuration and operation, developers are encouraged to consult the RP2040 datasheet, which provides detailed information on how the PLLs are calculated, their parameters, and their impact on the overall system performance.

Typedefs

typedef pll_hw_t

```
typedef pll_hw_t *PLL
```

This is a pointer type used in the PLL API of the Pico SDK. It represents a handle to a hardware PLL instance.

FUNCTIONS

pll_deinit()

```
void pll_deinit (PLL pll)
```

Release/uninitialize specified PLL. This will turn off the power to the specified PLL. Note this function does not currently check if the PLL is in use before powering it off so should be used with care.

Parameters

pll   pll_sys or pll_usb.

pll_init()

```
void pll_init (PLL pll, uint ref_div, uint vco_freq,
       uint post_div1, uint post_div2)
```

Initialize specified PLL.

Parameters

pll

pll_sys or pll_usb.

ref_div

Input clock divider.

vco_freq

Requested output from the VCO (voltage controlled oscillator).

post_div1

Post Divider 1 - range 1-7. Must be >= post_div2.

post_div2

Post Divider 2 - range 1-7.

PWM – PULSE WIDTH MODULATION

hardware_pwm

```
#include "hardware/pwm.h"
```

The PWM (Pulse Width Modulation) block in the RP2040 microcontroller offers versatile capabilities for controlling and measuring signals. With 8 identical slices, each slice of the PWM block can drive two PWM output signals or measure the frequency and duty cycle of an input signal. This provides a total of up to 16 controllable PWM outputs, enabling precise control over various applications. Additionally, all 30 GPIOs on the RP2040 can be driven by the PWM block, expanding its potential uses.

The PWM hardware functions by continuously comparing the input value to a free-running counter. This produces a toggling output where the amount of time spent at the high output level is proportional to the input value. The fraction of time spent at the high signal level is known as the duty cycle of the signal.

By default, a PWM slice counts upward from 0 until it reaches a specified wrap value (set using the pwm_config_set_wrap function). Once the wrap value is reached, the counter immediately wraps back to 0, creating a repeating pattern. Additionally, PWM slices offer a phase-correct mode where the counter counts downward after reaching the wrap value until it reaches 0 again. This mode allows for bidirectional control of devices or systems, enabling more flexible PWM applications.

This powerful feature set opens up a wide range of possibilities for controlling motors, generating analog signals, and implementing various other PWM-based applications with precision and efficiency.

STRUCTURES

struct pwm_config

uint32_t	csr
uint32_t	div
uint32_t	top

ENUMERATIONS

enum pwm_chan

PWM_CHAN_A	= 0
PWM_CHAN_B	= 1

enum pwm_clkdiv_mode

PWM Divider mode settings.

PWM_DIV_FREE_RUNNING   = 0

Free-running counting at rate dictated by fractional divider.

PWM_DIV_B_HIGH   = 1

Fractional divider is gated by the PWM B pin.

PWM_DIV_B_RISING   = 2

Fractional divider advances with each rising edge of the PWM B pin.

PWM_DIV_B_FALLING   = 3

Fractional divider advances with each falling edge of the PWM B pin.

FUNCTIONS

pwm_advance_count()   Inline Static

```
static void pwm_advance_count(uint slice_num)
```

Advance PWM count. Advance the phase of a running the counter by 1 count. This function will return once the increment is complete.

Parameters

slice_num   PWM slice number.

pwm_clear_irq()   Inline Static

```
static void pwm_clear_irq(uint slice_num)
```

Clear a single PWM channel interrupt.

Parameters

slice_num   PWM slice number.

pwm_config_set_clkdiv()   Inline Static

```
static void pwm_config_set_clkdiv(pwm_config *c, float div)
```

Set PWM clock divider in a PWM configuration. If the divide mode is free-running, the PWM counter runs at clk_sys / div. Otherwise, the divider reduces the rate of events seen on the B pin input (level or edge) before passing them on to the PWM counter.

Parameters

c

PWM configuration struct to modify.

div

Value to divide counting rate by. Must be greater than or equal to 1.

pwm_config_set_clkdiv_int() Inline Static

```
static void pwm_config_set_clkdiv_int(pwm_config *c,
        uint div)
```

Set PWM clock divider in a PWM configuration. If the divide mode is free-running, the PWM counter runs at clk_sys / div. Otherwise, the divider reduces the rate of events seen on the B pin input (level or edge) before passing them on to the PWM counter.

Parameters

c

> PWM configuration struct to modify.

div

> Integer value to reduce counting rate by. Must be greater than or equal to 1.

pwm_config_set_clkdiv_int_frac() Inline Static

```
static void pwm_config_set_clkdiv_int_frac(pwm_config *c,
        uint8_t integer, uint8_t fract)
```

Set PWM clock divider in a PWM configuration using an 8:4 fractional value. If the divide mode is free-running, the PWM counter runs at clk_sys / div. Otherwise, the divider reduces the rate of events seen on the B pin input (level or edge) before passing them on to the PWM counter.

Parameters

c

> PWM configuration struct to modify.

integer

> 8 bit integer part of the clock divider. Must be greater than or equal to 1.

fract

> 4 bit fractional part of the clock divider.

pwm_config_set_clkdiv_mode()   Inline Static

```
static void pwm_config_set_clkdiv_mode(pwm_config *c,
        num pwm_clkdiv_mode mode)
```

Set PWM counting mode in a PWM configuration. Configure which event gates the operation of the fractional divider. The default is always-on (free-running PWM). Can also be configured to count on high level, rising edge or falling edge of the B pin input.

Parameters

c   PWM configuration struct to modify.

mode   PWM divide/count mode.

pwm_config_set_output_polarity()   Inline Static

```
static void pwm_config_set_output_polarity(pwm_config *c,
        bool a, bool b)
```

Set output polarity in a PWM configuration.

Parameters

c   PWM configuration struct to modify.

a   True to invert output A.

b   True to invert output B.

pwm_config_set_phase_correct()   Inline Static

```
static void pwm_config_set_phase_correct(pwm_config *c,
        bool phase_correct)
```

Set phase correction in a PWM configuration. Setting phase control to true means that instead of wrapping back to zero when the wrap point is reached, the PWM starts counting back down. The output frequency is halved when phase-correct mode is enabled.

Parameters

c   PWM configuration struct to modify.

phase_correct   True to set phase correct modulation, false to set trailing edge.

pwm_config_set_wrap()   Inline Static

```
static void pwm_config_set_wrap(pwm_config *c,
        uint16_t wrap)
```

Set PWM counter wrap value in a PWM configuration. Set the highest value the counter will reach before returning to 0. Also known as TOP.

Parameters

c	PWM configuration struct to modify.
wrap	Value to set wrap to.

pwm_force_irq()   Inline Static

```
static void pwm_force_irq(uint slice_num)
```

Force PWM interrupt.

Parameters

slice_num	PWM slice number.

pwm_get_counter()   Inline Static

```
static uint16_t pwm_get_counter(uint slice_num)
```

Get PWM counter. Get current value of PWM counter

Parameters

slice_num	PWM slice number.

Returns

Current value of the PWM counter.

pwm_get_default_config()   Inline Static

```
static pwm_config pwm_get_default_config(void )
```

Get a set of default values for PWM configuration. PWM config is free-running at system clock speed, no phase correction, wrapping at 0xffff, with standard polarities for channels A and B.

Returns

Set of default values.

pwm_get_dreq()   Inline Static

```
static uint pwm_get_dreq(uint slice_num)
```

Return the DREQ to use for pacing transfers to a particular PWM slice. The DMA Request (DREQ) is a signal that indicates to the DMA controller when a particular peripheral or device is ready to send or receive data. It acts as a trigger for the DMA controller to initiate data transfers between memory and the peripheral without CPU intervention.

The pwm_get_dreq function is used to retrieve the DREQ number associated with a specific PWM slice. The DREQ number is used when setting up DMA transfers for the PWM peripheral. By providing the slice number as a parameter to this function, it returns the corresponding DREQ number that can be used for DMA configuration.

Parameters

slice_num   PWM slice number.

pwm_get_irq_status_mask()   Inline Static

```
static uint32_t pwm_get_irq_status_mask(void )
```

Get PWM interrupt status, raw.

Returns

Bitmask of all PWM interrup
ts currently set.

pwm_gpio_to_channel()   Inline Static

```
static uint pwm_gpio_to_channel(uint gpio)
```

Determine the PWM channel that is attached to the specified GPIO. Each slice 0 to 7 has two channels, A and B.

Returns

The PWM channel that controls the specified GPIO.

pwm_gpio_to_slice_num()   Inline Static

```
static uint pwm_gpio_to_slice_num(uint gpio)
```

Determine the PWM slice that is attached to the specified GPIO.

Returns

The PWM slice number that controls the specified GPIO.

pwm_init()   Inline Static

```
static void pwm_init(uint slice_num, pwm_config *c,
        bool start)
```

Initialize a PWM with settings from a configuration object. Use the pwm_get_default_config() function to Initialize a config structure, make changes as needed using the pwm_config_*functions, then call this function to set up the PWM.

Parameters

slice_num

PWM slice number.

c

The configuration to use.

start

If true the PWM will be started running once configured. If false you will need to start manually using pwm_set_enabled() or pwm_set_mask_enabled().

pwm_retard_count()   Inline Static

```
static void pwm_retard_count(uint slice_num)
```

Retard PWM count. Retard the phase of a running counter by 1 count. This function will return once the retardation is complete.

Parameters

slice_num   PWM slice number.

pwm_set_both_levels()   Inline Static

```
static void pwm_set_both_levels(uint slice_num,
        uint16_t level_a, uint16_t level_b)
```

Set the value of the PWM counter compare values, A and B. The counter compare register is double-buffered in hardware. This means that, when the PWM is running, a write to the counter compare values does not take effect until the next time the PWM slice wraps (or, in phase-correct mode, the next time the slice reaches 0). If the PWM is not running, the write is latched in immediately.

Parameters

slice_num

PWM slice number.

level_a

Value to set compare A to. When the counter reaches this value the A output is deasserted.

level_b

Value to set compare B to. When the counter reaches this value the B output is deasserted.

pwm_set_chan_level()   Inline Static

```
static void pwm_set_chan_level(uint slice_num, uint chan,
        uint16_t level)
```

Set the value of the PWM counter compare value, for either channel A or channel B. The counter compare register is double-buffered in hardware. This means that, when the PWM is running, a write to the counter compare values does not take effect until the next time the PWM slice wraps (or, in phase-correct mode, the next time the slice reaches 0). If the PWM is not running, the write is latched in immediately.

Parameters

slice_num	PWM slice number.
chan	Which channel to update. 0 for A, 1 for B.
level	New level for the selected output.

pwm_set_clkdiv()   Inline Static

```
static void pwm_set_clkdiv(uint slice_num, float divider)
```

Set PWM clock divider. Counter increment will be on sysclock divided by this value, taking into account the gating.

Parameters

slice_num	PWM slice number
divider	Floating point clock divider, 1.f <= value < 256.f.

pwm_set_clkdiv_int_frac()
Inline Static

```
static void pwm_set_clkdiv_int_frac(uint slice_num,
        uint8_t integer, uint8_t fract)
```

Set PWM clock divider using an 8:4 fractional value.Set the clock divider. Counter increment will be on sysclock divided by this value, taking into account the gating.

Parameters

slice_num	PWM slice number.
integer	8 bit integer part of the clock divider.
fract	4 bit fractional part of the clock divider.

pwm_set_clkdiv_mode()   Inline Static

```
static void pwm_set_clkdiv_mode(uint slice_num,
enum pwm_clkdiv_mode mode)
```

Set PWM divider mode.

Parameters

slice_num

PWM slice number.

mode

Required divider mode.

pwm_set_counter()   Inline Static

```
static void pwm_set_counter(uint slice_num, uint16_t c)
```

Set the value of the PWM counter.

Parameters

slice_num

PWM slice number.

c

Value to set the PWM counter to.

pwm_set_enabled() Inline Static

```
static void pwm_set_enabled(uint slice_num, bool enabled)
```

Enable/Disable PWM. When a PWM is disabled, it halts its counter, and the output pins are left high or low depending on exactly when the counter is halted. When re-enabled the PWM resumes immediately from where it left off.

If the PWM's output pins need to be low when halted: The counter compare can be set to zero whilst the PWM is enabled, and then the PWM disabled once both pins are seen to be low. The GPIO output overrides can be used to force the actual pins low.

The PWM can be run for one cycle (i.e. enabled then immediately disabled) with a TOP of 0, count of 0 and counter compare of 0, to force the pins low when the PWM has already been halted. The same method can be used with a counter compare value of 1 to force a pin high.

Note that, when disabled, the PWM can still be advanced one count at a time by pulsing the PH_ADV bit in its CSR. The output pins transition as though the PWM were enabled.

Parameters

slice_num	PWM slice number.
enabled	True to enable the specified PWM, false to disable.

pwm_set_gpio_level() Inline Static

```
static void pwm_set_gpio_level(uint gpio, uint16_t level)
```

Helper function to set the PWM level for the slice and channel associated with a GPIO. Look up the correct slice (0 to 7) and channel (A or B) for a given GPIO, and update the corresponding counter compare field. This PWM slice should already have been configured and set running. Also be careful of multiple GPIOs mapping to the same slice and channel (if GPIOs have a difference of 16).

The counter compare register is double-buffered in hardware. This means that, when the PWM is running, a write to the counter compare values does not take effect until the next time the PWM slice wraps (or, in phase-correct mode, the next time the slice reaches 0). If the PWM is not running, the write is latched in immediately.

Parameters

gpio	GPIO to set level of.
level	PWM level for this GPIO.

pwm_set_irq_enabled()   Inline Static

```
static void pwm_set_irq_enabled(uint slice_num,
       bool enabled)
```

Enable PWM instance interrupt. Used to enable a single PWM instance interrupt.

Parameters

slice_num	PWM block to enable/disable.
enabled	true to enable, false to disable.

pwm_set_irq_mask_enabled()   Inline Static

```
static void pwm_set_irq_mask_enabled(uint32_t slice_mask,
       bool enabled)
```

Enable multiple PWM instance interrupts. Use this to enable multiple PWM interrupts at once.

Parameters

slice_mask

Bitmask of all the blocks to enable/disable. Channel 0 = bit 0, channel 1 = bit 1 etc.

enabled

true to enable, false to disable.

pwm_set_mask_enabled()   Inline Static

```
static void pwm_set_mask_enabled(uint32_t mask)
```

Enable/Disable multiple PWM slices simultaneously.

Parameters

mask

Bitmap of PWMs to enable/disable. Bits 0 to 7 enable slices 0-7 respectively.

pwm_set_output_polarity()   Inline Static

```
static void pwm_set_output_polarity(uint slice_num,
        bool a, bool b)
```

Set PWM output polarity.

Parameters

slice_num	PWM slice number.
a	True to invert output A.
b	True to invert output B.

pwm_set_phase_correct()   Inline Static

```
static void pwm_set_phase_correct(uint slice_num,
        bool phase_correct)
```

Set PWM phase correct on/off. Setting phase control to true means that instead of wrapping back to zero when the wrap point is reached, the PWM starts counting back down. The output frequency is halved when phase-correct mode is enabled.

Parameters

slice_num

PWM slice number.

phase_correct

True to set phase correct modulation, false to set trailing edge.

pwm_set_wrap()   Inline Static

```
static void pwm_set_wrap(uint slice_num, uint16_t wrap)
```

Set the current PWM counter wrap value. Set the highest value the counter will reach before returning to 0. Also known as TOP.

The counter wrap value is double-buffered in hardware. This means that, when the PWM is running, a write to the counter wrap value does not take effect until after the next time the PWM slice wraps (or, in phase-correct mode, the next time the slice reaches 0). If the PWM is not running, the write is latched in immediately.

Parameters

slice_num

PWM slice number.

wrap

Value to set wrap to.

RESETS

hardware_resets

```
#include "hardware/resets.h"
```

The Resets section of the Pico API provides control over the reset behavior and configuration of various hardware components in the RP2040 microcontroller. Resets are mechanisms used to initialize or reconfigure specific modules, peripherals, or subsystems within the microcontroller.

In this section, you will find functions and definitions related to handling and configuring resets. These functions allow you to assert or de-assert resets, check the status of resets, and configure reset behavior for specific modules or peripherals. The Resets section of the Pico API provides you with the necessary tools to manage resets effectively and tailor the reset behavior according to your application's requirements.

It is important to consult the RP2040 datasheet and the Pico API documentation for detailed information on specific reset configurations and their impact on the microcontroller's functionality.

NOTE See the "src\rp2040\hardware_regs\include\hardware\regs\resets.h" for the full list of reset defines.

The Reset Bitmask - Multiple blocks are referred to using a bitmask as follows:

Block to Reset	Bit	Block to Reset	Bit
USB	24	PIO 1	11
UART 1	23	PIO 0	10
UART 0	22	Pads - QSPI	9
Timer	21	Pads - bank 0	8
TB Manager	20	JTAG	7
SysInfo	19	IO Bank 1	6
System Config	18	IO Bank 0	5
SPI 1	17	I2C 1	4
SPI 0	16	I2C 0	3
RTC	15	DMA	2
PWM	14	Bus Control	1
PLL USB	13	ADC 0	0
PLL System	12		

reset_block() Inline Static

```
static void reset_block (uint32_t bits)
```

Reset the specified HW blocks.

Parameters

bits

Bit pattern indicating blocks to reset. See reset_bitmask.

unreset_block() Inline Static

```
static void unreset_block (uint32_t bits)
```

Bring specified HW blocks out of reset.When a hardware block is in a reset state, it is effectively disabled, and its internal registers, state machines, and functionality are reset to their initial states. By bringing a hardware block out of reset, you are enabling its operation and allowing it to resume normal functionality. Once the reset is de-asserted, the hardware block becomes active and can be utilized for its intended purpose.

Parameters

bits

Bit pattern indicating blocks to unreset. See reset_bitmask.

unreset_block_wait() Inline Static

```
static void unreset_block_wait (uint32_t bits)
```

Bring specified HW blocks out of reset and wait for completion.

Parameters

bits

Bit pattern indicating blocks to unreset. See reset_bitmask.

RTC – REAL TIME CLOCK

hardware_rtc

```
#include "hardware/rtc.h"
```

The RTC keeps track of time in human readable format and generates events when the time is equal to a preset value. Think of a digital clock, not epoch time used by most computers. There are seven fields, one each for year (12 bit), month (4 bit), day (5 bit), day of the week (3 bit), hour (5 bit) minute (6 bit) and second (6 bit), storing the data in binary format.

TYPEDEFS

rtc_callback_t

```
typedef void(*rtc_callback_t) (void)
```

Callback function type for RTC alarms. See alsortc_set_alarm().

FUNCTIONS

rtc_get_datetime()

```
bool rtc_get_datetime (datetime_t *t)
```

Get the current time from the RTC.

Parameters

t

Pointer to a datetime_t structure to receive the current RTC time.

Returns

True if datetime is valid, false if the RTC is not running.

rtc_running()

```
bool rtc_running (void)
```

Is the RTC running?

Returns

True if the RTC is running,

rtc_set_alarm()

```
void rtc_set_alarm (datetime_t *t,
        rtc_callback_t  ser_callback)
```

Set a time in the future for the RTC to call a user provided callback.

Parameters

t

Pointer to a datetime_t structure containing a time in the future to fire the alarm. Any values set to -1 will not be matched on.

user_callback

Pointer to a rtc_callback_t to call when the alarm fires.

rtc_set_datetime()

```
bool rtc_set_datetime (datetime_t *t)
```

Set the RTC to the specified time. Note that after setting the RTC date and time, a subsequent read of the values (e.g. via rtc_get_datetime()) may not reflect the new setting until up to three cycles of the potentially-much-slower RTC clock domain have passed. This represents a period of 64 microseconds with the default RTC clock configuration.

Parameters

t   Pointer to a datetime_t structure contains time to set.

Returns

True if set, false if the passed in datetime was invalid.

SPI – Serial Periferal Interface

hardware_spi

```
#include "hardware/spi.h"
```

The Serial Peripheral Interface (SPI) is a widely used communication protocol for connecting microcontrollers and peripheral devices. It enables synchronous, full-duplex data transfer between a master device and one or more slave devices. The Serial Peripheral Interface (SPI) section of the Pico API provides support for the two identical instances of the SPI controller.

The SPI controller is based on the PrimeCell SSP (Synchronous Serial Port), which serves as a versatile interface for synchronous serial communication with peripheral devices. It supports popular protocols such as Motorola SPI, National Semiconductor Microwire, and Texas Instruments synchronous serial interfaces.

The API allows you to configure the SPI controller as either a master or a slave device. As a master, the microcontroller takes control of the communication, generating clock signals and transmitting data to connected slave devices. As a slave, the microcontroller responds to commands and data received from the master device.

The SPI controller can be connected to various GPIO pins, enabling flexible pin assignments for SPI communication. You can refer to the GPIO function selection table in the RP2040 datasheet for specific details on how to configure the GPIO pins for SPI functionality.

By using the SPI section of the Pico API, you can easily configure the SPI controller, set communication parameters such as clock frequency and data format, perform data transfers with connected devices, and configure the controller as a master or slave. This allows for seamless integration of SPI peripherals into your RP2040-based projects, enabling efficient and reliable communication with external devices supporting SPI protocols.

Macros

spi0

```
#define spi0    ((spi_inst_t *)spi0_hw)
```

Identifier for the first (SPI 0) hardware SPI instance (for use in SPI functions). e.g. spi_init(spi0, 48000).

spi1

```
#define spi1    ((spi_inst_t *)spi1_hw)
```

Identifier for the second (SPI 1) hardware SPI instance (for use in SPI functions). e.g. spi_init(spi1, 48000)

Enumerations

enum spi_cpha_t

Enumeration of SPI CPHA (clock phase) values.

SPI_CPHA_0	= 0
SPI_CPHA_1	= 1

enum spi_cpol_t

Enumeration of SPI CPOL (clock polarity) values.

SPI_CPOL_0	= 0
SPI_CPOL_1	= 1

enum spi_order_t

Enumeration of SPI bit-order values.

SPI_LSB_FIRST	= 0
SPI_MSB_FIRST	= 1

FUNCTIONS

spi_deinit()

```
void spi_deinit(spi_inst_t *spi)
```

Deinitialize SPI instancesPuts the SPI into a disabled state. Init will need to be called to reenable the device functions.

Parameters

spi   SPI instance specifier, either spi0 or spi1.

spi_get_baudrate()

```
uint spi_get_baudrate(const spi_inst_t *spi)
```

Get SPI baudrate. Get SPI baudrate which was set by spi_set_baudrate.

Parameters

spi   SPI instance specifier, either spi0 or spi1.

Returns

The actual baudrate set.

spi_get_dreq()   **Inline Static**

```
static uint spi_get_dreq(spi_inst_t *spi, bool is_tx)
```

Return the DREQ to use for pacing transfers to/from a particular SPI instance.

Parameters

spi
SPI instance specifier, either spi0 or spi1.
is_tx
True for sending data to the SPI instance, false for receiving data from the SPI instance.

spi_get_index()

```
static uint spi_get_index(const spi_inst_t *spi)
```

Convert SPI instance to hardware instance number.

Parameters

spi   SPI instance specifier, either spi0 or spi1.

Returns

 Number of SPI, 0 or 1.

spi_init()

```
uint spi_init(spi_inst_t *spi, uint baudrate)
```

Initialize SPI instances. Puts the SPI into a known state, and enable it. Must be called before other functions.

NOTE There is no guarantee that the baudrate requested can be achieved exactly; the nearest will be chosen and returned.

Parameters

spi   SPI instance specifier, either spi0 or spi1.
baudrate Baudrate requested in Hz.

Returns

 The actual baud rate set.

spi_is_busy() Inline Static

```
static bool spi_is_busy(const spi_inst_t *spi)
```

Check whether SPI is busy.

Parameters

spi   SPI instance specifier, either spi0 or spi1.

Returns

True if SPI is busy.

spi_is_readable() Inline Static

```
static bool spi_is_readable(const spi_inst_t *spi)
```

Check whether a read can be done on SPI device.

Parameters

spi   SPI instance specifier, either spi0 or spi1.

Returns

True if a read is possible i.e. data is present.

spi_is_writable() Inline Static

```
static bool spi_is_writable(const spi_inst_t *spi)
```

Check whether a write can be done on SPI device.

Parameters

spi   SPI instance specifier, either spi0 or spi1.

Returns

False if no space is available to write. True if a write is possible.

spi_read16_blocking()

```
int spi_read16_blocking(spi_inst_t *spi,
        uint16_t repeated_tx_data, uint16_t *dst,
        size_t len)
```

Read from an SPI device. Read len halfwords from SPI to dst. Blocks until all data is transferred. No timeout, as SPI hardware always transfers at a known data rate. repeated_tx_data is output repeatedly on TX as data is read in from RX. Generally this can be 0, but some devices require a specific value here, e.g. SD cards expect 0xff

NOTE SPI should be initialized with 16 data_bits using spi_set_format first, otherwise this function will only read 8 data_bits.

Parameters

spi	SPI instance specifier, either spi0 or spi1.
repeated_tx_data	Buffer of data to write.
dst	Buffer for read data.
len	Length of buffer dst.

Returns

Number of halfwords written/read.

spi_read_blocking()

```
int spi_read_blocking(spi_inst_t *spi,
        uint8_t repeated_tx_data, uint8_t *dst,
        size_t len)
```

Read from an SPI device. Read len bytes from SPI to dst. Blocks until all data is transferred. No timeout, as SPI hardware always transfers at a known data rate. repeated_tx_data is output repeatedly on TX as data is read in from RX. Generally this can be 0, but some devices require a specific value here, e.g. SD cards expect 0xff.

Parameters

spi	SPI instance specifier, either spi0 or spi1.
repeated_tx_data	Buffer of data to write.
dst	Buffer for read data.
len	Length of buffer dst.

Returns

Number of bytes written/read.

spi_set_baudrate()

```
uint spi_set_baudrate(spi_inst_t *spi, uint baudrate)
```

Set SPI baudrate. Set SPI frequency as close as possible to baudrate, and return the actual achieved rate.

Parameters

spi

SPI instance specifier, either spi0 or spi1.

baudrate

Baudrate required in Hz, should be capable of a bitrate of at least 2Mbps, or higher, depending on system clock settings.

Returns

The actual baudrate set.

spi_set_format() — Inline Static

```
static void spi_set_format(spi_inst_t *spi,
        int data_bits, spi_cpol_t cpol, spi_cpha_t cpha,
        __unused spi_order_t order)
```

Configure how the SPI serialises and deserialises data on the wire.

Parameters

spi
SPI instance specifier, either spi0 or spi1.

data_bits
Number of data bits per transfer. Valid values 4..16.

cpol
SSPCLKOUT polarity, applicable to Motorola SPI frame format only.

cpha
SSPCLKOUT phase, applicable to Motorola SPI frame format only.

order
Must be SPI_MSB_FIRST, no other values supported on the PL022.

spi_set_slave() — Inline Static

```
static void spi_set_slave(spi_inst_t *spi, bool slave)
```

Configure the SPI for master- or slave-mode operation. By default, spi_init() sets master-mode.

Parameters

spi   SPI instance specifier, either spi0 or spi1.
slave   True to set SPI device as a slave device, false for master.

spi_write16_blocking()

```
int spi_write16_blocking(spi_inst_t *spi, const uint16_t
        *src, size_t len)
```

Write to an SPI device. Write len halfwords from src to SPI. Discard any data received back. Blocks until all data is transferred. No timeout, as SPI hardware always transfers at a known data rate. *NOTE SPI should be initialized with 16 data_bits using spi_set_format first, otherwise this function will only write 8 data_bits.*

Parameters

spi	SPI instance specifier, either spi0 or spi1.
src	Buffer of data to write.
len	Length of buffers.

Returns

Number of halfwords written/read.

spi_write16_read16_blocking()

```
int spi_write16_read16_blocking(spi_inst_t *spi,
        const uint16_t *src, uint16_t *dst, size_t len)
```

Write/Read half words to/from an SPI device. Write len halfwords from src to SPI. Simultaneously read len halfwords from SPI to dst. Blocks until all data is transferred. No timeout, as SPI hardware always transfers at a known data rate. *NOTE SPI should be initialized with 16 data_bits using spi_set_format first, otherwise this function will only read/write 8 data_bits.*

Parameters

spi	SPI instance specifier, either spi0 or spi1.
src	Buffer of data to write.
dst	Buffer for read data.
len	Length of BOTH buffers in halfwords.

Returns

Number of halfwords written/read.

spi_write_blocking()

```
int spi_write_blocking(spi_inst_t *spi, const uint8_t
       *src, size_t len)
```

Write to an SPI device, blocking. Write len bytes from src to SPI, and discard any data received back Blocks until all data is transferred. No timeout, as SPI hardware always transfers at a known data rate.

Parameters

spi	SPI instance specifier, either spi0 or spi1.
src	Buffer of data to write.
len	Length of src.

Returns

Number of bytes written/read.

spi_write_read_blocking()

```
int spi_write_read_blocking(spi_inst_t *spi,
       const uint8_t *src, uint8_t *dst, size_t len)
```

Write/Read to/from an SPI device. Write len bytes from src to SPI. Simultaneously read len bytes from SPI to dst. Blocks until all data is transferred. No timeout, as SPI hardware always transfers at a known data rate.

Parameters

spi	SPI instance specifier, either spi0 or spi1.
src	Buffer of data to write.
dst	Buffer for read data.
len	Length of BOTH buffers.

Returns

Number of bytes written/read.

SYNC

hardware_sync

```
#include "hardware/sync.h"
```

The sync section of the API primarily focuses on providing spin lock functionality for synchronization purposes. The spin lock is a key component of the sync API and is used to protect critical sections of code or shared resources from concurrent access.

A spin lock, in this context, is a synchronization primitive that allows multiple threads or processes to take turns accessing a shared resource by spinning in a loop until the lock becomes available. It employs a busy-waiting approach, where a thread repeatedly checks the lock's status until it is acquired.

The Pico API's sync module provides functions to initialize, acquire, and release spin locks. Developers can use these functions to protect critical sections of their code from simultaneous execution by multiple threads. By acquiring a spin lock, a thread ensures exclusive access to the protected resource, while other threads spinning on the same lock wait until it becomes available.

Spin locks are suitable for scenarios where the expected wait time for the lock is short and contention is low. They can be more efficient than other synchronization primitives in situations where context switching and thread rescheduling overhead can be avoided. However, it's important to consider the characteristics of the specific application and adjust the usage of spin locks accordingly.

SPIN LOCKS

The RP2040 provides 32 hardware spin locks, which can be used to manage mutually-exclusive access to shared software and hardware resources.

Generally each spin lock itself is a shared resource, i.e. the same hardware spin lock can be used by multiple higher level primitives (as long as the spin locks are neither held for long periods, nor held concurrently with other spin locks by the same core - which could lead to deadlock). A hardware spin lock that is exclusively owned can be used individually without more flexibility and without regard to other software. Note that no hardware spin lock may be acquired re-entrantly (i.e. hardware spin locks are not on their own safe for use by both thread code and IRQs) however the default spinlock related methods here (e.g. spin_lock_blocking) always disable interrupts while the lock is held as use by IRQ handlers and user code is common/desirable, and spin locks are only expected to be held for brief periods

The SDK uses the following default spin lock assignments, classifying which spin locks are reserved for exclusive/special purposes vs those suitable for more general shared use:

Spin Lock ID

0 - 13

> Currently reserved for exclusive use by the SDK and other libraries. If you use these spin locks, you risk breaking SDK or other library functionality. Each reserved spin lock used individually has its own PICO_SPINLOCK_ID so you can search for those.

14, 15

> (PICO_SPINLOCK_ID_OS1 and PICO_SPINLOCK_ID_OS2). Currently reserved for exclusive use by an operating system (or other system level software) co-existing with the SDK.

16 - 23

> (PICO_SPINLOCK_ID_STRIPED_FIRST - PICO_SPINLOCK_ID_STRIPED_LAST). Spin locks from this range are assigned in a round-robin fashion via next_striped_spin_lock_num(). These spin locks are shared, but assigning numbers from a range reduces the probability that two higher level locking primitives using striped spin locks will actually be using the same spin lock.

24 - 31

> (PICO_SPINLOCK_ID_CLAIM_FREE_FIRST - PICO_SPINLOCK_ID_CLAIM_FREE_LAST). These are reserved for exclusive use and are allocated on a first come first served basis at runtime via spin_lock_claim_unused()

TYPEDEFS
spin_lock_t

```
typedef volatile uint32_t spin_lock_t
```

A spin lock identifier.

FUNCTIONS

__dmb()   Inline Static

```
static __force_inline void __dmb(void )
```

Insert a DMB instruction in to the code path. The DMB (data memory barrier) acts as a memory barrier, all memory accesses prior to this instruction will be observed before any explicit access after the instruction.

__dsb()   Inline Static

```
static __force_inline void __dsb(void )
```

Insert a DSB instruction in to the code path. The DSB (data synchronization barrier) acts as a special kind of data memory barrier (DMB). The DSB operation completes when all explicit memory accesses before this instruction complete.

__isb()   Inline Static

```
static __force_inline void __isb(void )
```

Insert a ISB instruction in to the code path.ISB acts as an instruction synchronization barrier. It flushes the pipeline of the processor, so that all instructions following the ISB are fetched from cache or memory again, after the ISB instruction has been completed.

__mem_fence_release()   Inline Static

```
static __force_inline void __mem_fence_release(void )
```

Release a memory fence.

__sev()   Inline Static

```
static __force_inline void __sev(void )
```

Insert a SEV instruction in to the code path. The SEV (send event) instruction sends an event to both cores.

__wfe()   Inline Static

```
static __force_inline void __wfe(void )
```

Insert a WFE instruction in to the code path. The WFE (wait for event) instruction waits until one of a number of events occurs, including events signalled by the SEV instruction on either core.

__wfi()   Inline Static

```
static __force_inline void __wfi(void )
```

Insert a WFI instruction in to the code path. The WFI (wait for interrupt) instruction waits for a interrupt to wake up the core.

is_spin_locked()   Inline Static

```
static bool is_spin_locked(spin_lock_t *lock)
```

Check to see if a spinlock is currently acquired elsewhere.

Parameters

lock   Spinlock instance.

next_striped_spin_lock_num()

```
uint next_striped_spin_lock_num(void )
```

Return a spin lock number from the striped range. Returns a spin lock number in the range PICO_SPINLOCK_ID_STRIPED_FIRST to PICO_SPINLOCK_ID_STRIPED_LAST in a round robin fashion. This does not grant the caller exclusive access to the spin lock, so the caller must:

• Abide (with other callers) by the contract of only holding this spin lock briefly (and with IRQs disabled - the default via spin_lock_blocking()), and not whilst holding other spin locks.

• Be OK with any contention caused by the - brief due to the above requirement - contention with other possible users of the spin lock.

See also   PICO_SPINLOCK_ID_STRIPED_FIRST
               PICO_SPINLOCK_ID_STRIPED_LAST.

Returns

A spin lock number the caller may use (non exclusively).

restore_interrupts()   Inline Static

```
static __force_inline void restore_interrupts
        (uint32_t status)
```

Restore interrupts to a specified state.

Parameters

status

Previous interrupt status from save_and_disable_interrupts().

save_and_disable_interrupts() — Inline Static

```
static __force_inline uint32_t save_and_disable_interrupts
    (void)
```

Save and disable interrupts.

Returns

The prior interrupt enable status for restoration later via restore_interrupts().

spin_lock_blocking() — Inline Static

```
static __force_inline uint32_t spin_lock_blocking
    (spin_lock_t *lock)
```

Acquire a spin lock safely. This function will disable interrupts prior to acquiring the spinlock.

Parameters

lock   Spinlock instance.

Returns

Interrupt status to be used when unlocking, to restore to original state.

spin_lock_claim()

```
void spin_lock_claim(uint lock_num)
```

Mark a spin lock as used. Method for cooperative claiming of hardware. Will cause a panic if the spin lock is already claimed. Use of this method by libraries detects accidental configurations that would fail in unpredictable ways.

Parameters

lock_num   The spin lock ID number.

spin_lock_claim_mask()

```
void spin_lock_claim_mask(uint32_t lock_num_mask)
```

Mark multiple spin locks as used. Method for cooperative claiming of hardware. Will cause a panic if any of the spin locks are already claimed. Use of this method by libraries detects accidental configurations that would fail in unpredictable ways.

Parameters

lock_num_mask

Bitfield of all required spin locks to claim (bit 0 == spin lock 0, bit 1 == spin lock 1 etc).

spin_lock_claim_unused()

```
int spin_lock_claim_unused(bool required)
```

Claim a free spin lock.

Parameters

required   If true the function will panic if none are available.

Returns

The spin lock number or -1 if required was false, and none were free.

spin_lock_get_num()   Inline Static

```
static __force_inline uint spin_lock_get_num
        (spin_lock_t *lock)
```

Get HW Spinlock number from instance.

Parameters

lock   Spinlock instance.

Returns

The Spinlock ID.

spin_lock_init()

```
spin_lock_t *spin_lock_init(uint lock_num)
```

Initialize a spin lock. The spin lock is initially unlocked.

Parameters

lock_num   The spin lock ID number.

Returns

The spin lock instance.

spin_lock_instance()   **Inline Static**

```
static __force_inline spin_lock_t *spin_lock_instance
       (uint lock_num)
```

Get HW Spinlock instance from number.

Parameters

lock_num   The spin lock ID number.

Returns

The spin lock instance.

spin_lock_is_claimed()

```
bool spin_lock_is_claimed(uint lock_num)
```

Determine if a spin lock is claimed. See also spin_lock_claim spin_lock_claim_mask.

Parameters

lock_num   The spin lock ID number.

Returns

True if claimed, false otherwise.

spin_lock_unclaim()

```
void spin_lock_unclaim(uint lock_num)
```

Mark a spin lock as no longer used. Method for cooperative claiming of hardware.

Parameters

lock_num   The spin lock ID number to release.

spin_lock_unsafe_blocking()   Inline Static

```
static __force_inline void spin_lock_unsafe_blocking
        (spin_lock_t *lock)
```

Acquire a spin lock without disabling interrupts (hence unsafe).

Parameters

lock   Spinlock instance.

spin_unlock()   Inline Static

```
static __force_inline void spin_unlock(spin_lock_t *lock,
        uint32_t saved_irq)
```

Release a spin lock safely. This function will re-enable interrupts according to the parameters. See also spin_lock_blocking().

Parameters

lock   Spinlock instance.

saved_irqReturn value from the spin_lock_blocking() function.

spin_unlock_unsafe() Inline Static

```
static __force_inline void spin_unlock_unsafe
        (spin_lock_t *lock)
```

Release a spin lock without re-enabling interrupts.

Parameters

lock   Spinlock instance.

TIMER

hardware_timer

#include "hardware/timer.h"

The timer section of the Pico API provides medium-level access to the timer hardware on the RP2040 microcontroller. It offers functionalities for managing timers and alarms to perform precise timing operations in your applications. It's important to note that for higher-level functionality utilizing the hardware timer, you may refer to the pico_time module.

The timer peripheral on RP2040 is equipped with a single 64-bit counter that increments at a rate of once per microsecond. This high-resolution counter allows for accurate time measurement and tracking within your application. To ensure race-free reading of the counter value over a 32-bit bus, the timer supports a latching two-stage read operation.

One of the key features of the timer is the support for four alarms. These alarms can be configured to match on the lower 32 bits of the counter and generate interrupts when a match occurs. Each alarm provides the capability to set specific time thresholds and trigger actions accordingly.

By default, the timer utilizes a one-microsecond reference that is generated in the Watchdog module, which, in turn, derives it from the clk_ref. This reference frequency ensures precise and consistent timing operations throughout your application.

It's important to understand that the timer's alarms operate within a 32-bit range of the 64-bit counter, allowing for alarms to be triggered a maximum of approximately 4,295 seconds (or about 72 minutes) into the future. Therefore, the timer is typically used for short sleep periods or timing operations. For longer alarms or more extensive real-time clock functionality, you may consider exploring the hardware_rtc functions within the Pico API.

TYPEDEFS

hardware_alarm_callback_t

```
typedef void(*hardware_alarm_callback_t) (uint alarm_num)
```

Callback function type for hardware alarms. See also hardware_alarm_set_callback().

Parameters

alarm_num   The hardware alarm number.

FUNCTIONS

busy_wait_ms()

```
void busy_wait_ms(uint32_t delay_ms)
```

Busy wait wasting cycles for the given number of milliseconds.

Parameters

delay_ms   Delay amount in milliseconds.

busy_wait_until()

```
void busy_wait_until(absolute_time_t t)
```

Busy wait wasting cycles until after the specified timestamp.

Parameters

t   Absolute time to wait until.

busy_wait_us()

```
void busy_wait_us(uint64_t delay_us)
```

Busy wait wasting cycles for the given (64 bit) number of microseconds.

Parameters

delay_ms   Delay amount in microseconds.

busy_wait_us_32()

```
void busy_wait_us_32(uint32_t delay_us)
```

Busy wait wasting cycles for the given (32 bit) number of microseconds.

Parameters

delay_ms   Delay amount in microseconds.

hardware_alarm_cancel()

```
void hardware_alarm_cancel(uint alarm_num)
```

Cancel an existing target (if any) for a given hardware_alarm.

Parameters

alarm_num   The hardware alarm number.

hardware_alarm_claim()

```
void hardware_alarm_claim(uint alarm_num)
```

Cooperatively claim the use of this hardware alarm_num. This method hard asserts if the hardware alarm is currently claimed. See also hardware_claiming.

Parameters

alarm_num   The hardware alarm to claim.

hardware_alarm_claim_unused()

```
int hardware_alarm_claim_unused(bool required)
```

Cooperatively claim the use of this hardware alarm_num. This method attempts to claim an unused hardware alarm. See also hardware_claiming.

Parameters

required   If true the function will panic if none are available.

Returns

The hardware alarm number claimed or -1 if requires was false, and none are available.

hardware_alarm_force_irq()

```
void hardware_alarm_force_irq(uint alarm_num)
```

Force and IRQ for a specific hardware alarm. This method will forcibly make sure the current alarm callback (if present) for the hardware alarm is called from an IRQ context after this call. If an actual callback is due at the same time then the callback may only be called once. Calling this method does not otherwise interfere with regular callback operations.

Parameters

alarm_num   The hardware alarm number.

hardware_alarm_is_claimed()

```
bool hardware_alarm_is_claimed(uint alarm_num)
```

Determine if a hardware alarm has been claimed. See also hardware_alarm_claim.

Parameters

alarm_num   The hardware alarm number.

Returns

True if claimed, false otherwise.

hardware_alarm_set_callback()

```
void hardware_alarm_set_callback(uint alarm_num,
        hardware_alarm_callback_t callback)
```

Enable/Disable a callback for a hardware timer on this core. This method enables/disables the alarm IRQ for the specified hardware alarm on the calling core, and set the specified callback to be associated with that alarm. This callback will be used for the timeout set via hardware_alarm_set_target. See also hardware_alarm_set_target().

NOTE This will install the handler on the current core if the IRQ handler isn't already set. Therefore the user has the opportunity to call this up from the core of their choice.

Parameters

alarm_num	The hardware alarm number.
callback	The callback to install, or NULL to unset.

hardware_alarm_set_target()

```
bool hardware_alarm_set_target(uint alarm_num,
        absolute_time_t t)
```

Set the current target for the specified hardware alarm. This will replace any existing target.

Parameters

alarm_num	The hardware alarm number.
t	The target timestamp.

Returns

True if the target was "missed"; i.e. it was in the past, or occurred before a future hardware timeout could be set.

hardware_alarm_unclaim()

```
void hardware_alarm_unclaim(uint alarm_num)
```

Cooperatively release the claim on use of this hardware alarm_num. See also hardware_claiming.

Parameters

alarm_num   The hardware alarm to unclaim.

Inline Static

time_reached()

```
static bool time_reached(absolute_time_t t)
```

Check if the specified timestamp has been reached.

Parameters

t   Absolute time to compare against current time.

Returns

True if it is now after the specified timestamp.

Inline Static

time_us_32()

```
static uint32_t time_us_32(void)
```

Return a 32 bit timestamp value in microseconds. Returns the low 32 bits of the hardware timer. This value wraps roughly every 1 hour 11 minutes and 35 seconds.

Returns

The 32 bit timestamp.

time_us_64()

```
uint64_t time_us_64(void)
```

Return the current 64 bit timestamp value in microseconds. Returns the full 64 bits of the hardware timer. The pico_time and other functions rely on the fact that this value monotonically increases from power up. As such it is expected that this value counts upwards and <u>never</u> wraps.

Returns

The 64 bit timestamp.

UART – Universal Asynchronous Receiver Transmitter

hardware_uart

`#include "hardware/uart.h"`

This section provides access to the UART peripherals on the RP2040 microcontroller. The RP2040 features two identical instances of the UART peripheral, which are based on the ARM PL011 UART. These UART peripherals offer versatile serial communication capabilities for your applications.

Each UART can be connected to a number of GPIO pins through GPIO muxing. This flexibility allows you to configure the UART's transmit (TX), receive (RX), request-to-send (RTS), and clear-to-send (CTS) signals to the desired GPIO pins based on your application requirements.

It's important to note that the RP2040 UART implementation focuses on the essential features, and therefore, some advanced modes of the PL011 UART, such as modem mode and IrDA mode, are not supported. However, you can still utilize the fundamental UART functionalities for reliable serial communication.

The UART section of the Pico API provides a range of functions and configurations to initialize, configure, and interact with the UART peripherals on the RP2040. Whether you need to transmit data, receive data, or control flow using hardware handshaking signals, the UART API enables seamless integration of serial communication capabilities into your RP2040-based projects.

Typedefs

uart_inst

```
typedef struct uart_inst uart_inst_t;
```

Currently always a pointer to hw but it might not be in the future

Macro

uart0

```
#define uart0    ((uart_inst_t *)uart0_hw)
```

Identifier for UART instance 0. A UART identifier for use in UART functions. e.g. uart_init(uart0, 48000).

uart1

```
#define uart1 ((uart_inst_t *)uart1_hw)
```

Identifier for UART instance 1. A UART identifier for use in UART functions. e.g. uart_init(uart1, 48000).

Enumerations

uart_parity_t

```
enum  uart_parity_t
```

UART Parity enumeration.

UART_PARITY_NONE	= 0
UART_PARITY_EVEN	= 1
UART_PARITY_ODD	= 2

FUNCTIONS

uart_deinit()

```
void uart_deinit(uart_inst_t *uart)
```

DeInitialize a UART. Disable the UART if it is no longer used. Must be reinitialised before being used again.

Parameters

uart   UART instance. uart0 or uart1.

uart_get_dreq()   Inline Static

```
static uint uart_get_dreq(uart_inst_t *uart, bool is_tx)
```

Return the DREQ to use for pacing transfers to/from a particular UART instance.

Parameters

uart

UART instance. uart0 or uart1.

is_tx

True for sending data to the UART instance, false for receiving data from the UART instance.

uart_get_index()   Inline Static

```
static uint uart_get_index(uart_inst_t *uart)
```

Convert UART instance to hardware instance number.

Parameters

uart   UART instance. uart0 or uart1.

Returns

Number of UART, 0 or 1.

uart_getc() Inline Static

```
static char uart_getc(uart_inst_t *uart)
```

Read a single character from the UART. This function will block until a character has been read.

Parameters

uart   UART instance. uart0 or uart1.

Returns

The character read.

uart_init()

```
uint uart_init(uart_inst_t *uart, uint baudrate)
```

Initialize a UART. Put the UART into a known state, and enable it. Must be called before other functions. This function always enables the FIFOs, and configures the UART for the following default line format: 8 data bits, No parity bit, One stop bit.

NOTE There is no guarantee that the baudrate requested will be possible, the nearest will be chosen, and this function will return the configured baud rate.

Parameters

uart   UART instance. uart0 or uart1.
baudrate   Baudrate of UART in Hz.

Returns

Actual set baudrate

uart_is_enabled()   Inline Static

```
static bool uart_is_enabled(uart_inst_t *uart)
```

Test if specific UART is enabled.

Parameters

uart   UART instance. uart0 or uart1.

Returns

True if the UART is enabled.

uart_is_readable()   Inline Static

```
static bool uart_is_readable(uart_inst_t *uart)
```

Determine whether data is waiting in the RX FIFO.

Parameters

uart   UART instance. uart0 or uart1.

Returns

True if the RX FIFO is not empty, otherwise false.

uart_is_readable_within_us()

```
bool uart_is_readable_within_us(uart_inst_t *uart,
        uint32_t us)
```

Wait for up to a certain number of microseconds for the RX FIFO to be non empty.

Parameters

uart

UART instance. uart0 or uart1.

us

the number of microseconds to wait at most (may be 0 for an instantaneous check).

Returns

True if the RX FIFO became non empty before the timeout, false otherwise.

uart_is_writable()   **Inline Static**

```
static bool uart_is_writable(uart_inst_t *uart)
```

Determine if space is available in the TX FIFO.

Parameters

uart   UART instance. uart0 or uart1.

Returns

False if no space available, true otherwise.

uart_putc()   Inline Static

```
static void uart_putc(uart_inst_t *uart, char c)
```

Write single character to UART for transmission, with optional CR/LF conversions. This function will block until the character has been sent.

Parameters

uart	UART instance. uart0 or uart1.
c	The character to send.

uart_putc_raw()   Inline Static

```
static void uart_putc_raw(uart_inst_t *uart, char c)
```

Write single character to UART for transmission. This function will block until the entire character has been sent

Parameters

uart	UART instance. uart0 or uart1.
c	The character to send.

uart_puts()   Inline Static

```
static void uart_puts(uart_inst_t *uart, const char *s)
```

Write string to UART for transmission, doing any CR/LF conversions. This function will block until the entire string has been sent.

Parameters

uart	UART instance. uart0 or uart1.
s	The null terminated string to send.

uart_read_blocking()   Inline Static

```
static void uart_read_blocking(uart_inst_t *uart,
         uint8_t *dst, size_t len)
```

Read from the UART. This function blocks until len characters have been read from the UART.

Parameters

uart	UART instance. uart0 or uart1.
dst	Buffer to accept received bytes.
len	The number of bytes to receive.

uart_set_baudrate()

```
uint uart_set_baudrate(uart_inst_t *uart, uint baudrate)
```

Set UART baud rate. Set baud rate as close as possible to requested, and return actual rate selected. The UART is paused for around two character periods whilst the settings are changed. Data received during this time may be dropped by the UART.

Any characters still in the transmit buffer will be sent using the new updated baud rate. uart_tx_wait_blocking() can be called before this function to ensure all characters at the old baud rate have been sent before the rate is changed.

This function should not be called from an interrupt context, and the UART interrupt should be disabled before calling this function.

Parameters

uart	UART instance. uart0 or uart1.
baudrate	Baudrate in Hz.

Returns

Actual set baudrate.

uart_set_break()

```
void uart_set_break(uart_inst_t *uart, bool en)
```

Assert a break condition on the UART transmission.

Parameters

uart

UART instance. uart0 or uart1.

en

Assert break condition (TX held low) if true. Clear break condition if false.

uart_set_fifo_enabled()

```
void uart_set_fifo_enabled(uart_inst_t *uart, bool enabled)
```

Enable/Disable the FIFOs on specified UART. The UART is paused for around two character periods whilst the settings are changed. Data received during this time may be dropped by the UART. Any characters still in the transmit FIFO will be lost if the FIFO is disabled. uart_tx_wait_blocking() can be called before this function to avoid this.

This function should not be called from an interrupt context, and the UART interrupt should be disabled when calling this function.

Parameters

uart	UART instance. uart0 or uart1.
enabled	True to enable FIFO (default), false to disable.

uart_set_format()

```
void uart_set_format(uart_inst_t *uart, uint data_bits,
        uint stop_bits, uart_parity_t parity)
```

Set UART data format. Configure the data format (bits etc) for the UART. The UART is paused for around two character periods whilst the settings are changed. Data received during this time may be dropped by the UART. Any characters still in the transmit buffer will be sent using the new updated data format. uart_tx_wait_blocking() can be called before this function to ensure all characters needing the old format have been sent before the format is changed.

This function should not be called from an interrupt context, and the UART interrupt should be disabled before calling this function.

Parameters

uart	UART instance. uart0 or uart1.
data_bits	Number of bits of data. 5..8.
stop_bits	Number of stop bits 1..2.
parity	Parity option.

uart_set_hw_flow()   Inline Static

```
static void uart_set_hw_flow(uart_inst_t *uart, bool cts,
        bool rts)
```

Set UART flow control CTS/RTS.

Parameters

uart

UART instance. uart0 or uart1.

cts

If true enable flow control of TX by clear-to-send input.

rts

If true enable assertion of request-to-send output by RX flow control.

uart_set_irq_enables() Inline Static

```
static void uart_set_irq_enables(uart_inst_t *uart,
        bool rx_has_data, bool tx_needs_data)
```

Setup UART interrupts. Enable the UART's interrupt output. An interrupt handler will need to be installed prior to calling this function.

Parameters

uart

UART instance. uart0 or uart1.

rx_has_data

If true an interrupt will be fired when the RX FIFO contains data.

tx_needs_data

If true an interrupt will be fired when the TX FIFO needs data.

uart_set_translate_crlf()

```
void uart_set_translate_crlf(uart_inst_t *uart,
        bool translate)
```

Set CR/LF conversion on UART.

Parameters

uart	UART instance. uart0 or uart1.
translate	If true, convert line feeds to carriage return on transmissions.

uart_tx_wait_blocking() Inline Static

```
static void uart_tx_wait_blocking(uart_inst_t *uart)
```

Wait for the UART TX fifo to be drained.

Parameters

uart	UART instance. uart0 or uart1.

uart_write_blocking()

```
static void uart_write_blocking(uart_inst_t *uart,
            const uint8_t *src, size_t len)
```

Write to the UART for transmission. This function will block until all the data has been sent to the UART.

Parameters

uart	UART instance. uart0 or uart1.
src	The bytes to send.
len	The number of bytes to send.

VREG – Voltage Regulator

hardware_vreg

```
#include "hardware/vreg.h"
```

The VREG (Voltage Regulator) API in the Pico SDK provides a function to control the voltage regulator on the RP2040 microcontroller. The voltage regulator is responsible for regulating the supply voltage to the core and peripherals of the chip.

Enumerations

vreg_voltage

enum vreg_voltage		
VREG_VOLTAGE_0_85	= 0b0110	0.85v
VREG_VOLTAGE_0_90	= 0b0111	0.90v
VREG_VOLTAGE_0_95	= 0b1000	0.95v
VREG_VOLTAGE_1_00	= 0b1001	1.00v
VREG_VOLTAGE_1_05	= 0b1010	1.05v
VREG_VOLTAGE_1_10	= 0b1011	1.10v
VREG_VOLTAGE_1_15	= 0b1100	1.15v
VREG_VOLTAGE_1_20	= 0b1101	1.20v
VREG_VOLTAGE_1_25	= 0b1110	1.25v
VREG_VOLTAGE_1_30	= 0b1111	1.30v
VREG_VOLTAGE_MIN	= VREG_VOLTAGE_0_85	
	Always the minimum possible voltage.	
VREG_VOLTAGE_DEFAULT	= VREG_VOLTAGE_1_10	
	Default voltage on power up.	
VREG_VOLTAGE_MAX	= VREG_VOLTAGE_1_30	
	Always the maximum possible voltage.	

FUNCTIONS

vreg_set_voltage()

```
void vreg_set_voltage(enum vreg_voltage voltage)
```

Set voltage.

Parameters

voltage

The voltage (from enumeration vreg_voltage) to apply to the voltage regulator.

WATCHDOG

hardware_watchdog

```
#include "hardware/watchdog.h"
```

Supporting functions for the Pico hardware watchdog timer.

The RP2040 has a built in HW watchdog Timer. This is a countdown timer that can restart parts of the chip if it reaches zero. For example, this can be used to restart the processor if the software running on it gets stuck in an infinite loop or similar. The programmer has to periodically write a value to the watchdog to stop it reaching zero.

watchdog_caused_reboot()

```
bool watchdog_caused_reboot(void )
```

Did the watchdog cause the last reboot?

Returns

> True If the watchdog timer or a watchdog force caused the last reboot. False If there has been no watchdog reboot since the last power on reset. A power on reset is typically caused by a power cycle or the run pin (reset button) being toggled.

watchdog_enable()

```
void watchdog_enable(uint32_t delay_ms,
            bool pause_on_debug)
```

Enable the watchdog. By default the SDK assumes a 12MHz XOSC and sets the watchdog_start_tick appropriately. This method sets a marker in the watchdog scratch register 4 that is checked by watchdog_enable_caused_reboot. If the device is subsequently reset via a call to watchdog_reboot (including for example by dragging a UF2 onto the RPI-RP2), then this value will be cleared, and so watchdog_enable_caused_reboot will return false.

NOTE If watchdog_start_tick value does not give a 1MHz clock to the watchdog system, then the delay_ms parameter will not be in microseconds. See the datasheet for more details.

Parameters

delay_ms

Number of milliseconds before watchdog will reboot without watchdog_update being called. Maximum of 0x7fffff, which is approximately 8.3 seconds

pause_on_debug

If the watchdog should be paused when the debugger is stepping through code

watchdog_enable_caused_reboot()

```
bool watchdog_enable_caused_reboot(void )
```

Did watchdog_enable cause the last reboot? Perform additional checking along with watchdog_caused_reboot to determine if a watchdog timeout initiated by watchdog_enable caused the last reboot. This method checks for a special value in watchdog scratch register 4 placed there by watchdog_enable. This would not be present if a watchdog reset is initiated by watchdog_reboot or by the RP2040 bootrom (e.g. dragging a UF2 onto the RPI-RP2 drive).

Returns

True If the watchdog timer or a watchdog force caused (see watchdog_caused_reboot) the last reboot and the watchdog reboot happened after watchdog_enable was called. False If there has been no watchdog reboot since the last power on reset, or the watchdog reboot was not caused by a watchdog timeout after watchdog_enable was called. A power on reset is typically caused by a power cycle or the run pin (reset button) being toggled.

watchdog_get_count()

```
uint32_t watchdog_get_count(void )
```

Returns the number of microseconds before the watchdog will reboot the chip.

Returns

The number of microseconds before the watchdog will reboot the chip.

watchdog_reboot()

```
void watchdog_reboot(uint32_t pc, uint32_t sp,
        uint32_t delay_ms)
```

Define actions to perform at watchdog timeout. By default the SDK assumes a 12MHz XOSC and sets the watchdog_start_tick appropriately.

NOTE If watchdog_start_tick value does not give a 1MHz clock to the watchdog system, then the delay_ms parameter will not be in microseconds. See the datasheet for more details.

Parameters

pc

If Zero, a standard boot will be performed, if non-zero this is the program counter to jump to on reset.

sp

If pc is non-zero, this will be the stack pointer used.

delay_ms

Initial load value. Maximum value 0x7fffff, approximately 8.3s.

watchdog_start_tick()

```
void watchdog_start_tick(uint cycles)
```

Start the watchdog tick.

Parameters

cycles

This needs to be a divider that when applied to the XOSC input, produces a 1MHz clock. So if the XOSC is 12MHz, this will need to be 12.

watchdog_update()

```
void watchdog_update(void )
```

Reload the watchdog counter with the amount of time set in watchdog_enable.

XOSC – CRYSTAL OSCILLATOR

hardware_xosc

```
#include "hardware/xosc.h"
```

Crystal Oscillator (XOSC) API.

xosc_disable()

```
void xosc_disable (void)
```

Disable the Crystal oscillator. Turns off the crystal oscillator source, and waits for it to become unstable

xosc_dormant()

```
void xosc_dormant (void)
```

Set the crystal oscillator system to dormant. Turns off the crystal oscillator until it is woken by an interrupt. This will block and hence the entire system will stop, until an interrupt wakes it up. This function will continue to block until the oscillator becomes stable after its wakeup.

xosc_init()

```
void xosc_init (void)
```

Initialize the crystal oscillator system. This function will block until the crystal oscillator has stabilized.

HIGH LEVEL

The High-Level API section of the Pico SDK consists of a collection of libraries that offer higher-level functionality beyond the basic hardware interfaces of the RP2040 microcontroller. These libraries provide a more abstracted and feature-rich set of functions, focusing on various aspects of application development. They aim to simplify common tasks, provide convenient abstractions, and offer additional functionality that is not directly tied to the hardware.

Async Context: Provides utilities for asynchronous programming and context management.

Flash: Offers APIs for accessing and manipulating flash memory on the RP2040.

I2C Slave: Enables the RP2040 to function as an I2C slave device, providing APIs for I2C communication.

Multicore: Facilitates multi-core programming on the RP2040, allowing parallel processing with both cores.

Rand: Provides functions for generating random numbers, serving as a source of randomness.

Stdlib: Includes standard C library functions for general-purpose programming tasks.

Sync: Offers synchronization primitives and utilities for managing concurrent access to shared resources.

Time: Provides functions for time-related operations, such as timing measurements and clock management.

Unique ID: Enables retrieval of a unique identifier for the RP2040 device.

Util: Includes various utility functions for common programming tasks, such as string formatting and data conversion.

ASYNC CONTEXT

pico_async_context

```
#include "async_context.h"

#include "async_context_base.h"

#include "async_context_freertos.h"

#include "async_context_poll.h"

#include "async_context_threadsafe_background.h"
```

An async_context provides a logically single-threaded context for performing work, and responding to asynchronous events. Thus an async_context instance is suitable for servicing third-party libraries that are not re-entrant.

The "context" in async_context refers to the fact that when calling workers or timeouts within the async_context various pre-conditions hold: That there is a single logical thread of execution; i.e. that the context does not call any worker functions concurrently. That the context always calls workers from the same processor core, as most uses of async_context rely on interaction with IRQs which are themselves core-specific.

The async_context provides two mechanisms for asynchronous work:

1. When pending workers (when_pending), which are processed whenever they have work pending. See async_context_add_when_pending_worker, async_context_remove_when_pending_worker, and async_context_set_work_pending, the latter of which can be used from an interrupt handler to signal that servicing work is required to be performed by the worker from the regular async_context.

2. At time workers (at_time), that are executed after at a specific time.

Note: "when pending" workers with work pending are executed before "at time" workers.

The async_context provides locking mechanisms, see async_context_acquire_lock_blocking, async_context_release_lock and async_context_lock_check which can be used by external code to ensure execution of external code does not happen concurrently with worker code. Locked code runs on the calling core, however async_context_execute_sync is provided to synchronously run a function from the core of the async_context.

The SDK ships with the following default async_contexts:

async_context_poll - this context is not thread-safe, and the user is responsible for calling async_context_poll periodically, and can use async_context_wait_for_work_until() to sleep between calls until work is needed if the user has nothing else to do.

async_context_threadsafe_background - in order to work in the background, a low priority IRQ is used to handle callbacks. Code is usually invoked from this IRQ context, but may be invoked after any other code that uses the async context in another (non-IRQ) context on the same core. Calling async_context_poll is not required, and is a no-op. This context implements async_context locking and is thus safe to call from either core, according to the specific notes on each API.

async_context_freertos - Work is performed from a separate "async_context" task, however once again, code may also be invoked after a direct use of the async_context on the same core that the async_context belongs to. Calling async_context_poll is not required, and is a no-op. This context implements async_context locking and is thus safe to call from any task, and from either core, according to the specific notes on each API.

Each async_context provides bespoke methods of instantiation which are provided in the corresponding headers (e.g. async_context_poll.h, async_context_threadsafe_background.h, asycn_context_freertos.h). async_contexts are de-initialized by the common async_context_deint() method.

Multiple async_context instances can be used by a single application, and they will operate independently.

TYPEDEFS

async_at_time_worker_t

```
typedef struct async_work_on_timeout
        async_at_time_worker_t
```

A "timeout" instance used by an async_context. A "timeout" represents some future action that must be taken at a specific time. Its methods are called from the async_context under lock at the given time.

See also async_context_add_worker_at async_context_add_worker_in_ms.

async_when_pending_worker_t

```
typedef struct async_when_pending_worker
        async_when_pending_worker_t
```

A "worker" instance used by an async_context. A "worker" represents some external entity that must do work in response to some external stimulus (usually an IRQ). Its methods are called from the async_context under lock at the given time.

See alsoasync_context_add_worker_at async_context_add_worker_in_ms.

async_context_type_t

```
typedef struct async_context_type async_context_type_t
```

Implementation of an async_context type, providing methods common to that type.

STRUCTURES

async_work_on_timeout

```
struct  async_work_on_timeout
```

```
#include <pico/async_context.h>
```

A "timeout" instance used by an async_context. A "timeout" represents some future action that must be taken at a specific time. Its methods are called from the async_context under lock at the given time. See also async_context_add_worker_at async_context_add_worker_in_ms.

Data Fields

struct async_work_on_timeout * next

> Private link list pointer.

void(* do_work)(async_context_t *context, struct async_work_on_timeout *timeout)

> Method called when the timeout is reached; may not be NULL. Note, that when this method is called, the timeout has been removed from the async_context, so if you want the timeout to repeat, you should re-add it during this callback.

> #### Parameters

>> context   The async_context.

>> timeout

absolute_time_t next_time

> The next timeout time; this should only be modified during the above methods or via async_context methods.

void * user_data

> User data associated with the timeout instance.

async_when_pending_worker

```
struct  async_when_pending_worker
```

`#include <pico/async_context.h>`

A "worker" instance used by an async_context. A "worker" instance used by an async_context. A "worker" represents some external entity that must do work in response to some external stimulus (usually an IRQ). Its methods are called from the async_context under lock at the given time.

See also async_context_add_worker_at, async_context_add_worker_in_ms.

Data Fields

struct async_when_pending_worker * next

Private link list pointer.

void(* do_work)(async_context_t *context, struct async_when_pending_worker *worker)

Called by the async_context when the worker has been marked as having "work pending".

Parameters

context	The async_context.
worker	The function to be called when work is pending.

bool work_pending

True if the worker need do_work called.

void * user_data

User data associated with the worker instance.

async_context_type

```
struct  async_context_type
```

```
#include <pico/async_context.h>
```

Implementation of an async_context type, providing methods common to that type.

Data Fields

uint16_t type

void(* acquire_lock_blocking)(async_context_t *self)

void(* release_lock)(async_context_t *self)

void(* lock_check)(async_context_t *self)

uint32_t(* execute_sync)(async_context_t *context, uint32_t(*func)(void *param), void *param)

bool(* add_at_time_worker)(async_context_t *self, async_at_time_worker_t *worker)

bool(* remove_at_time_worker)(async_context_t *self, async_at_time_worker_t *worker)

bool(* add_when_pending_worker)(async_context_t *self, async_when_pending_worker_t *worker)

bool(* remove_when_pending_worker)(async_context_t *self, async_when_pending_worker_t *worker)

void(* set_work_pending)(async_context_t *self, async_when_pending_worker_t *worker)

void(* poll)(async_context_t *self)

void(* wait_until)(async_context_t *self, absolute_time_t until)

void(* wait_for_work_until)(async_context_t *self, absolute_time_t until)

void(* deinit)(async_context_t *self)

async_context

```
struct  async_context
```

```
#include <pico/async_context.h>
```

Base structure type of all async_contexts. For details about its use, see pico_async_context. Individual async_context_types with additional state, should contain this structure at the start.

Data Fields

const async_context_type_t *type
async_when_pending_worker_t *when_pending_list
async_at_time_worker_t *at_time_list
absolute_time_t next_time
uint16_t flags
uint8_t core_num

Functions

async_context_acquire_lock_blocking()   Inline Static

```
static void async_context_acquire_lock_blocking
        (async_context_t * context)
```

Acquire the async_context lock. The owner of the async_context lock is the logic owner of the async_context and other work related to this async_context will not happen concurrently. This method may be called in a nested fashion by the the lock owner. For async_contexts that provide locking (not async_context_poll), this method is threadsafe. and may be called from within any worker method called by the async_context or from any other non-IRQ context. See also async_context_release_lock.

NOTE the async_context lock is nestable by the same caller, so an internal count is maintained.

Parameters

context   The async_context.

async_context_add_at_time_worker()   Inline Static

```
static bool async_context_add_at_time_worker
        (async_context_t * context,
        async_at_time_worker_t * worker)
```

Add an "at time" worker to a context. An "at time" worker will run at or after a specific point in time, and is automatically when (just before) it runs. The time to fire is specified in the next_time field of the worker. *NOTE for async_contexts that provide locking (not async_context_poll), this method is threadsafe. and may be called from within any worker method called by the async_context or from any other non-IRQ context.*

Parameters

context   The async_context.
worker   The "at time" worker to add

Returns

True if the worker was added, false if the worker was already present.

async_context_add_at_time_worker_at()   Inline Static

```
static bool async_context_add_at_time_worker_at
        (async_context_t *context,
         async_at_time_worker_t *worker,
         absolute_time_t at)
```

Add an "at time" worker to a context. An "at time" worker will run at or after a specific point in time, and is automatically when (just before) it runs. The time to fire is specified by the at parameter. *NOTE For async_contexts that provide locking (not async_context_poll), this method is threadsafe. and may be called from within any worker method called by the async_context or from any other non-IRQ context.*

Parameters

context	The async_context.
worker	The "at time" worker to add.
at	The time to fire at.

Returns

True if the worker was added, false if the worker was already present.

async_context_add_at_time_worker_in_ms()   Inline Static

```
static bool async_context_add_at_time_worker_in_ms
        (async_context_t *context,
         async_at_time_worker_t *worker, uint32_t ms)
```

Add an "at time" worker to a context. An "at time" worker will run at or after a specific point in time, and is automatically when (just before) it runs. The time to fire is specified by a delay via the ms parameter. *NOTE For async_contexts that provide locking (not async_context_poll), this method is threadsafe. and may be called from within any worker method called by the async_context or from any other non-IRQ context.*

Parameters

context	The async_context.
worker	The "at time" worker to add.
ms	The number of milliseconds from now to fire after.

Returns

True if the worker was added, false if the worker was already present.

async_context_add_when_pending_worker()   Inline Static

```
static bool async_context_add_when_pending_worker
        (async_context_t * context,
         async_when_pending_worker_t * worker)
```

Add a "when pending" worker to a context. An "when pending" worker will run when it is pending (can be set via async_context_set_work_pending), and is NOT automatically removed when it runs. The time to fire is specified by a delay via the ms parameter. *NOTE for async_contexts that provide locking (not async_context_poll), this method is threadsafe. and may be called from within any worker method called by the async_context or from any other non-IRQ context.*

Parameters

context   The async_context.
worker   The "when pending" worker to add.

Returns

True if the worker was added, false if the worker was already present.

async_context_core_num()   Inline Static

```
static uint async_context_core_num
        (const async_context_t * context)
```

Return the processor core this async_context belongs to.

Parameters

context   The async_context.

Returns

The physical core number.

async_context_deinit()   Inline Static

```
static void async_context_deinit
        (async_context_t * context)
```

End async_context processing, and free any resources. Note the user should clean up any resources associated with workers in the async_context themselves. Asynchronous (non-polled) async_contexts guarantee that no callback is being called once this method returns.

Parameters

context   The async_context.

async_context_execute_sync()   Inline Static

```
static uint32_t async_context_execute_sync
        (async_context_t * context,
        uint32_t(*)(void *param) func, void * param)
```

Execute work synchronously on the core the async_context belongs to. This method is intended for code external to the async_context (e.g. another thread/task) to execute a function with the same guarantees (single core, logical thread of execution) that async_context workers are called with.

NOTE You should NOT call this method while holding the async_context's lock.

Parameters

context   The async_context.
func   The function to call.
paramt   The paramter to pass to the function.

Returns

The return value from func.

async_context_freertos_default_config()   **Inline Static**

```
static async_context_freertos_config_t
        async_context_freertos_default_config(void)
```

Return a copy of the default configuration object used by async_context_freertos_init_with_defaults(). The caller can then modify just the settings it cares about, and call async_context_freertos_init().

Returns

The default configuration object.

async_context_freertos_init()

```
bool async_context_freertos_init
        (async_context_freertos_t * self,
        async_context_freertos_config_t * config)
```

Initialize an async_context_freertos instance using the specified configuration. If this method succeeds (returns true), then the async_context is available for use and can be de-initialized by calling async_context_deinit().

Parameters

self

A pointer to async_context_freertos structure to initialize.

config

The configuration object specifying characteristics for the async_context.

Returns

True if initialization is successful, false otherwise.

async_context_freertos_init_with_defaults()   Inline Static

```
static bool async_context_freertos_init_with_defaults
          (async_context_freertos_t * self)
```

Initialize an async_context_freertos instance with default values. If this method succeeds (returns true), then the async_context is available for use and can be de-initialized by calling async_context_deinit().

Parameters

self   A pointer to async_context_freertos structure to initialize.

Returns

True if initialization is successful, false otherwise.

async_context_lock_check()   Inline Static

```
static void async_context_lock_check
          (async_context_t * context)
```

Assert if the caller does not own the lock for the async_context. *NOTE this method is thread-safe.*

Parameters

context   The async_context.

async_context_poll()   Inline Static

```
static void async_context_poll(async_context_t * context)
```

Perform any pending work for polling style async_context. For a polled async_context (e.g. async_context_poll) the user is responsible for calling this method periodically to perform any required work. This method may immediately perform outstanding work on other context types, but is not required to.

Parameters

context   The async_context.

async_context_poll_init_with_defaults()

```
bool async_context_poll_init_with_defaults
          (async_context_poll_t * self)
```

Initialize an async_context_poll instance with default values. If this method succeeds (returns true), then the async_context is available for use and can be de-initialized by calling async_context_deinit().

Parameters

self   A pointer to async_context_freertos structure to initialize.

Returns

True if initialization is successful, false otherwise.

async_context_release_lock()   Inline Static

```
static void async_context_release_lock
          (async_context_t * context)
```

Release the async_context lock. For async_contexts that provide locking (not async_context_poll), this method is threadsafe. and may be called from within any worker method called by the async_context or from any other non-IRQ context. See also async_context_acquire_lock_blocking.

NOTE The async_context lock may be called in a nested fashion, so an internal count is maintained. On the outermost release, When the outermost lock is released, a check is made for work which might have been skipped while the lock was held, and any such work may be performed during this call IF the call is made from the same core that the async_context belongs to.

Parameters

context   The async_context.

async_context_remove_at_time_worker()   Inline Static

```
static bool async_context_remove_at_time_worker
        (async_context_t * context,
        async_at_time_worker_t * worker)
```

Remove an "at time" worker from a context.

NOTE For async_contexts that provide locking (not async_context_poll), this method is threadsafe. and may be called from within any worker method called by the async_context or from any other non-IRQ context.

Parameters

context   The async_context.
worker   The "at time" worker to remove.

Returns

True if the worker was removed, false if the instance not present.

async_context_remove_when_pending_worker()   Inline Static

```
static bool async_context_remove_when_pending_worker
        (async_context_t * context,
        async_when_pending_worker_t * worker)
```

Remove a "when pending" worker from a context.

NOTE For async_contexts that provide locking (not async_context_poll), this method is threadsafe. and may be called from within any worker method called by the async_context or from any other non-IRQ context.

Parameters

context   The async_context.
worker   The "when pending" worker to remove.

Returns

True if the worker was removed, false if the instance not present.

async_context_set_work_pending() Inline Static

```
static void async_context_set_work_pending
        (async_context_t * context,
        async_when_pending_worker_t * worker)
```

Mark a "when pending" worker as having work pending. The worker will be run from the async_context at a later time.

NOTE This method may be called from any context including IRQs.

Parameters

context   The async_context.

worker   The "when pending" worker to mark as pending.

async_context_threadsafe_background_default_config()

```
async_context_threadsafe_background_config_t
        async_context_threadsafe_background_default_config
        (void )
```

Return a copy of the default configuration object used by async_context_threadsafe_background_init_with_defaults(). The caller can then modify just the settings it cares about, and call async_context_threadsafe_background_init().

Returns

The default configuration object.

async_context_threadsafe_background_init()

```
Bool async_context_threadsafe_background_init
        (async_context_threadsafe_background_t * self,
        async_context_threadsafe_background_config_t *
        config)
```

Initialize an async_context_threadsafe_background instance using the specified configuration. If this method succeeds (returns true), then the async_context is available for use and can be de-initialized by calling async_context_deinit().

Parameters

self

A pointer to async_context_threadsafe_background structure to initialize.

config

The configuration object specifying characteristics for the async_context.

Returns

True if initialization is successful, false otherwise.

async_context_threadsafe_background_init_with_defaults()

Inline Static

```
static bool
        async_context_threadsafe_background_init_with_defau
        lts (async_context_threadsafe_background_t * self)
```

Initialize an async_context_threadsafe_background instance with default values. If this method succeeds (returns true), then the async_context is available for use and can be de-initialized by calling async_context_deinit().

Parameters

self

A pointer to async_context_threadsafe_background structure to initialize.

Returns

True if initialization is successful, false otherwise.

async_context_wait_for_work_ms()   Inline Static

```
static void async_context_wait_for_work_ms
          (async_context_t * context, uint32_t ms)
```

Block until work needs to be done or the specified number of milliseconds have passed.

NOTE This method should not be called from a worker callback.

Parameters

context

The async_context.

ms

The number of milliseconds to return after if no work is required.

async_context_wait_for_work_until()   Inline Static

```
static void async_context_wait_for_work_until
          (async_context_t * context, absolute_time_t until)
```

Block until work needs to be done or the specified time has been reached.

NOTE This method should not be called from a worker callback.

context

The async_context.

until

The time to return at if no work is required.

async_context_wait_until()   Inline Static

```
static void async_context_wait_until
        (async_context_t * context, absolute_time_t until)
```

Sleep until the specified time in an async_context callback safe way.

NOTE For async_contexts that provide locking (not async_context_poll), this method is threadsafe. and may be called from within any worker method called by the async_context or from any other non-IRQ context.

Parameters

context   The async_context.

until   The time to sleep until.

FLASH

pico_flash

```
#include "pico/flash.h"
```

Flash cannot be erased or written to when in XIP mode. However the system cannot directly access memory in the flash address space when not in XIP mode. It is therefore critical that no code or data is being read from flash while flash is been written or erased. If only one core is being used, then the problem is simple - just disable interrupts; however if code is running on the other core, then it has to be asked, nicely, to avoid flash for a bit. This is hard to do if you don't have complete control of the code running on that core at all times.

This library provides a flash_safe_execute method which calls a function back having sucessfully gotten into a state where interrupts are disabled, and the other core is not executing or reading from flash. How it does this is dependent on the supported environment (Free RTOS SMP or pico_multicore). Additionally the user can provide their own mechanism by providing a strong definition of get_flash_safety_helper(). Using the default settings, flash_safe_execute will only call the callback function if the state is safe otherwise returning an error (or an assert depending on PICO_FLASH_ASSERT_ON_UNSAFE).

There are conditions where safety would not be guaranteed:

FreeRTOS smp with configNUM_CORES=1 - FreeRTOS still uses pico_multicore in this case, so flash_safe_execute cannot know what the other core is doing, and there is no way to force code execution between a FreeRTOS core and a non FreeRTOS core.

FreeRTOS non SMP with pico_multicore - Again, there is no way to force code execution between a FreeRTOS and a non FreeRTOS core.

pico_multicore without flash_safe_execute_core_init() having been called on the other core - The flash_safe_execute method does not know if code is executing on the other core, so it has to assume it is. Either way, it is not able to intervene if flash_safe_execute_core_init() has not been called on the other core.

Fortunately, all is not lost in this situation, you may:

Set PICO_FLASH_ASSUME_CORE0_SAFE=1 to explicitly say that core 0 is never using flash.

Set PICO_FLASH_ASSUME_CORE1_SAFE=1 to explicitly say that core 1 is never using flash.flash_safe_execute()

The Pico C API Functionary

flash_safe_execute()

```
int flash_safe_execute (void(*)(void *) func,
        void * param, uint32_t enter_exit_timeout_ms)
```

Execute a function with IRQs disabled and with the other core also not executing/reading flash.

NOTE If PICO_FLASH_ASSERT_ON_UNSAFE is 1, this function will assert in debug mode vs returning PICO_ERROR_NOT_PERMITTED.

Parameters

func

The function to call.

param

The parameter to pass to the function.

enter_exit_timeout_ms

The timeout for each of the enter/exit phases when coordinating with the other core.

Returns

PICO_OK on success (the function will have been called). PICO_TIMEOUT on timeout (the function may have been called).
PICO_ERROR_NOT_PERMITTED if safe execution is not possible (the function will not have been called).
PICO_ERROR_INSUFFICIENT_RESOURCES if the method fails due to dynamic resource exhaustion (the function will not have been called)

flash_safe_execute_core_deinit()

```
bool flash_safe_execute_core_deinit (void)
```

De-initialize work done by flash_safe_execute_core_init.

Returns

True on success.

flash_safe_execute_core_init()

```
bool flash_safe_execute_core_init (void)
```

Initialize a core such that the other core can lock it out during flash_safe_execute.

NOTE This is not necessary for FreeRTOS SMP, but should be used when launching via multicore_launch_core1

Returns

True on success; there is no need to call flash_safe_execute_core_deinit() on failure.

get_flash_safety_helper()

```
flash_safety_helper_t * get_flash_safety_helper (void)
```

Internal method to return the flash safety helper implementation. Advanced users can provide their own implementation of this function to perform different inter-core coordination before disabling XIP mode.

Returns

The flash_safety_helper_t.

I2C SLAVE

pico_i2c_slave

```
#include "pico/i2c_slave.h"
```

Functions providing an interrupt driven I2C slave interface. This I2C slave helper library configures slave mode and hooks the relevant I2C IRQ so that a user supplied handler is called with enumerated I2C events.

TYPEDEFS

i2c_slave_event_t

```
typedef enum i2c_slave_event_t i2c_slave_event_t
```

I2C slave event types.

i2c_slave_handler_t

```
typedef void(* i2c_slave_handler_t) (i2c_inst_t *i2c,
        i2c_slave_event_t event)
```

I2C slave event handler.

ENUMERATIONS

i2c_slave_event_t

`enum i2c_slave_event_t`

I2C slave event types.

I2C_SLAVE_RECEIVE

Data from master is available for reading. Slave must read from Rx FIFO.

I2C_SLAVE_REQUEST

Master is requesting data. Slave must write into Tx FIFO.

I2C_SLAVE_FINISH

Master has sent a Stop or Restart signal. Slave may prepare for the next transfer.

FUNCTIONS

i2c_slave_deinit()

`void i2c_slave_deinit (i2c_inst_t *i2c)`

Restore an I2C instance to master mode.

Parameters

i2c	Either i2c0 or i2c1.

i2c_slave_init()

`void i2c_slave_init (i2c_inst_t *i2c, uint8_t address, i2c_slave_handler_t handler)`

Configure an I2C instance for slave mode.

Parameters

i2c	Either i2c0 or i2c1.
address	7-bit slave address.
handler	Callback for events from I2C master. It will run from the I2C ISR, on the CPU core where the slave was initialised.

MULTICORE

pico_multicore

```
#include "pico/multicore.h"
```

The multicore section of the API provides support for running code on the second processor core (core 1) of the RP2040. It introduces inter-core FIFOs, which are 32 bits wide and 8 entries deep, enabling data, messages, or ordered events to be passed between the two cores. One FIFO is dedicated to core 0 for writing and core 1 for reading, while the other FIFO is dedicated to core 1 for writing and core 0 for reading.

In addition to the inter-core FIFOs, the multicore API offers functions for entering critical sections on both cores simultaneously. These "lockout" functions utilize the FIFOs to interrupt one core from the other and manage the waiting process until the other core enters a "locked out" state. This allows for cooperative execution synchronization between the cores.

It's important to note that when a core is "locked out," it enters a paused state with interrupts disabled, typically executing a tight loop with code stored in RAM. This makes the lockout functions suitable for scenarios such as writing to flash, where no code can be executing from flash memory.

To initiate a lockout, the core wishing to lock out the other core calls functions like multicore_lockout_start_blocking or multicore_lockout_start_timeout_us to interrupt the "victim" core and wait for it to enter the "locked out" state. Once the lockout is no longer needed, the core calls multicore_lockout_end_blocking or multicore_lockout_end_timeout_us to release the lockout and wait for confirmation.

It's also worth noting that due to the utilization of inter-core FIFOs by multicore lockout, the FIFOs cannot be used for any other purpose simultaneously. Therefore, it's recommended to avoid using the FIFOs for custom data transfer between the cores unless it's necessary and doesn't conflict with the mentioned concerns.

multicore_fifo_clear_irq()   Inline Static

```
static void multicore_fifo_clear_irq(void )
```

Clear FIFO interrupt. Note that this only clears an interrupt that was caused by the ROE or WOF flags. To clear the VLD flag you need to use one of the 'pop' or 'drain' functions. See the note in the fifo section for considerations regarding use of the inter-core FIFOs. See alsomulticore_fifo_get_status.

multicore_fifo_drain()   Inline Static

```
static void multicore_fifo_drain(void )
```

Discard any data in the read FIFO. See the note in the fifo section for considerations regarding use of the inter-core FIFOs

multicore_fifo_get_status()   Inline Static

```
static uint32_t multicore_fifo_get_status(void )
```

Get FIFO statuses.

Returns

The statuses as a bitfield.

Bit	Description
3	Sticky flag indicating the RX FIFO was read when empty (ROE). This read was ignored by the FIFO.
2	Sticky flag indicating the TX FIFO was written when full (WOF). This write was ignored by the FIFO.
1	Value is 1 if this core's TX FIFO is not full (i.e. if FIFO_WR is ready for more data)
0	Value is 1 if this core's RX FIFO is not empty (i.e. if FIFO_RD is valid)

See the note in the fifo section for considerations regarding use of the inter-core FIFOs.

multicore_fifo_pop_blocking()

```
uint32_t multicore_fifo_pop_blocking(void )
```

Pop data from the read FIFO (data from the other core). This function will block until there is data ready to be read Use multicore_fifo_rvalid() to check if data is ready to be read if you don't want to block. See the note in the fifo section for considerations regarding use of the inter-core FIFOs.

Returns

32 bit data from the read FIFO.

multicore_fifo_pop_timeout_us()

```
bool multicore_fifo_pop_timeout_us(uint64_t timeout_us,
        uint32_t * out)
```

Pop data from the read FIFO (data from the other core) with timeout. This function will block until there is data ready to be read or the timeout is reached. See the note in the fifo section for considerations regarding use of the inter-core FIFOs.

Parameters

timeout_us   The timeout in microseconds.
out   The location to store the popped data if available.

Returns

True if the data was popped and a value copied into out, false if the timeout occurred before data could be popped.

multicore_fifo_push_blocking()

```
void multicore_fifo_push_blocking(uint32_t data)
```

Push data on to the write FIFO (data to the other core). This function will block until there is space for the data to be sent. Use multicore_fifo_wready() to check if it is possible to write to the FIFO if you don't want to block. See the note in the fifo section for considerations regarding use of the inter-core FIFOs.

Parameters

data	A 32 bit value to push on to the FIFO.

multicore_fifo_push_timeout_us()

```
bool multicore_fifo_push_timeout_us(uint32_t data, uint64_t
    timeout_us)
```

Push data on to the write FIFO (data to the other core) with timeout. This function will block until there is space for the data to be sent or the timeout is reached.

Parameters

data	A 32 bit value to push on to the FIFO.
timeout_us	The timeout in microseconds.

Returns

True if the data was pushed, false if the timeout occurred before data could be pushed.

multicore_fifo_rvalid()   Inline Static

```
static bool multicore_fifo_rvalid(void )
```

Check the read FIFO to see if there is data available (sent by the other core). See the note in the fifo section for considerations regarding use of the inter-core FIFOs.

Returns

True if the FIFO has data in it, false otherwise.

multicore_fifo_wready()   Inline Static

```
static bool multicore_fifo_wready(void )
```

Check the write FIFO to see if it has space for more data. See the note in the fifo section for considerations regarding use of the inter-core FIFOs.

Returns

True if the FIFO has room for more data, false otherwise.

multicore_launch_core1()

```
void multicore_launch_core1(void(*)(void) entry)
```

Run code on core 1. Wake up (a previously reset) core 1 and enter the given function on core 1 using the default core 1 stack (below core 0 stack). Core 1 must previously have been reset either as a result of a system reset or by calling multicore_reset_core1. Core 1 will use the same vector table as core 0. See also multicore_reset_core1.

Parameters

entry   Function entry point.

multicore_launch_core1_raw()

```
void multicore_launch_core1_raw(void(*)(void) entry,
        uint32_t * sp, uint32_t vector_table)
```

Launch code on core 1 with no stack protection. Wake up (a previously reset) core 1 and start it executing with a specific entry point, stack pointer and vector table. This is a low level function that does not provide a stack guard even if USE_STACK_GUARDS is defined. Core 1 must previously have been reset either as a result of a system reset or by calling multicore_reset_core1. See also multicore_reset_core1.

Parameters

entry	Function entry point.
sp	Pointer to the top of the core 1 stack.
vector_table	Address of the vector table to use for core 1.

multicore_launch_core1_with_stack()

```
void multicore_launch_core1_with_stack
        (void(*)(void) entry, uint32_t * stack_bottom,
        size_t stack_size_bytes)
```

Launch code on core 1 with stack. Wake up (a previously reset) core 1 and enter the given function on core 1 using the passed stack for core 1. Core 1 must previously have been reset either as a result of a system reset or by calling multicore_reset_core1. Core 1 will use the same vector table as core 0. See also multicore_reset_core1.

Parameters

entry	Function entry point.
stack_bottom	The bottom (lowest address) of the stack.
stack_size_bytes	The size of the stack in bytes (must be a multiple of 4).

multicore_lockout_end_blocking()

```
void multicore_lockout_end_blocking(void )
```

Release the other core from a locked out state amd wait for it to acknowledge.

NOTE The other core must previously have been "locked out" by calling a multicore_lockout_start_ function from this core.

multicore_lockout_end_timeout_us()

```
bool multicore_lockout_end_timeout_us(uint64_t timeout_us)
```

Release the other core from a locked out state amd wait up to a time limit for it to acknowledge. The other core must previously have been "locked out" by calling a multicore_lockout_start_ function from this core.

NOTE Be very careful using small timeout values, as a timeout here will leave the "lockout" functionality in a bad state. It is probably preferable to use multicore_lockout_end_blocking anyway as if you have already waited for the victim core to enter the lockout state, then the victim core will be ready to exit the lockout state very quickly.

Parameters

timeout_us   The timeout in microseconds.

Returns

True if the other core successfully exited locked out state within the timeout, false otherwise.

multicore_lockout_start_blocking()

```
void multicore_lockout_start_blocking(void )
```

Request the other core to pause in a known state and wait for it to do so. The other (victim) core must have previously executed multicore_lockout_victim_init().

NOTE Multicore_lockout_start_ functions are not nestable, and must be paired with a call to a corresponding multicore_lockout_end_blocking.

multicore_lockout_start_timeout_us()

```
bool multicore_lockout_start_timeout_us(uint64_t
        timeout_us)
```

Request the other core to pause in a known state and wait up to a time limit for it to do so. The other core must have previously executed multicore_lockout_victim_init().

NOTE Multicore_lockout_start_ functions are not nestable, and must be paired with a call to a corresponding multicore_lockout_end_blocking.

Parameters

timeout_us   The timeout in microseconds.

Returns

True if the other core entered the locked out state within the timeout, false otherwise.

multicore_lockout_victim_init()

```
void multicore_lockout_victim_init(void )
```

Initialize the current core such that it can be a "victim" of lockout (i.e. forced to pause in a known state by the other core). This code hooks the intercore FIFO IRQ, and the FIFO may not be used for any other purpose after this.

multicore_lockout_victim_is_initialized()

```
bool multicore_lockout_victim_is_initialized
          (uint core_num)
```

Determine if multicore_victim_init() has been called on the specified core.

NOTE This state persists even if the core is subsequently reset; therefore you are advised to always call multicore_lockout_victim_init() again after resetting a core, which had previously been initialized.

Parameters

core_num   The core number (0 or 1).

Returns

True if multicore_victim_init() has been called on the specified core, false otherwise.

multicore_reset_core1()

```
void multicore_reset_core1(void )
```

Reset core 1. This function can be used to reset core 1 into its initial state (ready for launching code against via multicore_launch_core1 and similar methods).

NOTE This function should only be called from core 0.

RAND

pico_rand

```
#include "pico/rand.h"
```

This module provides functionality for generating random numbers at runtime. It utilizes various entropy sources to modify the state of a 128-bit Pseudo Random Number Generator (PRNG) implemented in software.

The module supports generating random numbers ranging from 32 to 128 bits. These numbers are read from the PRNG, which helps ensure a large number space.

Multiple sources of entropy are available, each enabled by a define directive:

• The Ring Oscillator (ROSC) is one source of entropy. It gathers bits from the ring oscillator's "random bit" and mixes them into the PRNG state. Note that this should only be used if the ROSC is enabled and the processor is running from the ROSC.

• Time-based entropy is another source where the 64-bit microsecond timer is mixed into the PRNG state.

• The Bus Performance Counter provides another source of entropy. One of the bus fabric's performance counters is mixed into the PRNG state.

It's important to note that all entropy sources are hashed before being applied to the PRNG state machine, ensuring their effectiveness.

When requesting a random number for the first time, the 128-bit PRNG state must be seeded. Multiple entropy sources are available for the seeding operation:

• The Ring Oscillator (ROSC) can contribute 64 bits from its "random bit" to the seed.

• Time-based entropy includes the 64-bit microsecond timer mixed into the seed.

• The Board Identifier, obtained via pico_get_unique_board_id, can be mixed into the seed.

RAM hash entropy allows the hashed contents of a subset of RAM to be mixed into the seed. By default, the last 1K of RAM (often containing the core 0 stack) is hashed, providing entropy based on differences after each warm reset.

With the default settings, seed generation takes approximately 1 millisecond, while subsequent random number generation generally takes between 10 and 20 microseconds.

The pico_rand methods can be safely called from either core or an interrupt service routine (IRQ), but caution should be exercised when calling them from an IRQ, as the calls may block for microseconds while waiting for more entropy.

get_rand_128()

```
void get_rand_128 (rng_128_t *rand128)
```

Get 128-bit random number. This method may be safely called from either core or from an IRQ, but be careful in the latter case as the call may block for a number of microseconds waiting on more entropy.

Parameters

rand128   Pointer to storage to accept a 128-bit random number.

get_rand_32()

```
uint32_t get_rand_32 (void)
```

Get 32-bit random number. This method may be safely called from either core or from an IRQ, but be careful in the latter case as the call may block for a number of microseconds waiting on more entropy.

Returns

32-bit random number.

get_rand_64()

```
uint64_t get_rand_64 (void)
```

Get 64-bit random number. This method may be safely called from either core or from an IRQ, but be careful in the latter case as the call may block for a number of microseconds waiting on more entropy.

Returns

64-bit random number.

STDLIB

pico_stdlib

```
#include "pico/stdlib.h"
```

Aggregation of a core subset of Raspberry Pi Pico SDK libraries used by most executables along with some additional utility methods. Including pico_stdlib gives you everything you need to get a basic program running which prints to stdout or flashes a LED

This library aggregates:

- hardware_uart

- hardware_gpio

- pico_binary_info

- pico_runtime

- pico_platform

- pico_printf

- pico_stdio

- pico_standard_link

- pico_util

There are some basic default values used by these functions that will default to usable values, however, they can be customized in a board definition header via config.h or similar.

check_sys_clock_khz()

```
bool check_sys_clock_khz (uint32_t freq_khz,
        uint *vco_freq_out, uint *post_div1_out, uint
        *post_div2_out)
```

Check if a given system clock frequency is valid/attainable.

Parameters

freq_khz

Requested frequency

vco_freq_out

On success, the voltage controlled oscillator frequency to be used by the SYS PLL.

post_div1_out

On success, The first post divider for the SYS PLL.

post_div2_out

On success, The second post divider for the SYS PLL.

Returns

True if the frequency is possible and the output parameters have been written.

set_sys_clock_48mhz()

```
void set_sys_clock_48mhz (void)
```

Initialize the system clock to 48MHz. Set the system clock to 48MHz, and set the peripheral clock to match.

set_sys_clock_khz()   Inline Static

```
static bool set_sys_clock_khz (uint32_t freq_khz,
        bool required)
```

Attempt to set a system clock frequency in khz. Note that not all clock frequencies are possible; it is preferred that you use src/rp2_common/hardware_clocks/scripts/vcocalc.py to calculate the parameters for use with set_sys_clock_pll.

Parameters

freq_khz

Requested frequency.

required

If true then this function will assert if the frequency is not attainable.

Returns

True if the clock was configured.

set_sys_clock_pll()

```
void set_sys_clock_pll (uint32_t vco_freq, uint post_div1,
        uint post_div2)
```

Initialize the system clock. See the PLL documentation in the datasheet for details of driving the PLLs.

Parameters

vco_freq

The voltage controller oscillator frequency to be used by the SYS PLL

post_div1

The first post divider for the SYS PLL

post_div2

The second post divider for the SYS PLL.

The Pico C API Functionary

setup_default_uart()

```
void setup_default_uart(void)
```

Set up the default UART and assign it to the default GPIOs. By default this will use UART 0, with TX to pin GPIO 0, RX to pin GPIO 1, and the baudrate to 115200. Calling this method also initializes stdin/stdout over UART if the pico_stdio_uart library is linked. Defaults can be changed using configuration defines:

- **PICO_DEFAULT_UART_INSTANCE**
- **PICO_DEFAULT_UART_BAUD_RATE**
- **PICO_DEFAULT_UART_TX_PIN**
- **PICO_DEFAULT_UART_RX_PIN.**

SYNC

pico_sync

```
#include "pico/sync.h"
```

This API provides synchronization primitives and mutual exclusion mechanisms for safe and controlled access to shared resources.

Critical Sections

The Critical Section API offers short-lived mutual exclusion that is safe for both interrupt service routines (IRQ) and multi-core environments. A critical section ensures non-reentrant behavior by utilizing a spin-lock to prevent access from the other core and higher-priority interrupts on the same core. The spin-lock mechanism protects the critical section from concurrent access. Additionally, interrupts are disabled on the calling core to prevent interruptions during critical section execution.

It is important to keep critical sections as short as possible since interrupts are disabled while the critical section is owned.

Lock Core

```
#include "lock_core.h"
```

The pico_sync API includes lock_core-based structures, which function by acquiring the spin lock, checking the state, and determining whether blocking or notification is necessary upon release of the spin lock. In the case of blocking, the thread will be awakened in the future to re-evaluate the lock state.

By default, the SDK utilizes the processors' events for notification and blocking, as they are suitable for cross-core operations and notification from interrupt handlers. However, macros are provided in the pico_sync API to abstract the wait and notify mechanisms, allowing the SDK locking functions to be effectively used within a real-time operating system (RTOS) or other environments.

When integrating with an RTOS, it is desirable for the SDK synchronization primitives that wait to block the calling task and yield immediately, while those that notify should awaken blocked tasks that are not running on the processor. The wait macro implementation should be atomic with the spin lock unlock operation from the caller's perspective, ensuring the task unlocks the spin lock when it starts waiting. The RTOS integration determines the specific implementation, but the macros are designed to combine these operations into a single call, even though the default implementation may not require it, as the Wait for Event (WFE) instruction following the corresponding Send Event (SEV) instruction is not missed.

Mutex

The Mutex API provides non-IRQ mutual exclusion between cores. Mutexes are locks used to protect data structures that may be accessed by multiple threads of execution. Unlike critical sections, the code protected by a mutex is not necessarily expected to complete quickly, as no other system-wide locks are held while the mutex is acquired.

When a mutex is acquired, it has an owner, which, in the plain SDK, is typically the acquiring core. However, in an RTOS environment, the owner could be a task or an IRQ handler context.

Two variants of mutexes are provided: mutex_t (and associated mutex_ functions) represent regular mutexes that cannot be acquired recursively by the same owner, as it would result in a deadlock. recursive_mutex_t (and associated recursive_mutex_ functions) are recursive mutexes that allow recursive acquisition by the same caller, albeit with some additional overhead during acquisition and release.

It is generally not recommended to call blocking mutex functions from within an IRQ handler. However, calling mutex_try_enter or recursive_mutex_try_enter from an IRQ handler is valid if the operation that would be performed under the lock can be skipped if the mutex is already locked by the same owner.

NOTE: For backward compatibility with version 1.2.0 of the SDK, the regular mutex_ functions can also be used for recursive mutexes if the PICO_MUTEX_ENABLE_SDK120_COMPATIBILITY define is set to 1. This flag will be removed in a future version of the SDK.

Refer to critical_section.h for protecting access between multiple cores and IRQ handlers.

Semaphore

Semaphore API for restricting access to a resource. A semaphore holds a number of available permits. sem_acquire methods will acquire a permit if available (reducing the available count by 1) or block if the number of available permits is 0. sem_release() increases the number of available permits by one potentially unblocking a sem_acquire method.

Note that sem_release() may be called an arbitrary number of times, however the number of available permits is capped to the max_permit value specified during semaphore initialization.

Although these semaphore related functions can be used from IRQ handlers, it is obviously preferable to only release semaphores from within an IRQ handler (i.e. avoid blocking)

The pico_sync API provides a comprehensive set of synchronization primitives and mutual exclusion mechanisms to ensure safe and controlled access to shared resources in various scenarios.

MACROS

auto_init_mutex()

```
#define auto_init_mutex(name)
```

Helper macro for static definition of mutexes.

auto_init_recursive_mutex()

```
#define auto_init_recursive_mutex(name)
```

Helper macro for static definition of recursive mutexes.

lock_get_caller_owner_id()

```
#define lock_get_caller_owner_id()
        ((lock_owner_id_t)get_core_num())
```

Return the owner id for the caller. By default this returns the calling core number, but may be overridden (e.g. to return an RTOS task id)

lock_internal_spin_unlock_with_best_effort_wait_or_timeout()

```
#define
        lock_internal_spin_unlock_with_best_effort_wait_or_t
        imeout (lock, save, until)
```

Atomically unlock the lock's spin lock, and wait for a notification or a timeout. Atomic here refers to the fact that it should not be possible for a concurrent lock_internal_spin_unlock_with_notify to insert itself between the spin unlock and this wait in a way that the wait does not see the notification (i.e. causing a missed notification). In other words this method should always wake up in response to a lock_internal_spin_unlock_with_notify for the same lock, which completes after this call starts.

In an ideal implementation, this method would return exactly after the corresponding lock_internal_spin_unlock_with_notify has subsequently been called on the same lock instance or the timeout has been reached, however this method is free to return at any point before that; this macro is always used in a loop which locks the spin lock, checks the internal locking primitive state and then waits again if the calling thread should not proceed.

By default this simply unlocks the spin lock, and then calls best_effort_wfe_or_timeout but may be overridden (e.g. to actually block the RTOS task with a timeout).

Parameters

lock

The lock_core for the primitive which needs to block.

save

The uint32_t value that should be passed to spin_unlock when the spin lock is unlocked. (i.e. the PRIMASK state when the spin lock was acquire).

until

The absolute_time_t value.

Returns

True if the timeout has been reached.

lock_internal_spin_unlock_with_notify()

```
#define lock_internal_spin_unlock_with_notify(lock, save)
        spin_unlock ((lock)->spin_lock, save), __sev()
```

Atomically unlock the lock's spin lock, and send a notification. Atomic here refers to the fact that it should not be possible for this notification to happen during a lock_internal_spin_unlock_with_wait in a way that that wait does not see the notification (i.e. causing a missed notification). In other words this method should always wake up any lock_internal_spin_unlock_with_wait which started before this call completes.

In an ideal implementation, this method would wake up only the corresponding lock_internal_spin_unlock_with_wait that has been called on the same lock instance, however it is free to wake up any of them, as they will check their condition and then re-wait if necessary/

By default this macro simply unlocks the spin lock, and then performs a SEV, but may be overridden (e.g. to actually un-block RTOS task(s)).

Parameters

lock

>The lock_core for the primitive which needs to block.

save

>The uint32_t value that should be passed to spin_unlock when the spin lock is unlocked. (i.e. the PRIMASK state when the spin lock was acquire).

lock_internal_spin_unlock_with_wait()

```
#define lock_internal_spin_unlock_with_wait(lock, save)
        spin_unlock((lock)->spin_lock, save), __wfe()
```

Atomically unlock the lock's spin lock, and wait for a notification. Atomic here refers to the fact that it should not be possible for a concurrent lock_internal_spin_unlock_with_notify to insert itself between the spin unlock and this wait in a way that the wait does not see the notification (i.e. causing a missed notification). In other words this method should always wake up in response to a lock_internal_spin_unlock_with_notify for the same lock, which completes after this call starts.

In an ideal implementation, this method would return exactly after the corresponding lock_internal_spin_unlock_with_notify has subsequently been called on the same lock instance, however this method is free to return at any point before that; this macro is always used in a loop which locks the spin lock, checks the internal locking primitive state and then waits again if the calling thread should not proceed.

By default this macro simply unlocks the spin lock, and then performs a WFE, but may be overridden (e.g. to actually block the RTOS task).

Parameters

lock

> The lock_core for the primitive which needs to block.

save

> The uint32_t value that should be passed to spin_unlock when the spin lock is unlocked. (i.e. the PRIMASK state when the spin lock was acquire.

LOCK_INVALID_OWNER_ID

```
#define LOCK_INVALID_OWNER_ID    ((lock_owner_id_t)-1)
```

Marker value to use for a lock_owner_id_t which does not refer to any valid owner.

lock_owner_id_t

```
#define lock_owner_id_t    int8_t
```

Type to use to store the 'owner' of a lock.By default this is int8_t as it only needs to store the core number or -1, however it may be overridden if a larger type is required (e.g. for an RTOS task id).

sync_internal_yield_until_before()

```
#define sync_internal_yield_until_before(until)    ((void)0)
```

Yield to other processing until some time before the requested time. This method is provided for cases where the caller has no useful work to do until the specified time. By default this method does nothing, however it can be overridden (for example by an RTOS which is able to block the current task until the scheduler tick before the given time)

Parameters

until   The absolute_time_t value.

TYPEDEFS

mutex_t

```
typedef struct __packed_aligned mutex mutex_t
```

Regular (non recursive) mutex instance.

recursive_mutex_t

```
typedef struct __packed_aligned recursive_mutex_t
```

Recursive mutex instance.

STRUCTURES

mutex

```
typedef struct __packed_aligned mutex
```

`#include <mutex.h>`

Regular (non recursive) mutex instance.

Data Fields

lock_core_t	core
lock_owner_id_t	owner

recursive_mutex

```
typedef struct __packed_aligned recursive_mutex
```

`#include <mutex.h>`

Recursive mutex instance. *NOTE This structure is not actually named in the API and just defined as the data type recursive_mutex_t.*

Data Fields

lock_core_t	core
lock_owner_id_t	owner
uint8_t	enter_count

FUNCTIONS

critical_section_deinit()

```
void critical_section_deinit(critical_section_t *
     crit_sec)
```

De-Initialize a critical_section created by the critical_section_init method. This method is only used to free the associated spin lock allocated via the critical_section_init method (it should not be used to de-initialize a spin lock created via critical_section_init_with_lock_num). After this call, the critical section is invalid.

Parameters

crit_sec   Pointer to critical_section structure.

critical_section_enter_blocking()   Inline Static

```
static void critical_section_enter_blocking
     (critical_section_t * crit_sec)
```

Enter a critical_section. If the spin lock associated with this critical section is in use, then this method will block until it is released.

Parameters

crit_sec   Pointer to critical_section structure.

critical_section_exit()   Inline Static

```
static void critical_section_exit
     (critical_section_t * crit_sec)
```

Release a critical_section.

Parameters

crit_sec   Pointer to critical_section structure.

critical_section_init()

```
void critical_section_init(critical_section_t * crit_sec)
```

Initialize a critical_section structure allowing the system to assign a spin lock number. The critical section is initialized ready for use, and will use a (possibly shared) spin lock number assigned by the system. Note that in general it is unlikely that you would be nesting critical sections, however if you do so you must use critical_section_init_with_lock_num to ensure that the spin locks used are different.

Parameters

crit_sec   Pointer to critical_section structure.

critical_section_init_with_lock_num()

```
void critical_section_init_with_lock_num
        (critical_section_t * crit_sec, uint lock_num)
```

Initialize a critical_section structure assigning a specific spin lock number.

Parameters

crit_sec   Pointer to critical_section structure.
lock_num   The specific spin lock number to use.

critical_section_is_initialized()   Inline Static

```
static bool critical_section_is_initialized
        (critical_section_t * crit_sec)
```

Test whether a critical_section has been initialized.

Parameters

crit_sec   Pointer to critical_section structure.

Returns

True if the critical section is initialized, false otherwise.

lock_init()

```
void lock_init(lock_core_t * core, uint lock_num)
```

Initialize a lock structure. Initialize a lock structure, providing the spin lock number to use for protecting internal state.

Parameters

core

    Pointer to the lock_core to initialize.

lock_num

    Spin lock number to use for the lock. As the spin lock is only used internally to the locking primitive method implementations, this does not need to be globally unique, however could suffer contention.

mutex_enter_block_until()

```
bool mutex_enter_block_until(mutex_t * mtx,
          absolute_time_t until)
```

Wait for mutex until a specific time. Wait until the specific time to take ownership of the mutex. If the caller can be granted ownership of the mutex before the timeout expires, then true will be returned and the caller will own the mutex, otherwise false will be returned and the caller will NOT own the mutex.

Parameters

mtx

    Pointer to mutex structure.

until

    The time after which to return if the caller cannot be granted ownership of the mutex.

Returns

    True if mutex now owned, false if timeout occurred before ownership could be granted.

mutex_enter_blocking()

```
void mutex_enter_blocking(mutex_t * mtx)
```

Take ownership of a mutex. This function will block until the caller can be granted ownership of the mutex. On return the caller owns the mutex.

Parameters

mtx   Pointer to mutex structure.

mutex_enter_timeout_ms()

```
bool mutex_enter_timeout_ms (mutex_t * mtx,
       uint32_t timeout_ms)
```

Wait for mutex with timeout. Wait for up to the specific time to take ownership of the mutex. If the caller can be granted ownership of the mutex before the timeout expires, then true will be returned and the caller will own the mutex, otherwise false will be returned and the caller will NOT own the mutex.

Parameters

mtx   Pointer to mutex structure.
timeout_ms   The timeout in milliseconds.

Returns

True if mutex now owned, false if timeout occurred before ownership could be granted.

mutex_enter_timeout_us()

```
bool mutex_enter_timeout_us(mutex_t * mtx,
        uint32_t timeout_us)
```

Wait for mutex with timeout. Wait for up to the specific time to take ownership of the mutex. If the caller can be granted ownership of the mutex before the timeout expires, then true will be returned and the caller will own the mutex, otherwise false will be returned and the caller will NOT own the mutex.

Parameters

mtx	Pointer to mutex structure.
timeout_us	The timeout in microseconds.

Returns

True if mutex now owned, false if timeout occurred before ownership could be granted.

mutex_exit()

```
void mutex_exit(mutex_t * mtx)
```

Release ownership of a mutex.

Parameters

mtx	Pointer to mutex structure.

mutex_init()

```
void mutex_init(mutex_t * mtx)
```

Initialize a mutex structure.

Parameters

mtx	Pointer to mutex structure.

mutex_is_initialized() Inline Static

```
static bool mutex_is_initialized(mutex_t * mtx)
```

Test for mutex initialized state.

Parameters

mtx   Pointer to mutex structure.

Returns

True if the mutex is initialized, false otherwise.

mutex_try_enter()

```
bool mutex_try_enter(mutex_t * mtx, uint32_t * owner_out)
```

Attempt to take ownership of a mutex. If the mutex wasn't owned, this will claim the mutex for the caller and return true. Otherwise (if the mutex was already owned) this will return false and the caller will NOT own the mutex.

Parameters

mtx

Pointer to mutex structure.

owner_out

If mutex was already owned, and this pointer is non-zero, it will be filled in with the owner id of the current owner of the mutex

Returns

True if mutex now owned, false otherwise.

mutex_try_enter_block_until()

```
bool mutex_try_enter_block_until(mutex_t * mtx,
        absolute_time_t until)
```

Attempt to take ownership of a mutex until the specified time. If the mutex wasn't owned, this method will immediately claim the mutex for the caller and return true. If the mutex is owned by the caller, this method will immediately return false, If the mutex is owned by someone else, this method will try to claim it until the specified time, returning true if it succeeds, or false on timeout.

Parameters

mtx   Pointer to mutex structure.

until   The time after which to return if the caller cannot be granted ownership of the mutex.

Returns

True if mutex now owned, false otherwise.

recursive_mutex_enter_block_until()

```
bool recursive_mutex_enter_block_until
        (recursive_mutex_t * mtx, absolute_time_t until)
```

Wait for mutex until a specific time. Wait until the specific time to take ownership of the mutex. If the caller already has ownership of the mutex or can be granted ownership of the mutex before the timeout expires, then true will be returned and the caller will own the mutex, otherwise false will be returned and the caller will NOT own the mutex.

Parameters

mtx   Pointer to recursive mutex structure.

until   The time after which to return if the caller cannot be granted ownership of the mutex.

Returns

True if the recursive mutex (now) owned, false if timeout occurred before ownership could be granted.

recursive_mutex_enter_blocking()

```
void recursive_mutex_enter_blocking(recursive_mutex_t *
        mtx)
```

Take ownership of a recursive mutex. This function will block until the caller can be granted ownership of the mutex. On return the caller owns the mutex.

Parameters

mtx   Pointer to recursive mutex structure.

recursive_mutex_enter_timeout_ms()

```
bool recursive_mutex_enter_timeout_ms
        (recursive_mutex_t * mtx, uint32_t timeout_ms )
```

Wait for recursive mutex with timeout. Wait for up to the specific time to take ownership of the recursive mutex. If the caller already has ownership of the mutex or can be granted ownership of the mutex before the timeout expires, then true will be returned and the caller will own the mutex, otherwise false will be returned and the caller will NOT own the mutex.

Parameters

mtx   Pointer to recursive mutex structure.
timeout_ms   The timeout in milliseconds.

Returns

True if the recursive mutex (now) owned, false if timeout occurred before ownership could be granted.

recursive_mutex_enter_timeout_us()

```
bool recursive_mutex_enter_timeout_us
        (recursive_mutex_t * mtx, uint32_t timeout_us)
```

Wait for recursive mutex with timeout. Wait for up to the specific time to take ownership of the recursive mutex. If the caller already has ownership of the mutex or can be granted ownership of the mutex before the timeout expires, then true will be returned and the caller will own the mutex, otherwise false will be returned and the caller will NOT own the mutex.

Parameters

mtx	Pointer to recursive mutex structure.
timeout_us	The timeout in microseconds.

Returns

True if the recursive mutex (now) owned, false if timeout occurred before ownership could be granted.

recursive_mutex_exit()

```
void recursive_mutex_exit(recursive_mutex_t * mtx)
```

Release ownership of a recursive mutex.

Parameters

mtx	Pointer to recursive mutex structure.

recursive_mutex_init()

```
void recursive_mutex_init(recursive_mutex_t * mtx)
```

Initialize a recursive mutex structure. A recursive mutex may be entered in a nested fashion by the same owner.

Parameters

mtx	Pointer to recursive mutex structure.

recursive_mutex_is_initialized()   Inline Static

```
static bool recursive_mutex_is_initialized
          (recursive_mutex_t * mtx)
```

Test for recursive mutex initialized state.

Parameters

mtx   Pointer to recursive mutex structure.

Returns

True if the recursive mutex is initialized, false otherwise.

recursive_mutex_try_enter()

```
bool recursive_mutex_try_enter(recursive_mutex_t * mtx,
          uint32_t * owner_out)
```

Attempt to take ownership of a recursive mutex. If the mutex wasn't owned or was owned by the caller, this will claim the mutex and return true. Otherwise (if the mutex was already owned by another owner) this will return false and the caller will NOT own the mutex.

Parameters

mtx

Pointer to recursive mutex structure.

owner_out

If mutex was already owned by another owner, and this pointer is non-zero, it will be filled in with the owner id of the current owner of the mutex

Returns

True if the recursive mutex (now) owned, false otherwise.

sem_acquire_block_until()

```
bool sem_acquire_block_until(semaphore_t * sem,
        absolute_time_t until)
```

Wait to acquire a permit from a semaphore until a specific time. This function will block and wait if no permits are available, until the specified timeout time. If the timeout is reached the function will return false, otherwise it will return true.

Parameters

sem	Pointer to semaphore structure.
until	The time after which to return if the sem is not available.

Returns

True if permit was acquired, false if the until time was reached before acquiring.

sem_acquire_blocking()

```
void sem_acquire_blocking(semaphore_t * sem)
```

Acquire a permit from the semaphore. This function will block and wait if no permits are available.

Parameters

sem	Pointer to semaphore structure.

sem_acquire_timeout_ms()

```
bool sem_acquire_timeout_ms(semaphore_t * sem,
          uint32_t timeout_ms)
```

Acquire a permit from a semaphore, with timeout. This function will block and wait if no permits are available, until the defined timeout has been reached. If the timeout is reached the function will return false, otherwise it will return true.

Parameters

sem	Pointer to semaphore structure.
timeout_ms	Time to wait to acquire the semaphore, in milliseconds.

Returns

False if timeout reached, true if permit was acquired.

sem_acquire_timeout_us()

```
bool sem_acquire_timeout_us(semaphore_t * sem,
          uint32_t timeout_us)
```

Acquire a permit from a semaphore, with timeout. This function will block and wait if no permits are available, until the defined timeout has been reached. If the timeout is reached the function will return false, otherwise it will return true.

Parameters

sem	Pointer to semaphore structure.
timeout_ms	Time to wait to acquire the semaphore, in milliseconds.

Returns

False if timeout reached, true if permit was acquired.

sem_available()

```
int sem_available(semaphore_t * sem)
```

Return number of available permits on the semaphore.

Parameters

sem   Pointer to semaphore structure.

Returns

The number of permits available on the semaphore.

sem_init()

```
void sem_init(semaphore_t * sem, int16_t initial_permits,
        int16_t max_permits)
```

Initialize a semaphore structure.

Parameters

sem   Pointer to semaphore structure.
initial_permits   How many permits are initially acquired.
max_permits   Total number of permits allowed for this semaphore.

sem_release()

```
bool sem_release(semaphore_t * sem)
```

Release a permit on a semaphore. Increases the number of permits by one (unless the number of permits is already at the maximum). A blocked sem_acquire will be released if the number of permits is increased.

Parameters

sem   Pointer to semaphore structure.

Returns

True if the number of permits available was increased.

sem_reset()

```
void sem_reset(semaphore_t * sem, int16_t permits)
```

Reset semaphore to a specific number of available permits. Reset value should be from 0 to the max_permits specified in the init function.

Parameters

sem	Pointer to semaphore structure.
permits	The new number of available permits.

sem_try_acquire()

```
bool sem_try_acquire(semaphore_t * sem)
```

Attempt to acquire a permit from a semaphore without blocking. This function will return false without blocking if no permits are available, otherwise it will acquire a permit and return true.

Parameters

sem	Pointer to semaphore structure.

Returns

True if permit was acquired.

TIME

pico_time

```
#include "pico/time.h"
```

The Pico Time API provides a comprehensive set of functions for accurate timestamps, sleeping, and time-based callbacks. This API offers a powerful and user-friendly wrapping around the low-level hardware timer functionality, simplifying the handling of time-related operations. To ensure proper functioning of these functions, it is crucial not to modify the hardware timer, as it is expected to increment monotonically at a rate of one microsecond per tick. However, if there is a need to introduce additional functionality that is not already covered by the API, it can easily be achieved by adding or subtracting a constant value from the unmodified hardware timer. For more information, refer to the hardware_timer documentation.

Timestamp

The Time API includes functions for managing timestamps, which represent specific points in time. These functions operate on the absolute_time_t type, which is designed to prevent accidental mixing of timestamps and relative time values.

Sleep

The Sleep functions allow for delaying execution by putting the calling core into a lower power state. This sleep mode wakes up and rechecks the time on every processor event using the Wait for Event (WFE) instruction, reducing power consumption. It is important to note that the sleep functions rely on the default alarm pool, which can be disabled using the PICO_TIME_DEFAULT_ALARM_POOL_DISABLED define or may be currently full, in which case the functions act as busy waits instead. It is recommended not to call these sleep functions from an interrupt service routine (IRQ) handler. For alternative busy wait functions, see busy_wait_until(), busy_wait_us(), and busy_wait_us_32().

Alarm

The Alarm functions enable the scheduling of future executions. Alarms are added to alarm pools, which can hold a fixed number of active alarms. Each alarm pool corresponds to one of the four underlying hardware alarms, allowing for up to four alarm pools in total. The callbacks associated with alarms are executed on the core from which the alarm pool was created. It is important to handle the implementation of callbacks with care, as they are executed from the hardware alarm's interrupt handler. By default, a pool is created on the core specified by PICO_TIME_DEFAULT_ALARM_POOL_HARDWARE_ALARM_NUM on core 0, and this default pool can be used by the function variants that do not require an explicit alarm pool parameter. For more information, refer to the struct alarm_pool and hardware_timer documentation.

Repeating Timer

The Repeating Timer functions provide a simple way to schedule repeated execution of a task. While regular alarm functionality can be used to create repeating alarms by returning a non-zero value from the callback function, the Repeating Timer methods further abstract this functionality at the cost of requiring a user-defined structure to store the repeat delay, as the underlying alarm framework does not have space for it.

The Pico Time API offers a convenient and efficient solution for managing timestamps, implementing sleep functionality, scheduling alarms, and handling repeating tasks. By utilizing this API, developers can easily incorporate accurate time-based operations into their applications.

DEFINITIONS

PICO_TIME_DEFAULT_ALARM_POOL_DISABLED

```
#define PICO_TIME_DEFAULT_ALARM_POOL_DISABLED    0
```

If 1 then the default alarm pool is disabled (so no hardware alarm is claimed for the pool).

PICO_TIME_DEFAULT_ALARM_POOL_HARDWARE_ALARM_NUM

```
#define PICO_TIME_DEFAULT_ALARM_POOL_HARDWARE_ALARM_NUM    3
```

Selects which hardware alarm is used for the default alarm pool.

PICO_TIME_DEFAULT_ALARM_POOL_MAX_TIMERS

```
#define PICO_TIME_DEFAULT_ALARM_POOL_MAX_TIMERS    16
```

Selects the maximum number of concurrent timers in the default alarm pool.

TYPEDEFS

alarm_callback_t

```
typedef int64_t(* alarm_callback_t) (alarm_id_t id,
        void *user_data)
```

User alarm callback.

Parameters

id	The alarm_id as returned when the alarm was added.
user_data	The user data passed when the alarm was added.

Returns

A negative number to reschedule the same alarm this many us from the time the alarm was previously scheduled to fire.

A positive number greater than zero to reschedule the same alarm this many us from the time this method returns.

Zero to not reschedule the alarm.

alarm_id_t

```
typedef int32_t alarm_id_t
```

The identifier for an alarm. Alarm IDs may be reused, however for convenience the implementation makes an attempt to defer reusing as long as possible. You should certainly expect it to be hundreds of ids before one is reused, although in most cases it is more. Nonetheless care must still be taken when cancelling alarms or other functionality based on alarms when the alarm may have expired, as eventually the alarm id may be reused for another alarm.

NOTE This identifier is signed because -1 is used as an error condition when creating alarms.

repeating_timer_callback_t

```
typedef bool(* repeating_timer_callback_t)
        (repeating_timer_t *rt)
```

Callback for a repeating timer.

Parameters

rt

> Repeating time structure containing information about the repeating time. user_data is of primary important to the user.

Returns

> True to continue repeating, false to stop.

STRUCTURES

repeating_timer

```
struct repeating_timer
```

```
#include <time.h>
```

Information about a repeating timer.

Data Fields

int64_t	delay_us
alarm_pool_t *	pool
alarm_id_t	alarm_id
repeating_timer_callback_t	callback
void *	user_data

VARIABLES

at_the_end_of_time

```
const absolute_time_t at_the_end_of_time
```

The timestamp representing the end of time; this is actually not the maximum possible timestamp, but is set to 0x7fffffff_ffffffff microseconds to avoid sign overflows with time arithmetic. This is almost 300,000 years, so it should be sufficient.

nil_time

```
const absolute_time_t nil_time
```

The timestamp representing a null timestamp.

FUNCTIONS

absolute_time_diff_us()   **Inline Static**

```
static int64_t absolute_time_diff_us(absolute_time_t from,
        absolute_time_t to)
```

Return the difference in microseconds between two timestamps.

NOTE Be careful when diffing against large timestamps (e.g. at_the_end_of_time) as the signed integer may overflow.

Parameters

from   The first timestamp.
to   Tthe second timestamp.

Returns

The number of microseconds between the two timestamps (positive if to is after from except in case of overflow).

absolute_time_min() Inline Static

```
static absolute_time_t absolute_time_min
        (absolute_time_t a, absolute_time_t b)
```

Return the earlier of two timestamps.

Parameters

a   The first timestamp.
b   The second timestamp.

Returns

The earlier of the two timestamps.

best_effort_wfe_or_timeout()

```
bool best_effort_wfe_or_timeout
        (absolute_time_t timeout_timestamp)
```

Helper method for blocking on a timeout. This method will return in response to an event (as per __wfe) or when the target time is reached, or at any point before. This method can be used to implement a lower power polling loop waiting on some condition signalled by an event (__sev()).

This is called best_effort because under certain circumstances (notably the default timer pool being disabled or full) the best effort is simply to return immediately without a __wfe, thus turning the calling code into a busy wait.

Parameters

timeout_timestamp   The timeout time.

Returns

True if the target time is reached, false otherwise.

add_alarm_at()   Inline Static

```
static alarm_id_t add_alarm_at(absolute_time_t time,
        alarm_callback_t callback, void * user_data,
        bool fire_if_past)
```

Add an alarm callback to be called at a specific time. Generally the callback is called as soon as possible after the time specified from an IRQ handler on the core of the default alarm pool (generally core 0). If the callback is in the past or happens before the alarm setup could be completed, then this method will optionally call the callback itself and then return a return code to indicate that the target time has passed.

NOTE It is safe to call this method from an IRQ handler (including alarm callbacks), and from either core.

Parameters

time

> The timestamp when (after which) the callback should fire.

callback

> The callback function.

user_data

> User data to pass to the callback function.

fire_if_past

> If true, and the alarm time falls before or during this call before the alarm can be set, then the callback should be called during (by) this function instead.

Returns

> A positive number is the alarm id.

> A zero (0) is returned if the alarm time passed before or during the call AND there is no active alarm to return the id of. The latter can either happen because fire_if_past was false (i.e. no timer was ever created), or if the callback was called during this method but the callback canceled itself by returning 0.

> A negative one (-1) is returned if there were no alarm slots available.

add_alarm_in_ms()

```
static alarm_id_t add_alarm_in_ms(uint32_t ms,
        alarm_callback_t callback, void * user_data,
        bool fire_if_past)
```

Add an alarm callback to be called after a delay specified in milliseconds. Generally the callback is called as soon as possible after the time specified from an IRQ handler on the core of the default alarm pool (generally core 0). If the callback is in the past or happens before the alarm setup could be completed, then this method will optionally call the callback itself and then return a return code to indicate that the target time has passed.

NOTE It is safe to call this method from an IRQ handler (including alarm callbacks), and from either core.

Parameters

ms

> The delay (from now) in milliseconds when (after which) the callback should fire.

callback

> The callback function.

user_data

> User data to pass to the callback function.

fire_if_past

> If true, and the alarm time falls during this call before the alarm can be set, then the callback should be called during (by) this function instead.

Returns

> A positive number is the alarm id.

> A zero (0) is returned if the alarm time passed before or during the call AND there is no active alarm to return the id of. The latter can either happen because fire_if_past was false (i.e. no timer was ever created), or if the callback was called during this method but the callback canceled itself by returning 0.

> A negative one (-1) is returned if there were no alarm slots available.

add_alarm_in_us()

```
static alarm_id_t add_alarm_in_us(uint64_t us,
        alarm_callback_t callback, void * user_data,
        bool fire_if_past)
```

Add an alarm callback to be called after a delay specified in microseconds. Generally the callback is called as soon as possible after the time specified from an IRQ handler on the core of the default alarm pool (generally core 0). If the callback is in the past or happens before the alarm setup could be completed, then this method will optionally call the callback itself and then return a return code to indicate that the target time has passed.

NOTE It is safe to call this method from an IRQ handler (including alarm callbacks), and from either core.

Parameters

us

> The delay (from now) in microseconds when (after which) the callback should fire.

callback

> The callback function.

user_data

> User data to pass to the callback function.

fire_if_past

> If true, and the alarm time falls during this call before the alarm can be set, then the callback should be called during (by) this function instead.

Returns

> A positive number is the alarm id.

> A zero (0) is returned if the alarm time passed before or during the call AND there is no active alarm to return the id of. The latter can either happen because fire_if_past was false (i.e. no timer was ever created), or if the callback was called during this method but the callback canceled itself by returning 0.

> A negative one (-1) is returned if there were no alarm slots available.

alarm_pool_add_alarm_at()

```
alarm_id_t alarm_pool_add_alarm_at(alarm_pool_t * pool,
        absolute_time_t time, alarm_callback_t callback,
        void * user_data, bool fire_if_past)
```

Add an alarm callback to be called at a specific time. Generally the callback is called as soon as possible after the time specified from an IRQ handler on the core the alarm pool was created on. If the callback is in the past or happens before the alarm setup could be completed, then this method will optionally call the callback itself and then return a return code to indicate that the target time has passed.

NOTE It is safe to call this method from an IRQ handler (including alarm callbacks), and from either core.

Parameters

pool

> The alarm pool to use for scheduling the callback (this determines which hardware alarm is used, and which core calls the callback).

time

> The timestamp when (after which) the callback should fire

callback

> The callback function

user_data

> User data to pass to the callback function.

fire_if_past

> If true, and the alarm time falls before or during this call before the alarm can be set, then the callback should be called during (by) this function instead.

Returns

> A positive number is the alarm id for an active (at the time of return) alarm.

> A zero (0) is returned if the alarm time passed before or during the call AND there is no active alarm to return the id of. The latter can either happen because fire_if_past was false (i.e. no timer was ever created), or if the callback was called during this method but the callback canceled itself by returning 0.

> A negative one (-1) is returned if there were no alarm slots available.

alarm_pool_add_alarm_at_force_in_context()

```
alarm_id_t alarm_pool_add_alarm_at_force_in_context
        (alarm_pool_t * pool, absolute_time_t time,
        alarm_callback_t callback, void * user_data)
```

Add an alarm callback to be called at or after a specific time. The callback is called as soon as possible after the time specified from an IRQ handler on the core the alarm pool was created on. Unlike alarm_pool_add_alarm_at, this method guarantees to call the callback from that core even if the time is during this method call or in the past.

NOTE It is safe to call this method from an IRQ handler (including alarm callbacks), and from either core.

Parameters

pool

The alarm pool to use for scheduling the callback (this determines which hardware alarm is used, and which core calls the callback).

time

The timestamp when (after which) the callback should fire.

callback

The callback function.

user_data

User data to pass to the callback function.

Returns

A positive number is the alarm id for an active (at the time of return) alarm.

A negative one (-1) is returned if there were no alarm slots available.

alarm_pool_add_alarm_in_ms() Inline Static

```
static alarm_id_t alarm_pool_add_alarm_in_ms
        (alarm_pool_t * pool, uint32_t ms,
         alarm_callback_t callback, void * user_data,
         bool fire_if_past)
```

Add an alarm callback to be called after a delay specified in milliseconds. Generally the callback is called as soon as possible after the time specified from an IRQ handler on the core the alarm pool was created on. If the callback is in the past or happens before the alarm setup could be completed, then this method will optionally call the callback itself and then return a return code to indicate that the target time has passed.

NOTE It is safe to call this method from an IRQ handler (including alarm callbacks), and from either core.

Parameters

pool

The alarm pool to use for scheduling the callback (this determines which hardware alarm is used, and which core calls the callback).

ms

The delay (from now) in milliseconds when (after which) the callback should fire.

callback

The callback function.

user_data

User data to pass to the callback function.

fire_if_past

If true, and the alarm time falls before or during this call before the alarm can be set, then the callback should be called during (by) this function instead.

Returns

A positive number is the alarm id.

A zero (0) is returned if the alarm time passed before or during the call AND there is no active alarm to return the id of. The latter can either happen because fire_if_past was false (i.e. no timer was ever created), or if the callback was called during this method but the callback canceled itself by returning 0.

A negative one (-1) is returned if there were no alarm slots available.

alarm_pool_add_alarm_in_us()   Inline Static

```
static alarm_id_t alarm_pool_add_alarm_in_us
        (alarm_pool_t * pool, uint64_t us,
        alarm_callback_t callback, void * user_data,
        bool fire_if_past)
```

Add an alarm callback to be called after a delay specified in microseconds. Generally the callback is called as soon as possible after the time specified from an IRQ handler on the core the alarm pool was created on. If the callback is in the past or happens before the alarm setup could be completed, then this method will optionally call the callback itself and then return a return code to indicate that the target time has passed.

NOTE It is safe to call this method from an IRQ handler (including alarm callbacks), and from either core.

Parameters

pool

The alarm pool to use for scheduling the callback (this determines which hardware alarm is used, and which core calls the callback).

us

The delay (from now) in microseconds when (after which) the callback should fire.

callback

The callback function.

user_data

User data to pass to the callback function.

fire_if_past

If true, and the alarm time falls before or during this call before the alarm can be set, then the callback should be called during (by) this function instead.

Returns

A positive number is the alarm id.

A zero (0) is returned if the alarm time passed before or during the call AND there is no active alarm to return the id of. The latter can either happen because fire_if_past was false (i.e. no timer was ever created), or if the callback was called during this method but the callback canceled itself by returning 0

A negative   one (-1) is returned if there were no alarm slots available.

add_repeating_timer_ms()   Inline Static

```
static bool add_repeating_timer_ms(int32_t delay_ms,
        repeating_timer_callback_t callback,
        void * user_data, repeating_timer_t * out)
```

Add a repeating timer that is called repeatedly at the specified interval in milliseconds. Generally the callback is called as soon as possible after the time specified from an IRQ handler on the core of the default alarm pool (generally core 0). If the callback is in the past or happens before the alarm setup could be completed, then this method will optionally call the callback itself and then return a return code to indicate that the target time has passed.

NOTE It is safe to call this method from an IRQ handler (including alarm callbacks), and from either core.

Parameters

delay_ms

The repeat delay in milliseconds; if >0 then this is the delay between one callback ending and the next starting; if <0 then this is the negative of the time between the starts of the callbacks. The value of 0 is treated as 1 microsecond.

callback

The repeating timer callback function.

user_data

User data to pass to store in the repeating_timer structure for use by the callback.

out

The pointer to the user owned structure to store the repeating timer info in. BEWARE this storage location must outlive the repeating timer, so be careful of using stack space.

Returns

False if there were no alarm slots available to create the timer, true otherwise.

add_repeating_timer_us()

```
static bool add_repeating_timer_us(int64_t delay_us,
        repeating_timer_callback_t callback,
        void * user_data, repeating_timer_t * out)
```

Add a repeating timer that is called repeatedly at the specified interval in microseconds. Generally the callback is called as soon as possible after the time specified from an IRQ handler on the core of the default alarm pool (generally core 0). If the callback is in the past or happens before the alarm setup could be completed, then this method will optionally call the callback itself and then return a return code to indicate that the target time has passed.

NOTE It is safe to call this method from an IRQ handler (including alarm callbacks), and from either core.

Parameters

delay_us

The repeat delay in microseconds; if >0 then this is the delay between one callback ending and the next starting; if <0 then this is the negative of the time between the starts of the callbacks. The value of 0 is treated as 1

callback

The repeating timer callback function.

user_data

User data to pass to store in the repeating_timer structure for use by the callback.

out

The pointer to the user owned structure to store the repeating timer info in. BEWARE this storage location must outlive the repeating timer, so be careful of using stack space.

Returns

False if there were no alarm slots available to create the timer, true otherwise.

alarm_pool_add_repeating_timer_ms()   Inline Static

```
static bool alarm_pool_add_repeating_timer_ms
        (alarm_pool_t * pool, int32_t delay_ms,
        repeating_timer_callback_t callback,
        void * user_data, repeating_timer_t * out)
```

Add a repeating timer that is called repeatedly at the specified interval in milliseconds. Generally the callback is called as soon as possible after the time specified from an IRQ handler on the core the alarm pool was created on. If the callback is in the past or happens before the alarm setup could be completed, then this method will optionally call the callback itself and then return a return code to indicate that the target time has passed.

NOTE It is safe to call this method from an IRQ handler (including alarm callbacks), and from either core.

Parameters

pool

The alarm pool to use for scheduling the repeating timer (this determines which hardware alarm is used, and which core calls the callback).

delay_ms

The repeat delay in milliseconds; if >0 then this is the delay between one callback ending and the next starting; if <0 then this is the negative of the time between the starts of the callbacks. The value of 0 is treated as 1 microsecond.

callback

The repeating timer callback function.

user_data

User data to pass to store in the repeating_timer structure for use by the callback.

out

The pointer to the user owned structure to store the repeating timer info in. BEWARE this storage location must outlive the repeating timer, so be careful of using stack space.

Returns

False if there were no alarm slots available to create the timer, true otherwise.

alarm_pool_add_repeating_timer_us()

```
bool alarm_pool_add_repeating_timer_us
        (alarm_pool_t * pool, int64_t delay_us,
        repeating_timer_callback_t callback,
        void * user_data, repeating_timer_t * out)
```

Add a repeating timer that is called repeatedly at the specified interval in microseconds. Generally the callback is called as soon as possible after the time specified from an IRQ handler on the core the alarm pool was created on. If the callback is in the past or happens before the alarm setup could be completed, then this method will optionally call the callback itself and then return a return code to indicate that the target time has passed.

NOTE It is safe to call this method from an IRQ handler (including alarm callbacks), and from either core.

Parameters

pool

The alarm pool to use for scheduling the repeating timer (this determines which hardware alarm is used, and which core calls the callback).

delay_us

The repeat delay in microseconds; if >0 then this is the delay between one callback ending and the next starting; if <0 then this is the negative of the time between the starts of the callbacks. The value of 0 is treated as 1.

callback

The repeating timer callback function.

user_data

User data to pass to store in the repeating_timer structure for use by the callback.

out

The pointer to the user owned structure to store the repeating timer info in. BEWARE this storage location must outlive the repeating timer, so be careful of using stack space.

Returns

False if there were no alarm slots available to create the timer, true otherwise.

alarm_pool_cancel_alarm()

```
bool alarm_pool_cancel_alarm(alarm_pool_t * pool,
        alarm_id_t alarm_id)
```

Cancel an alarm. See also alarm_id_t for a note on reuse of Ids.

Parameters

pool	The alarm_pool containing the alarm.
alarm_id	The alarm.

Returns

True if the alarm was canceled , false if it didn't exist.

alarm_pool_core_num()

```
uint alarm_pool_core_num(alarm_pool_t * pool)
```

Return the core number the alarm pool was initialized on (and hence callbacks are called on).

Parameters

pool	The pool.

Returns

Tthe core used by the pool.

alarm_pool_create()

alarm_pool_t * alarm_pool_create(uint hardware_alarm_num, uint max_timers)

Create an alarm pool. The alarm pool will call callbacks from an alarm IRQ Handler on the core of this function is called from. In many situations there is never any need for anything other than the default alarm pool, however you might want to create another if you want alarm callbacks on core 1 or require alarm pools of different priority (IRQ priority based preemption of callbacks). For implementation reasons this is limited to PICO_PHEAP_MAX_ENTRIES which defaults to 255. See also alarm_pool_get_default() hardware_claiming.

NOTE This method will hard assert if the hardware alarm is already claimed.

Parameters

hardware_alarm_num

> The hardware alarm to use to back this pool.

max_timers

> The maximum number of timers.

alarm_pool_create_with_unused_hardware_alarm()

```
alarm_pool_t *
        alarm_pool_create_with_unused_hardware_alarm
        (uint max_timers)
```

Create an alarm pool, claiming an used hardware alarm to back it. The alarm pool will call callbacks from an alarm IRQ Handler on the core of this function is called from.In many situations there is never any need for anything other than the default alarm pool, however you might want to create another if you want alarm callbacks on core 1 or require alarm pools of different priority (IRQ priority based preemption of callbacks) For implementation reasons this is limited to PICO_PHEAP_MAX_ENTRIES which defaults to 255. See also alarm_pool_get_default() hardware_claiming.

NOTE This method will hard assert if the there is no free hardware to claim.

Parameters

max_timers

> The maximum number of timers.

alarm_pool_destroy()

```
void alarm_pool_destroy(alarm_pool_t * pool)
```

Destroy the alarm pool, canceling all alarms and freeing up the underlying hardware alarm.

Parameters

pool   The pool.

alarm_pool_get_default()

```
alarm_pool_t * alarm_pool_get_default (void )
```

The default alarm pool used when alarms are added without specifying an alarm pool, and also used by the SDK to support lower power sleeps and timeouts. See also PICO_TIME_DEFAULT_ALARM_POOL_HARDWARE_ALARM_NUM.

Returns

The default alarm pool used when alarms are added without specifying an alarm pool.

alarm_pool_hardware_alarm_num()

```
uint alarm_pool_hardware_alarm_num (alarm_pool_t * pool)
```

Return the hardware alarm used by an alarm pool.

Parameters

pool   The pool.

Returns

The hardware alarm used by the pool.

cancel_alarm() Inline Static

```
static bool cancel_alarm(alarm_id_t alarm_id)
```

Cancel an alarm from the default alarm pool. See also alarm_id_t for a note on reuse of IDs.

Parameters

alarm_id   The alarm.

Returns

True if the alarm was canceled , false if it didn't exist.

cancel_repeating_timer()

```
bool cancel_repeating_timer (repeating_timer_t * timer)
```

Cancel a repeating timer. See also alarm_id_t for a note on reuse of IDs.

Parameters

timer   The repeating timer to cancel.

Returns

True if the repeating timer was canceled , false if it didn't exist.

delayed_by_ms()   Inline Static

```
static absolute_time_t delayed_by_ms
        (const absolute_time_t t, uint32_t ms)
```

Return a timestamp value obtained by adding a number of milliseconds to another timestamp.

Parameters

t   The base timestamp.

ms   The number of milliseconds to add.

Returns

The timestamp representing the resulting time.

delayed_by_us()   Inline Static

```
static absolute_time_t delayed_by_us
        (const absolute_time_t t, uint64_t us)
```

Return a timestamp value obtained by adding a number of microseconds to another timestamp.

Parameters

t   The base timestamp.

us   The number of microseconds to add.

Returns

The timestamp representing the resulting time.

from_us_since_boot()   Inline Static

```
static absolute_time_t from_us_since_boot
          (uint64_t us_since_boot)
```

Convert a number of microseconds since boot to an absolute_time_t.

Parameters

us_since_boot   Number of microseconds since boot.

Returns

An absolute time equivalent to us_since_boot.

get_absolute_time()   Inline Static

```
static absolute_time_t get_absolute_time(void )
```

Return a representation of the current time. Returns an opaque high fidelity representation of the current time sampled during the call. See also absolute_time_t sleep_until() time_us_64().

Returns

The absolute time (now) of the hardware timer.

is_at_the_end_of_time()   Inline Static

```
static bool is_at_the_end_of_time(absolute_time_t t)
```

Determine if the given timestamp is "at_the_end_of_time". See also at_the_end_of_time.

Parameters

t   The timestamp.

Returns

True if the timestamp is at_the_end_of_time.

is_nil_time()   Inline Static

```
static bool is_nil_time(absolute_time_t t)
```

Determine if the given timestamp is nil. See also nil_time.

Parameters

t   The timestamp.

Returns

True if the timestamp is nil

make_timeout_time_ms()   Inline Static

```
static absolute_time_t make_timeout_time_ms(uint32_t ms)
```

Convenience method to get the timestamp a number of milliseconds from the current time.

Parameters

ms   The number of milliseconds to add to the current timestamp.

Returns

The future timestamp.

make_timeout_time_us()   Inline Static

```
static absolute_time_t make_timeout_time_us(uint64_t us)
```

Convenience method to get the timestamp a number of microseconds from the current time.

Parameters

us

The number of microseconds to add to the current timestamp.

Returns

The future timestamp.

sleep_ms()

```
void sleep_ms(uint32_t ms)
```

Wait for the given number of milliseconds before returning.

NOTE This method attempts to perform a lower power sleep (using WFE) as much as possible.

Parameters

ms   The number of milliseconds to sleep.

sleep_until()

```
void sleep_until(absolute_time_t target)
```

Wait until after the given timestamp to return.

NOTE This method attempts to perform a lower power (WFE) sleep. See also sleep_us() busy_wait_until().

Parameters

target   The time after which to return.

sleep_us()

```
void sleep_us(uint64_t us)
```

Wait for the given number of microseconds before returning. See also busy_wait_us().

NOTE This method attempts to perform a lower power (WFE) sleep.

Parameters

us   The number of microseconds to sleep.

to_ms_since_boot()   **Inline Static**

```
static uint32_t to_ms_since_boot(absolute_time_t t)
```

Convert a timestamp into a number of milliseconds since boot. See also to_us_since_boot().

Parameters

t   An absolute_time_t value to convert.

Returns

The number of milliseconds since boot represented by t.

to_us_since_boot()   **Inline Static**

```
static uint64_t to_us_since_boot(absolute_time_t t)
```

Convert an absolute_time_t into a number of microseconds since boot.

Parameters

t   The absolute time to convert.

Returns

A number of microseconds since boot, equivalent to t.

update_us_since_boot()   Inline Static

```
static void update_us_since_boot(absolute_time_t * t,
        uint64_t us_since_boot)
```

Update an absolute_time_t value to represent a given number of microseconds since boot.

Parameters

t

The absolute time value to update.

us_since_boot

The number of microseconds since boot to represent. Note this should be representable as a signed 64 bit integer.

UNIQUE ID

pico_unique_id

```
#include "pico/unique_id.h"
```

Unique device ID access API. RP2040 does not have an on-board unique identifier (all instances of RP2040 silicon are identical and have no persistent state). However, RP2040 boots from serial NOR flash devices which have a 64-bit unique ID as a standard feature, and there is a 1:1 association between RP2040 and flash, so this is suitable for use as a unique identifier for an RP2040-based board.

This library injects a call to the flash_get_unique_id function from the hardware_flash library, to run before main, and stores the result in a static location which can safely be accessed at any time via pico_get_unique_id().

This avoids some pitfalls of the hardware_flash API, which requires any flash-resident interrupt routines to be disabled when called into.

STRUCTURES

pico_unique_board_id_t

```
struct  pico_unique_board_id_t
```

```
#include <unique_id.h>
```

This struct is suitable for holding the unique identifier of a NOR flash device on an RP2040-based board. It contains an array of PICO_UNIQUE_BOARD_ID_SIZE_BYTES identifier bytes.

Data Fields

uint8_t	id [8]	Unique board identifier.

FUNCTIONS

pico_get_unique_board_id()

```
void pico_get_unique_board_id
       (pico_unique_board_id_t *id_out)
```

Get unique ID. Get the unique 64-bit device identifier which was retrieved from the external NOR flash device at boot. On PICO_NO_FLASH builds the unique identifier is set to all 0xEE.

Parameters

id_out

> A pointer to a pico_unique_board_id_t struct, to which the identifier will be written.

pico_get_unique_board_id_string()

void pico_get_unique_board_id_string (char *id_out, uint len)

Get unique ID in string format. Get the unique 64-bit device identifier which was retrieved from the external NOR flash device at boot, formatted as an ASCII hex string. Will always 0-terminate. On PICO_NO_FLASH builds the unique identifier is set to all 0xEE.

Parameters

id_out

> A pointer to a char buffer of size len, to which the identifier will be written.

len

> The size of id_out. For full serial, len >= 2 * PICO_UNIQUE_BOARD_ID_SIZE_BYTES + 1.

UTIL

pico_util

```
#include "pico/util.h"
```

The Pico API's Util section offers useful utility functions to aid in the development of your applications. These components provide efficient and reliable ways to handle various tasks and manage data.

One such component is the Pairing Heap Implementation (pheap), which defines a simple pairing heap. This implementation keeps track of array indexes, requiring the user to provide storage for heap entries and a comparison function. It offers an efficient way to organize and manipulate data within the heap. However, it's important to note that this class is not inherently safe for concurrent usage. It should be externally protected if used in a concurrent context. Additionally, concurrent users need to be cautious when accessing returned IDs, as subsequent operations on the heap may reuse these IDs, potentially leading to data overwriting.

Another valuable component in the Util section is the Queue implementation. This queue is designed to be safe for use in multi-core and IRQ scenarios, offering a reliable way to store and retrieve values of a specified size. When values are pushed into the queue, they are copied into the internal storage, ensuring data integrity and consistency.

By utilizing the provided data structures and utility functions from the Util section, you can enhance the efficiency and reliability of your code. Whether you need to manage a pairing heap or handle data storage with a multi-core and IRQ safe queue, these components offer the necessary tools to streamline your development process and improve the performance of your applications.

STRUCTURES

datetime_t

`struct datetime_t`

`#include <types.h>`

Structure containing date and time information. When setting an RTC alarm, set a field to -1 tells the RTC to not match on this field.

Data Fields

int16_t	year	0..4095
int8_t	month	1..12, 1 is January
int8_t	day	1..28,29,30,31 depending on month
int8_t	dotw	0..6, 0 is Sunday
int8_t	hour	0..23
int8_t	min	0..59
int8_t	sec	0..59

FUNCTIONS

datetime_to_str()

```
void datetime_to_str(char * buf, uint buf_size,
        const datetime_t * t)
```

Convert a datetime_t structure to a string.

Parameters

buf	Character buffer to accept generated string.
buf_size	The size of the passed in buffer.
t	The datetime to be converted.

queue_add_blocking()

```
void queue_add_blocking(queue_t * q, const void * data)
```

Blocking add of value to queue. If the queue is full this function will block, until a removal happens on the queue.

Parameters

q	Pointer to a queue_t structure, used as a handle.
data	Pointer to value to be copied into the queue.

queue_free()

```
void queue_free (queue_t * q)
```

Destroy the specified queue. Does not deallocate the queue_t structure itself.

Parameters

q	Pointer to a queue_t structure, used as a handle.

queue_get_level()   Inline Static

```
static uint queue_get_level (queue_t * q)
```

Check of level of the specified queue.

Parameters

q	Pointer to a queue_t structure, used as a handle.

Returns

Number of entries in the queue.

queue_get_level_unsafe()   Inline Static

```
static uint queue_get_level_unsafe (queue_t * q)
```

Unsafe check of level of the specified queue. This does not use the spinlock, so may return incorrect results if the spin lock is not externally locked.

Parameters

q   Pointer to a queue_t structure, used as a handle.

Returns

Number of entries in the queue.

queue_init()   Inline Static

static void queue_init(queue_t * q, uint element_size, uint element_count)

Initialize a queue, allocating a (possibly shared) spinlock.

Parameters

q   Pointer to a queue_t structure, used as a handle.
element_size   Size of each value in the queue.
element_count   Maximum number of entries in the queue.

queue_init_with_spinlock()

```
void queue_init_with_spinlock (queue_t * q,
        uint element_size, uint element_count,
        uint spinlock_num)
```

Initialize a queue with a specific spinlock for concurrency protection.

Parameters

q   Pointer to a queue_t structure, used as a handle.
element_size   Size of each value in the queue.
element_count   Maximum number of entries in the queue.
spinlock_num   The spin ID used to protect the queue.

queue_is_empty()   Inline Static

```
static bool queue_is_empty (queue_t * q)
```

Check if queue is empty. This function is interrupt and multicore safe.

Parameters

q   Pointer to a queue_t structure, used as a handle.

Returns

True if queue is empty, false otherwise.

queue_is_full()   Inline Static

```
static bool queue_is_full (queue_t * q)
```

Check if queue is full. This function is interrupt and multicore safe.

Parameters

q   Pointer to a queue_t structure, used as a handle.

Returns

True if queue is full, false otherwise.

queue_peek_blocking()

```
void queue_peek_blocking(queue_t * q, void * data)
```

Blocking peek at next value to be removed from queue. If the queue is empty function will block until a value is added.

Parameters

q   Pointer to a queue_t structure, used as a handle.
data   Pointer to the location to receive the peeked value.

queue_remove_blocking()

```
void queue_remove_blocking (queue_t * q, void * data)
```

Blocking remove entry from queue. If the queue is empty this function will block until a value is added.

Parameters

q	Pointer to a queue_t structure, used as a handle.
data	Pointer to the location to receive the removed value.

queue_try_add()

```
bool queue_try_add(queue_t * q, const void * data)
```

Non-blocking add value queue if not full. If the queue is full this function will return immediately with false, otherwise the data is copied into a new value added to the queue, and this function will return true.

Parameters

q	Pointer to a queue_t structure, used as a handle.
data	Pointer to value to be copied into the queue.

Returns

True if the value was added.

queue_try_peek()

```
bool queue_try_peek (queue_t * q, void * data)
```

Non-blocking peek at the next item to be removed from the queue. If the queue is not empty this function will return immediately with true with the peeked entry copied into the location specified by the data parameter, otherwise the function will return false.

Parameters

q   Pointer to a queue_t structure, used as a handle.

data   Pointer to the location to receive the peeked value.

Returns

True if there was a value to peek

queue_try_remove()

```
bool queue_try_remove(queue_t * q, void * data)
```

Non-blocking removal of entry from the queue if non empty. If the queue is not empty function will copy the removed value into the location provided and return immediately with true, otherwise the function will return immediately with false.

Parameters

q   Pointer to a queue_t structure, used as a handle.

data   Pointer to the location to receive the removed value.

Returns

True if a value was removed.

NETWORKING

The Networking Libraries of the Pico API provides a set of powerful tools and libraries to facilitate networking and communication tasks in your applications. These libraries offer convenient and efficient solutions for handling various networking protocols and functionalities, allowing you to build robust and connected systems.

Whether you need to establish network connections, exchange data with remote devices, or implement network protocols, the Networking Libraries section offers a range of capabilities to meet your requirements. These libraries are designed to be flexible, reliable, and optimized for performance, enabling seamless integration of networking functionalities into your Pico-based projects.

• Some of the key features and functionalities provided by the Networking Libraries include:

• TCP/IP and UDP Support: The libraries offer support for Transmission Control Protocol (TCP) and User Datagram Protocol (UDP), two fundamental protocols used for reliable and connectionless communication over IP networks.

• Socket Management: You can create, manage, and interact with network sockets using the provided socket APIs. These APIs allow you to establish connections, send and receive data, and handle network events.

• Network Protocols: The Networking Libraries include support for various network protocols, such as HTTP, DNS, MQTT, and more. These protocols enable seamless integration with web services, cloud platforms, and IoT ecosystems.

• Security and Encryption: To ensure secure communication, the libraries offer encryption and authentication mechanisms, including SSL/TLS support. These features help protect sensitive data and establish secure connections with remote devices or servers.

• Asynchronous Networking: Asynchronous programming models are supported, allowing you to handle network operations efficiently without blocking the execution flow of your application. This enables you to build responsive and scalable networking applications.

By leveraging the Networking Libraries in the Pico API, you can simplify the implementation of networking functionality in your projects. Whether you're developing IoT devices, networked applications, or connected systems, these libraries provide the necessary tools to establish reliable and efficient communication over networks, enabling seamless integration with the broader Internet ecosystem.

BTSTACK

pico_btstack

Integration/wrapper libraries for BTstack the documentation for which is at **https://bluekitchen-gmbh.com/btstack/**. A supplemental license for BTstack (in addition to the stock BTstack licensing terms) is provided at **https://github.com/raspberrypi/pico-sdk/blob/master/src/rp2_common/pico_btstack/LICENSE.RP**.

The pico_btstack_ble library adds the support needed for Bluetooth Low Energy (BLE). The pico_btstack_classic library adds the support needed for Bluetooth Classic. You can link to either library individually, or to both libraries thus enabling dual-mode support provided by BTstack.

To use BTstack you need to provide a btstack_config.h file in your source tree and add its location to your include path. The BTstack configuration macros ENABLE_CLASSIC and ENABLE_BLE are defined for you when you link the pico_btstack_classic and pico_btstack_ble libraries respectively, so you should not define them yourself.

For more details, see How to configure BTstack and the relevant pico-examples.

The follow libraries are provided for you to link.

* pico_btstack_ble - Adds Bluetooth Low Energy (LE) support.

* pico_btstack_classic - Adds Bluetooth Classic support.

* pico_btstack_sbc_encoder - Adds Bluetooth Sub Band Coding (SBC) encoder support.

* pico_btstack_sbc_decoder - Adds Bluetooth Sub Band Coding (SBC) decoder support.

* pico_btstack_bnep_lwip - Adds Bluetooth Network Encapsulation Protocol (BNEP) support using LwIP.

* pico_btstack_bnep_lwip_sys_freertos - Adds Bluetooth Network Encapsulation Protocol (BNEP) support using LwIP with FreeRTOS for NO_SYS=0.

NOTE The CMake function pico_btstack_make_gatt_header can be used to run the BTstack compile_gatt tool to make a GATT header file from a BTstack GATT file.

See also pico_btstack_cyw43 in pico_cyw43_driver, which adds the cyw43 driver support needed for BTstack including BTstack run loop support.

btstack_run_loop_async_context_get_instance()

```
const btstack_run_loop_t
        *btstack_run_loop_async_context_get_instance
        (async_context_t *context)
```

Initialize and return the singleton BTstack run loop instance that integrates with the async_context API.

Parameters

context

The async_context instance that provides the abstraction for handling asynchronous work.

Returns

The BTstack run loop instance.

pico_flash_bank_instance()

```
const hal_flash_bank_t * pico_flash_bank_instance (void)
```

Return the singleton BTstack HAL flash instance, used for non-volatile storage.

NOTE By default two sectors at the end of flash are used (see PICO_FLASH_BANK_STORAGE_OFFSET and PICO_FLASH_BANK_TOTAL_SIZE).

Returns

The singleton BTstack HAL flash instance.

LWIP - LIGHTWEIGHT IP

Pico_lwip

Integration/wrapper libraries for lwIP the documentation for which is located at **https://www.nongnu.org/lwip/2_1_x/index.html**. The main pico_lwip library itself aggregates the lwIP RAW API: pico_lwip_core, pico_lwip_core4, pico_lwip_core6, pico_lwip_api, pico_lwip_netif, pico_lwip_sixlowpan and pico_lwip_ppp.

If you wish to run in NO_SYS=1 mode, then you can link pico_lwip along with pico_lwip_nosys.

If you wish to run in NO_SYS=0 mode, then you can link pico_lwip with (for instance) pico_lwip_freertos, and also link in pico_lwip_api for the additional blocking/thread-safe APIs.

Additionally you must link in pico_lwip_arch unless you provide your own compiler bindings for lwIP. Additional individual pieces of lwIP functionality are available à la cart, by linking any of the libraries below.

The following libraries are provided that contain exactly the equivalent lwIP functionality groups:

pico_lwip_core   **pico_lwip_sixlowpan**
pico_lwip_core4   **pico_lwip_ppp**
pico_lwip_core6   **pico_lwip_api**
pico_lwip_netif

The following libraries are provided that contain exactly the equivalent lwIP application support:

pico_lwip_snmp   **pico_lwip_mdns**
pico_lwip_http   **pico_lwip_netbios**
pico_lwip_makefsdata   **pico_lwip_tftp**
pico_lwip_iperf   **pico_lwip_mbedtls**
pico_lwip_smtp   **pico_lwip_mqtt**
pico_lwip_sntp

PICO_LWIP_ARCH

lwIP compiler adapters. This is not included by default in pico_lwip in case you wish to implement your own.

The "pico_lwip_arch" component in the Pico SDK refers to the lightweight IP (lwIP) architecture specifically tailored for the Raspberry Pi Pico microcontroller. lwIP is an open-source TCP/IP networking stack widely used in embedded systems and provides the necessary protocols for network communication.

The pico_lwip_arch module serves as an adaptation layer between the lwIP stack and the underlying hardware and operating environment of the Raspberry Pi Pico. It provides the necessary functions, configurations, and hooks to integrate lwIP with the Pico SDK and enable network communication capabilities on the Pico board.

The pico_lwip_arch component takes into account the specific characteristics and constraints of the Pico microcontroller to optimize the lwIP stack for efficient operation in resource-constrained environments. It includes platform-specific implementations of key components such as network interfaces, timers, memory management, and synchronization primitives.

Including the pico_lwip_arch link library allows you to call functions from the external lwIP API. The library serves as a bridge between the Pico SDK and the lwIP stack, providing an interface that enables you to interact with lwIP functions and features.

The lwIP stack itself is an independent open-source TCP/IP networking stack widely used in embedded systems and other resource-constrained environments. It provides a comprehensive set of protocols and functionality for network communication, including IP, TCP, UDP, ICMP, DHCP, DNS, and more.

The pico_lwip_arch library integrates the lwIP stack with the Pico SDK and provides an abstraction layer to simplify the usage of lwIP functions within Pico-based projects. By including this library, you can leverage the rich set of lwIP features and APIs to build network-enabled applications on the Raspberry Pi Pico microcontroller.

See https://www.nongnu.org/lwip/2_1_x/index.html

PICO_LWIP_FREERTOS

```
#include "pico/lwip_freertos.h"
```

Glue library for integration lwIP in NO_SYS=0 mode with the SDK. Simple init and deinit are all that is required to hook up lwIP (with full blocking API support) via an async_context instance.

lwip_freertos_deinit()

```
void lwip_freertos_deinit (async_context_t *context)
```

De-initialize lwIP (NO_SYS=0 mode) support for FreeRTOS. Note that since lwIP may only be initialized once, and doesn't itself provide a shutdown mechanism, lwIP itself may still consume resources. It is however safe to call lwip_freertos_init again later.

Parameters

context

> The async_context the lwip_freertos support was added to via lwip_freertos_init.

lwip_freertos_init()

```
bool lwip_freertos_init (async_context_t *context)
```

Initializes lwIP (NO_SYS=0 mode) support support for FreeRTOS using the provided async_context. If the initialization succeeds, lwip_freertos_deinit() can be called to shutdown lwIP support.

Parameters

context

> The async_context instance that provides the abstraction for handling asynchronous work. Note in general this would be an async_context_freertos instance, though it doesn't have to be.

Returns

> True if the initialization succeeded.

PICO_LWIP_NOSYS

```
#include "pico/lwip_nosys.h"
```

Glue library for integration lwIP in NO_SYS=1 mode with the SDK. Simple init and deinit are all that is required to hook up lwIP via an async_context instance.

lwip_nosys_deinit()

```
void lwip_nosys_deinit (async_context_t * context)
```

De-initialize lwIP (NO_SYS=1 mode) support. Note that since lwIP may only be initialized once, and doesn't itself provide a shutdown mechanism, lwIP itself may still consume resources. It is however safe to call lwip_nosys_init again later.

Parameters

context

> The async_context the lwip_nosys support was added to via lwip_nosys_init.

lwip_nosys_init()

```
bool lwip_nosys_init (async_context_t * context)
```

Initializes lwIP (NO_SYS=1 mode) support support using the provided async_context. If the initialization succeeds, lwip_nosys_deinit() can be called to shutdown lwIP support.

Parameters

context

> The async_context instance that provides the abstraction for handling asynchronous work.

Returns

> True if the initialization succeeded.

The Cyw43 Chip Driver API

pico_cyw43_driver

The Cyw43 Chip Driver API provides a set of functions for initializing the CYW4343W Wi-Fi and Bluetooth chip on the Raspberry Pi Pico microcontroller. The CYW4343W chip is a highly capable wireless module that supports both Wi-Fi (802.11b/g/n) and Bluetooth (4.2) connectivity.

cyw43_driver_deinit()

```
void cyw43_driver_deinit      (async_context_t *context)
```

```
#include "pico/cyw43_driver.h"
```

De-initialize the lowever level cyw43_driver and unhooks it from the async_context.

Parameters

context

> The async_context the cyw43_driver support was added to via cyw43_driver_init.

cyw43_driver_init()

```
bool cyw43_driver_init (async_context_t *context)
```

```
#include "pico/cyw43_driver.h"
```

Initializes the lower level cyw43_driver and integrates it with the provided async_context. If the initialization succeeds, lwip_nosys_deinit() can be called to shutdown lwIP support.

Parameters

context

The async_context instance that provides the abstraction for handling asynchronous work.

Returns

True if the initialization succeeded.

hci_transport_cyw43_instance()

```
const hci_transport_t * hci_transport_cyw43_instance
         (void)
```

```
#include "pico/btstack_hci_transport_cyw43.h"
```

Get the Bluetooth HCI transport instance for cyw43.

Returns

An instantiation of the hci_transport_t interface for the cyw43 chipset.

THE CYW43 CHIP ARCHITECTURE API

pico_cyw43_arch

```
#include "pico/cyw43_arch.h"
```

The pico_cyw43_arch section of the Pico API is a fundamental module responsible for seamlessly integrating the CYW43 driver, which enables wireless communication on the Raspberry Pi Pico W, and the lwIP (Lightweight IP) stack, which serves as the TCP/IP protocol implementation. Additionally, it facilitates access to the on-board LED on the Pico W.

The integration of both the low-level CYW43 driver and the lwIP stack poses challenges, particularly in handling periodic servicing and addressing limitations concerning multiple cores/threads. To overcome these complexities, pico_cyw43_arch provides several behavioral groups:

- 'poll': This mode is not multi-core/IRQ safe, requiring the user to call cyw43_arch_poll periodically from their main loop.

- 'thread_safe_background': This mode ensures multi-core/thread/task safety, and maintenance of the driver and TCP/IP stack occurs automatically in the background.

- 'freertos': In this mode, multi-core/thread/task safety is also guaranteed, employing a separate FreeRTOS task to handle lwIP and driver operations.

While the pico_cyw43_arch primarily supports lwIP as the TCP/IP stack, it aims to remain independent of the specific stack or Bluetooth stack used in the future. The integration of lwIP is handled based on the #define CYW43_LWIP used by the cyw43_driver.

It's important to note that starting from version 1.5.0 of the Pico SDK, pico_cyw43_arch no longer directly implements distinct behavioral abstractions. Instead, it relies on the more general pico_async_context library to handle this. Nevertheless, pico_cyw43_arch still offers specific Pico W APIs for connection management, locking, and GPIO interaction. The connection management APIs may eventually be moved to a more generic library in future releases.

For users' convenience, several wrapper libraries are provided to aggregate defines and dependencies, making it easier to use pico_cyw43_arch together with other components:

pico_cyw43_arch_lwip_poll: For using the RAW lwIP API without any background processing or multi-core/thread safety.

pico_cyw43_arch_lwip_threadsafe_background: For using the RAW lwIP API with multi-core/thread safety and automatic servicing of the cyw43_driver and lwIP in the background.

pico_cyw43_arch_lwip_sys_freertos: For using the full lwIP API, including blocking sockets in OS (NO_SYS=0) mode, along with multi-core/task/thread safety and automatic servicing of the cyw43_driver and the lwIP stack.

pico_cyw43_arch_none: For projects that do not require the TCP/IP stack but still wish to utilize the on-board LED.

By utilizing the pico_cyw43_arch module and its associated wrapper libraries, developers can seamlessly integrate wireless communication capabilities into their Pico W projects, while the low-level complexities of the CYW43 driver and lwIP integration are abstracted, enabling easier and more efficient development of Wi-Fi and Bluetooth-enabled applications.

MACROS

CYW43_AGGRESSIVE_PM

```
#define CYW43_AGGRESSIVE_PM
        cyw43_pm_value(CYW43_PM2_POWERSAVE_MODE, 2000, 1,
        1, 10)
```

Aggressive power management mode for optimal power usage at the cost of performance.

cyw43_arch_lwip_check

```
void cyw43_arch_lwip_check (void)
```

Checks the caller has any locks required for calling into lwIP. The lwIP API is not thread safe. You should surround calls into the lwIP API with calls to cyw43_arch_lwip_begin and this method. Note these calls are not necessary (but harmless) when you are calling back into the lwIP API from an lwIP callback.

This method will assert in debug mode, if the above conditions are not met (i.e. it is not safe to call into the lwIP API) See alsocyw43_arch_lwip_begin cyw43_arch_lwip_protect async_context_lock_check cyw43_arch_async_context.

NOTE As of SDK release 1.5.0, this is now equivalent to calling async_context_lock_check on the async_context associated with cyw43_arch and lwIP.

CYW43_COUNTRY()

```
#define CYW43_COUNTRY(A, B, REV)
        ((unsigned char)(A) | ((unsigned char)(B) << 8) |
        ((REV) << 16))
```

Create a country code from the two character country and revision number.

CYW43_DEFAULT_PM

```
#define CYW43_DEFAULT_PM
        cyw43_pm_value (CYW43_PM2_POWERSAVE_MODE, 200, 1,
        1, 10)
```

Default power management mode.

CYW43_PERFORMANCE_PM

```
#define CYW43_PERFORMANCE_PM
        cyw43_pm_value(CYW43_PM2_POWERSAVE_MODE, 20, 1, 1,
        1)
```

Performance power management mode where more power is used to increase performance.

DEFINITIONS

Authorization types

Used when setting up an access point, or connecting to an access point

#define CYW43_AUTH_OPEN   (0)
   No authorization required (open).

#define CYW43_AUTH_WPA_TKIP_PSK   (0x00200002)
   WPA authorization.

#define CYW43_AUTH_WPA2_AES_PSK   (0x00400004)
   WPA2 authorization (preferred).

#define CYW43_AUTH_WPA2_MIXED_PSK (0x00400006)
   WPA2/WPA mixed authorization.

Country Code Definitions

#define CYW43_COUNTRY_WORLDWIDE	CYW43_COUNTRY('X', 'X', 0)
#define CYW43_COUNTRY_AUSTRALIA	CYW43_COUNTRY('A', 'U', 0)
#define CYW43_COUNTRY_AUSTRIA	CYW43_COUNTRY('A', 'T', 0)
#define CYW43_COUNTRY_BELGIUM	CYW43_COUNTRY('B', 'E', 0)
#define CYW43_COUNTRY_BRAZIL	CYW43_COUNTRY('B', 'R', 0)
#define CYW43_COUNTRY_CANADA	CYW43_COUNTRY('C', 'A', 0)
#define CYW43_COUNTRY_CHILE	CYW43_COUNTRY('C', 'L', 0)
#define CYW43_COUNTRY_CHINA	CYW43_COUNTRY('C', 'N', 0)
#define CYW43_COUNTRY_COLOMBIA	CYW43_COUNTRY('C', 'O', 0)
#define CYW43_COUNTRY_CZECH_REPUBLIC	CYW43_COUNTRY('C', 'Z', 0)
#define CYW43_COUNTRY_DENMARK	CYW43_COUNTRY('D', 'K', 0)
#define CYW43_COUNTRY_ESTONIA	CYW43_COUNTRY('E', 'E', 0)
#define CYW43_COUNTRY_FINLAND	CYW43_COUNTRY('F', 'I', 0)
#define CYW43_COUNTRY_FRANCE	CYW43_COUNTRY('F', 'R', 0)
#define CYW43_COUNTRY_GERMANY	CYW43_COUNTRY('D', 'E', 0)
#define CYW43_COUNTRY_GREECE	CYW43_COUNTRY('G', 'R', 0)
#define CYW43_COUNTRY_HONG_KONG	CYW43_COUNTRY('H', 'K', 0)
#define CYW43_COUNTRY_HUNGARY	CYW43_COUNTRY('H', 'U', 0)
#define CYW43_COUNTRY_ICELAND	CYW43_COUNTRY('I', 'S', 0)
#define CYW43_COUNTRY_INDIA	CYW43_COUNTRY('I', 'N', 0)
#define CYW43_COUNTRY_ISRAEL	CYW43_COUNTRY('I', 'L', 0)
#define CYW43_COUNTRY_ITALY	CYW43_COUNTRY('I', 'T', 0)
#define CYW43_COUNTRY_JAPAN	CYW43_COUNTRY('J', 'P', 0)
#define CYW43_COUNTRY_KENYA	CYW43_COUNTRY('K', 'E', 0)
#define CYW43_COUNTRY_LATVIA	CYW43_COUNTRY('L', 'V', 0)
#define CYW43_COUNTRY_LIECHTENSTEIN	CYW43_COUNTRY('L', 'I', 0)
#define CYW43_COUNTRY_LITHUANIA	CYW43_COUNTRY('L', 'T', 0)
#define CYW43_COUNTRY_LUXEMBOURG	CYW43_COUNTRY('L', 'U', 0)
#define CYW43_COUNTRY_MALAYSIA	CYW43_COUNTRY('M', 'Y', 0)
#define CYW43_COUNTRY_MALTA	CYW43_COUNTRY('M', 'T', 0)
#define CYW43_COUNTRY_MEXICO	CYW43_COUNTRY('M', 'X', 0)
#define CYW43_COUNTRY_NETHERLANDS	CYW43_COUNTRY('N', 'L', 0)
#define CYW43_COUNTRY_NEW_ZEALAND	CYW43_COUNTRY('N', 'Z', 0)
#define CYW43_COUNTRY_NIGERIA	CYW43_COUNTRY('N', 'G', 0)
#define CYW43_COUNTRY_NORWAY	CYW43_COUNTRY('N', 'O', 0)

#define CYW43_COUNTRY_PERU	CYW43_COUNTRY('P', 'E', 0)
#define CYW43_COUNTRY_PHILIPPINES	CYW43_COUNTRY('P', 'H', 0)
#define CYW43_COUNTRY_POLAND	CYW43_COUNTRY('P', 'L', 0)
#define CYW43_COUNTRY_PORTUGAL	CYW43_COUNTRY('P', 'T', 0)
#define CYW43_COUNTRY_SINGAPORE	CYW43_COUNTRY('S', 'G', 0)
#define CYW43_COUNTRY_SLOVAKIA	CYW43_COUNTRY('S', 'K', 0)
#define CYW43_COUNTRY_SLOVENIA	CYW43_COUNTRY('S', 'I', 0)
#define CYW43_COUNTRY_SOUTH_AFRICA	CYW43_COUNTRY('Z', 'A', 0)
#define CYW43_COUNTRY_SOUTH_KOREA	CYW43_COUNTRY('K', 'R', 0)
#define CYW43_COUNTRY_SPAIN	CYW43_COUNTRY('E', 'S', 0)
#define CYW43_COUNTRY_SWEDEN	CYW43_COUNTRY('S', 'E', 0)
#define CYW43_COUNTRY_SWITZERLAND	CYW43_COUNTRY('C', 'H', 0)
#define CYW43_COUNTRY_TAIWAN	CYW43_COUNTRY('T', 'W', 0)
#define CYW43_COUNTRY_THAILAND	CYW43_COUNTRY('T', 'H', 0)
#define CYW43_COUNTRY_TURKEY	CYW43_COUNTRY('T', 'R', 0)
#define CYW43_COUNTRY_UK	CYW43_COUNTRY('G', 'B', 0)
#define CYW43_COUNTRY_USA	CYW43_COUNTRY('U', 'S', 0)

CYW43 General Definitions

#define CYW43_IOCTL_GET_SSID	(0x32)
#define CYW43_IOCTL_GET_CHANNEL	(0x3a)
#define CYW43_IOCTL_SET_DISASSOC	(0x69)
#define CYW43_IOCTL_GET_ANTDIV	(0x7e)
#define CYW43_IOCTL_SET_ANTDIV	(0x81)
#define CYW43_IOCTL_SET_MONITOR	(0xd9)
#define CYW43_IOCTL_GET_RSSI	(0xfe)
#define CYW43_IOCTL_GET_VAR	(0x20c)
#define CYW43_IOCTL_SET_VAR	(0x20f)
#define CYW43_EV_SET_SSID	(0)
#define CYW43_EV_JOIN	(1)
#define CYW43_EV_AUTH	(3)
#define CYW43_EV_DEAUTH	(5)
#define CYW43_EV_DEAUTH_IND	(6)
#define CYW43_EV_ASSOC	(7)

```
#define CYW43_EV_DISASSOC                    (11)
#define CYW43_EV_DISASSOC_IND                (12)
#define CYW43_EV_LINK                        (16)
#define CYW43_EV_PRUNE                       (23)
#define CYW43_EV_PSK_SUP                     (46)
#define CYW43_EV_ESCAN_RESULT                (69)
#define CYW43_EV_CSA_COMPLETE_IND            (80)
#define CYW43_EV_ASSOC_REQ_IE                (87)
#define CYW43_EV_ASSOC_RESP_IE               (88)


#define CYW43_STATUS_SUCCESS                 (0)
#define CYW43_STATUS_FAIL                    (1)
#define CYW43_STATUS_TIMEOUT                 (2)
#define CYW43_STATUS_NO_NETWORKS             (3)
#define CYW43_STATUS_ABORT                   (4)
#define CYW43_STATUS_NO_ACK                  (5)
#define CYW43_STATUS_UNSOLICITED             (6)
#define CYW43_STATUS_ATTEMPT                 (7)
#define CYW43_STATUS_PARTIAL                 (8)
#define CYW43_STATUS_NEWSCAN                 (9)
#define CYW43_STATUS_NEWASSOC                (10)


#define CYW43_SUP_DISCONNECTED               (0)
#define CYW43_SUP_CONNECTING                 (1)
#define CYW43_SUP_IDREQUIRED                 (2)
#define CYW43_SUP_AUTHENTICATING             (3)
#define CYW43_SUP_AUTHENTICATED              (4)
#define CYW43_SUP_KEYXCHANGE                 (5)
#define CYW43_SUP_KEYED                      (6)
#define CYW43_SUP_TIMEOUT                    (7)
#define CYW43_SUP_LAST_BASIC_STATE           (8)
#define CYW43_SUP_KEYXCHANGE_WAIT_M1
                         CYW43_SUP_AUTHENTICATED
#define CYW43_SUP_KEYXCHANGE_PREP_M2
                         CYW43_SUP_KEYXCHANGE
#define CYW43_SUP_KEYXCHANGE_WAIT_M3
                         CYW43_SUP_LAST_BASIC_STATE
```

```
#define CYW43_SUP_KEYXCHANGE_PREP_M4            (9)
#define CYW43_SUP_KEYXCHANGE_WAIT_G1            (10)
#define CYW43_SUP_KEYXCHANGE_PREP_G2            (11)


#define CYW43_REASON_INITIAL_ASSOC             (0)
#define CYW43_REASON_LOW_RSSI                  (1)
#define CYW43_REASON_DEAUTH                    (2)
#define CYW43_REASON_DISASSOC                  (3)
#define CYW43_REASON_BCNS_LOST                 (4)
#define CYW43_REASON_FAST_ROAM_FAILED          (5)
#define CYW43_REASON_DIRECTED_ROAM             (6)
#define CYW43_REASON_TSPEC_REJECTED            (7)
#define CYW43_REASON_BETTER_AP                 (8)
#define CYW43_REASON_PRUNE_ENCR_MISMATCH       (1)
#define CYW43_REASON_PRUNE_BCAST_BSSID         (2)
#define CYW43_REASON_PRUNE_MAC_DENY            (3)
#define CYW43_REASON_PRUNE_MAC_NA              (4)
#define CYW43_REASON_PRUNE_REG_PASSV           (5)
#define CYW43_REASON_PRUNE_SPCT_MGMT           (6)
#define CYW43_REASON_PRUNE_RADAR               (7)
#define CYW43_REASON_RSN_MISMATCH              (8)
#define CYW43_REASON_PRUNE_NO_COMMON_RATES     (9)
#define CYW43_REASON_PRUNE_BASIC_RATES         (10)
#define CYW43_REASON_PRUNE_CCXFAST_PREVAP      (11)
#define CYW43_REASON_PRUNE_CIPHER_NA           (12)
#define CYW43_REASON_PRUNE_KNOWN_STA           (13)
#define CYW43_REASON_PRUNE_CCXFAST_DROAM       (14)
#define CYW43_REASON_PRUNE_WDS_PEER            (15)
#define CYW43_REASON_PRUNE_QBSS_LOAD           (16)
#define CYW43_REASON_PRUNE_HOME_AP             (17)
#define CYW43_REASON_PRUNE_AP_BLOCKED          (18)
#define CYW43_REASON_PRUNE_NO_DIAG_SUPPORT     (19)
#define CYW43_REASON_SUP_OTHER                 (0)
#define CYW43_REASON_SUP_DECRYPT_KEY_DATA      (1)
#define CYW43_REASON_SUP_BAD_UCAST_WEP128      (2)
#define CYW43_REASON_SUP_BAD_UCAST_WEP40       (3)
```

```
#define CYW43_REASON_SUP_UNSUP_KEY_LEN          (4)
#define CYW43_REASON_SUP_PW_KEY_CIPHER          (5)
#define CYW43_REASON_SUP_MSG3_TOO_MANY_IE       (6)
#define CYW43_REASON_SUP_MSG3_IE_MISMATCH       (7)
#define CYW43_REASON_SUP_NO_INSTALL_FLAG        (8)
#define CYW43_REASON_SUP_MSG3_NO_GTK            (9)
#define CYW43_REASON_SUP_GRP_KEY_CIPHER         (10)
#define CYW43_REASON_SUP_GRP_MSG1_NO_GTK        (11)
#define CYW43_REASON_SUP_GTK_DECRYPT_FAIL       (12)
#define CYW43_REASON_SUP_SEND_FAIL              (13)
#define CYW43_REASON_SUP_DEAUTH                 (14)
#define CYW43_REASON_SUP_WPA_PSK_TMO            (15)


#define CYW43_WPA_AUTH_PSK                      (0x0004)
#define CYW43_WPA2_AUTH_PSK                     (0x0080)
#define CYW43_NO_POWERSAVE_MODE                 (0)
```

Power save mode parameter passed to cyw43_ll_wifi_pm.

```
#define CYW43_PM1_POWERSAVE_MODE                (1)
```

Powersave mode on specified interface without regard for throughput reduction.

```
#define CYW43_PM2_POWERSAVE_MODE                (2)
```

Powersave mode on specified interface with High throughput.

```
#define CYW43_BUS_MAX_BLOCK_SIZE                16384
#define CYW43_BACKPLANE_READ_PAD_LEN_BYTES      0
#define CYW43_LL_STATE_SIZE_WORDS               526 + 5
#define CYW43_CHANNEL_NONE                      (0xffffffff)
```

To indicate no specific channel when calling cyw43_ll_wifi_join with bssid specified.

CYW43 Driver Version Definitions

Current version of the CYW43 driver as major/minor/micro components.

#define **CYW43_VERSION_MAJOR**	0
#define **CYW43_VERSION_MINOR**	9
#define **CYW43_VERSION_MICRO**	0
#define **CYW43_VERSION**	(CYW43_VERSION_MAJOR << 16 | CYW43_VERSION_MINOR << 8 | CYW43_VERSION_MICRO)

CYW43_VERSION combines CYW43 driver versions as a 32-bit number.

Link Status Definitions

See also status_name() to get a user readable name of the status for debug cyw43_wifi_link_status() to get the wifi status cyw43_tcpip_link_status() to get the overall link status.

#define **CYW43_LINK_DOWN**	(0)	Link is down.
#define **CYW43_LINK_JOIN**	(1)	Connected to wifi.
#define **CYW43_LINK_NOIP**	(2)	Connected to wifi, but no IP address.
#define **CYW43_LINK_UP**	(3)	Connect to wifi with an IP address.
#define **CYW43_LINK_FAIL**	(-1)	Connection failed.
#define **CYW43_LINK_NONET**	(-2)	No matching SSID found (could be out of range, or down).
#define **CYW43_LINK_BADAUTH**	(-3)	Authentication failure.

Trace Flag Definitions

#define **CYW43_TRACE_ASYNC_EV**	(0x0001)
#define **CYW43_TRACE_ETH_TX**	(0x0002)
#define **CYW43_TRACE_ETH_RX**	(0x0004)
#define **CYW43_TRACE_ETH_FULL**	(0x0008)
#define **CYW43_TRACE_MAC**	(0x0010)

The Pico C API Functionary

ENUMERATIONS

anonymous enum of interface modes

Network interface types .

Enumerator

CYW43_ITF_STA	Client interface STA mode.
CYW43_ITF_AP	Access point (AP) interface mode.

STRUCTURES

_cyw43_t

`struct _cyw43_t`

Data Fields

cyw43_ll_t	**cyw43_ll**
uint8_t	**itf_state**
uint32_t	**trace_flags**
volatile uint32_t	**wifi_scan_state**
uint32_t	**wifi_join_state**
void *	**wifi_scan_env**
int(* wifi_scan_cb)(void *, const cyw43_ev_scan_result_t *)	
bool	**initted**
bool	**pend_disassoc**
bool	**pend_rejoin**
bool	**pend_rejoin_wpa**
uint32_t	**ap_auth**
uint8_t	**ap_channel**
uint8_t	**ap_ssid_len**
uint8_t	**ap_key_len**
uint8_t	**ap_ssid [32]**
uint8_t	**ap_key [64]**
struct	**netif netif [2]**
uint8_t	**mac [6]**

_cyw43_ev_scan_result_t

struct _cyw43_ev_scan_result_t

Structure to return wifi scan results.

Data Fields

uint32_t	_0 [5]	
uint8_t	bssid [6]	Access point mac address.
uint16_t	_1 [2]	
uint8_t	ssid_len	Length of wlan access point name.
uint8_t	ssid [32]	wlan access point name.
uint32_t	_2 [5]	
uint16_t	channel	Wifi channel.
uint16_t	_3	
uint8_t	auth_mode	Wifi auth mode CYW43_AUTH_
int16_t	rssi	Signal strength.

_cyw43_async_event_t

struct _cyw43_async_event_t

Data Fields

uint16_t	_0
uint16_t	flags
uint32_t	event_type
uint32_t	status
uint32_t	reason
uint8_t	_1 [30]
uint8_t	interface
uint8_t	_2
union {	
cyw43_ev_scan_result_t scan_result	
} u	

_cyw43_wifi_scan_options_t

```
struct   _cyw43_wifi_scan_options_t
```

wifi scan options passed to cyw43_wifi_scan.

Data Fields

uint32_t	**version**	version (not used)
uint16_t	**action**	action (not used)
uint16_t	**_**	not used
uint32_t	**ssid_len**	ssid length, 0=all
uint8_t	**ssid** [32]	ssid name
uint8_t	**bssid** [6]	bssid (not used)
int8_t	**bss_type**	bssid type (not used)
int8_t	**scan_type**	scan type 0=active, 1=passive
int32_t	**nprobes**	number of probes (not used)
int32_t	**active_time**	active time (not used)
int32_t	**passive_time**	passive time (not used)
int32_t	**home_time**	home time (not used)
int32_t	**channel_num**	number of channels (not used)
uint16_t	**channel_list** [1]	channel list (not used)

_cyw43_ll_t

```
struct   _cyw43_ll_t
```

Data Fields

uint32_t	**opaque** [526+5]	See cyw43_ll_init.
	cb_data	
	cur_backplane_window	
	wwd_sdpcm_packet_transmit_sequence_number	
	wwd_sdpcm_last_bus_data_credit	
	wlan_flow_control	
	wwd_sdpcm_requested_ioctl_id	
	bus_is_up	
	had_successful_packet	
	bus_data	

TYPEDEFS

cyw43_t

```
typedef struct _cyw43_t cyw43_t
```

This is a type definition of the _cyw43_t data structure.

cyw43_async_event_t

```
typedef struct _cyw43_async_event_t cyw43_async_event_t
```

This is a type definition of the _cyw43_async_event_t data structure.

cyw43_ll_t

```
typedef struct _cyw43_ll_t cyw43_ll_t
```

This is a type definition of the _cyw43_ll_t data structure.

cyw43_ev_scan_result_t

```
typedef struct _cyw43_ev_scan_result_t
         cyw43_ev_scan_result_t
```

Structure to return wifi scan results.

cyw43_wifi_scan_options_t

```
typedef struct _cyw43_wifi_scan_options_t
         cyw43_wifi_scan_options_t
```

Wifi scan options passed to cyw43_wifi_scan.

VARIABLES

cyw43_state

```
cyw43_t cyw43_state
```

The cyw43_state structure is part of the CYW43 Chip Driver API in the Pico API. It represents the state of the CYW43 wireless chip and contains various fields and parameters that store information related to the chip's configuration and operation.

cyw43_poll

```
void(* cyw43_poll )(void)
```

The cyw43_poll is a function pointer in the CYW43 Chip Driver API of the Pico API. It represents a callback function that is responsible for periodically polling the CYW43 wireless chip for any updates or events.

cyw43_sleep

```
uint32_t cyw43_sleep
```

The cyw43_sleep is a variable in the CYW43 Chip Driver API of the Pico API. It represents the sleep duration for the CYW43 wireless chip in milliseconds.

By setting the cyw43_sleep variable to a specific value, the application can control the sleep duration of the CYW43 chip. This allows for efficient power management by adjusting the sleep period based on the desired trade-off between power consumption and responsiveness to incoming wireless communication.

FUNCTIONS

cyw43_arch_async_context()

```
async_context_t * cyw43_arch_async_context (void)
```

Return the current async_context currently in use by the cyw43_arch code.

Returns

The async_context.

cyw43_arch_deinit()

```
void cyw43_arch_deinit (void)
```

De-initialize the CYW43 architecture. This method de-initializes the cyw43_driver code and de-initializes the lwIP stack (if it was enabled at build time). Note this method should always be called from the same core (or RTOS task, depending on the environment) as cyw43_arch_init. Additionally if the cyw43_arch is using its own async_context instance, then that instance is de-initialized.

cyw43_arch_disable_ap_mode()

```
void cyw43_arch_disable_ap_mode (void)
```

Disables Wi-Fi AP (Access point) mode. This Disbles the Wi-Fi in Access Point mode.

cyw43_arch_disable_sta_mode()

```
void cyw43_arch_disable_sta_mode (void)
```

Disables Wi-Fi STA (Station) mode. This disables the Wi-Fi in Station mode, disconnecting any active connection. You should subsequently check the status by calling cyw43_wifi_link_status.

cyw43_arch_enable_ap_mode()

```
void cyw43_arch_enable_ap_mode(const char * ssid,
        const char * password, uint32_t auth)
```

Enables Wi-Fi AP (Access point) mode. This enables the Wi-Fi in Access Point mode such that connections can be made to the device by other Wi-Fi clients

Parameters

ssid   The name for the access point.

password The password to use or NULL for no password.

auth   The authorization type to use when the password is enabled.
              Values are CYW43_AUTH_WPA_TKIP_PSK,
              CYW43_AUTH_WPA2_AES_PSK, or
              CYW43_AUTH_WPA2_MIXED_PSK (see CYW43_AUTH_).

cyw43_arch_enable_sta_mode()

```
void cyw43_arch_enable_sta_mode (void)
```

Enables Wi-Fi STA (Station) mode. This enables the Wi-Fi in Station mode such that connections can be made to other Wi-Fi Access Points

cyw43_arch_get_country_code()

```
uint32_t cyw43_arch_get_country_code (void)
```

Return the country code used to initialize cyw43_arch.

Returns

The country code (see CYW43_COUNTRY_)

cyw43_arch_gpio_get()

```
bool cyw43_arch_gpio_get (uint wl_gpio)
```

Read the value of a GPIO pin on the wireless chip.

NOTE This method does not check for errors setting the GPIO. You can use the lower level cyw43_gpio_get instead if you wish to check for errors.

Parameters

wl_gpio   The GPIO number on the wireless chip.

Returns

True if the GPIO is high, false otherwise.

cyw43_arch_gpio_put()

```
void cyw43_arch_gpio_put(uint wl_gpio, bool value)
```

Set a GPIO pin on the wireless chip to a given value.

NOTE This method does not check for errors setting the GPIO. You can use the lower level cyw43_gpio_set instead if you wish to check for errors.

Parameters

wl_gpio   The GPIO number on the wireless chip.
value   True to set the GPIO, false to clear it.

cyw43_arch_init()

```
int cyw43_arch_init (void)
```

Initialize the CYW43 architecture. This method initializes the cyw43_driver code and initializes the lwIP stack (if it was enabled at build time). This method must be called prior to using any other pico_cyw43_arch, cyw43_driver or lwIP functions. By default this method initializes the cyw43_arch code's own async_context by calling cyw43_arch_init_default_async_context, however the user can specify use of their own async_context by calling cyw43_arch_set_async_context() before calling this method. See also pico_error_codes.

NOTE This method initializes wireless with a country code of PICO_CYW43_ARCH_DEFAULT_COUNTRY_CODE which defaults to CYW43_COUNTRY_WORLDWIDE. Worldwide settings may not give the best performance; consider setting PICO_CYW43_ARCH_DEFAULT_COUNTRY_CODE to a different value or calling cyw43_arch_init_with_country.

Returns

0 if the initialization is successful, an error code otherwise.

cyw43_arch_init_default_async_context()

```
async_context_t * cyw43_arch_init_default_async_context
       (void )
```

Initialize the default async_context for the current cyw43_arch type. This method initializes and returns a pointer to the static async_context associated with cyw43_arch. This method is called by cyw43_arch_init automatically if a different async_context has not been set by cyw43_arch_set_async_context

Returns

The context or NULL if initialization failed.

cyw43_arch_init_with_country()

```
int cyw43_arch_init_with_country (uint32_t country)
```

Initialize the CYW43 architecture for use in a specific country. This method initializes the cyw43_driver code and initializes the lwIP stack (if it was enabled at build time). This method must be called prior to using any other pico_cyw43_arch, cyw43_driver or lwIP functions.

By default this method initializes the cyw43_arch code's own async_context by calling cyw43_arch_init_default_async_context, however the user can specify use of their own async_context by calling cyw43_arch_set_async_context() before calling this method. See also pico_error_codes.

Parameters

country   The country code to use (see CYW43_COUNTRY_).

Returns

0 if the initialization is successful, an error code otherwise.

cyw43_arch_lwip_begin()   **Inline Static**

```
cyw43_arch_lwip_begin (void )
```

Acquire any locks required to call into lwIP. The lwIP API is not thread safe. You should surround calls into the lwIP API with calls to this method and cyw43_arch_lwip_end. Note these calls are not necessary (but harmless) when you are calling back into the lwIP API from an lwIP callback. If you are using single-core polling only (pico_cyw43_arch_poll) then these calls are no-ops anyway it is good practice to call them anyway where they are necessary.

See also cyw43_arch_lwip_end cyw43_arch_lwip_protect async_context_acquire_lock_blocking cyw43_arch_async_context.

NOTE As of SDK release 1.5.0, this is now equivalent to calling async_context_acquire_lock_blocking on the async_context associated with cyw43_arch and lwIP.

cyw43_arch_lwip_end()   **Inline Static**

```
void cyw43_arch_lwip_end (void)
```

Release any locks required for calling into lwIP. The lwIP API is not thread safe. You should surround calls into the lwIP API with calls to cyw43_arch_lwip_begin and this method. Note these calls are not necessary (but harmless) when you are calling back into the lwIP API from an lwIP callback. If you are using single-core polling only (pico_cyw43_arch_poll) then these calls are no-ops anyway it is good practice to call them anyway where they are necessary. See also cyw43_arch_lwip_begin cyw43_arch_lwip_protect async_context_release_lock cyw43_arch_async_context.

NOTE As of SDK release 1.5.0, this is now equivalent to calling async_context_release_lock on the async_context associated with cyw43_arch and lwIP.

cyw43_arch_lwip_protect()   **Inline Static**

```
int cyw43_arch_lwip_protect(int(*)(void *param) func,
        void * param)
```

Release any locks required for calling into lwIP. The lwIP API is not thread safe. You can use this method to wrap a function with any locking required to call into the lwIP API. If you are using single-core polling only (pico_cyw43_arch_poll) then there are no locks to required, but it is still good practice to use this function. See also cyw43_arch_lwip_begin cyw43_arch_lwip_end.

Parameters

func   The function ta call with any required locks held.
param   Parameter to pass to func.

Returns

the return value from func

cyw43_arch_poll()

```
void cyw43_arch_poll(void )
```

Perform any processing required by the cyw43_driver or the TCP/IP stack. This method must be called periodically from the main loop when using a polling style pico_cyw43_arch (e.g. pico_cyw43_arch_lwip_poll). It may be called in other styles, but it is unnecessary to do so.

cyw43_arch_set_async_context()

```
void cyw43_arch_set_async_context
            (async_context_t * context)
```

Set the async_context to be used by the cyw43_arch_init.

NOTE This method must be called before calling cyw43_arch_init or cyw43_arch_init_with_country if you wish to use a custom async_context instance.

Parameters

context   The async_context to be used.

cyw43_arch_wait_for_work_until()

```
void cyw43_arch_wait_for_work_until(absolute_time_t until)
```

Sleep until there is cyw43_driver work to be done. This method may be called by code that is waiting for an event to come from the cyw43_driver, and has no work to do, but would like to sleep without blocking any background work associated with the cyw43_driver.

Parameters

until   The time to wait until if there is no work to do.

cyw43_arch_wifi_connect_async()

```
int cyw43_arch_wifi_connect_async(const char * ssid, const
        char * pw, uint32_t auth)
```

Start attempting to connect to a wireless access point.This method tells the CYW43 driver to start connecting to an access point. You should subsequently check the status by calling cyw43_wifi_link_status. See also pico_error_codes.

Parameters

ssid

The network name to connect to.

pw

The network password or NULL if there is no password required.

auth

The authorization type to use when the password is enabled. Values are CYW43_AUTH_WPA_TKIP_PSK, CYW43_AUTH_WPA2_AES_PSK, or CYW43_AUTH_WPA2_MIXED_PSK (see CYW43_AUTH_).

Returns

0 if the scan was started successfully, an error code otherwise

cyw43_arch_wifi_connect_blocking()

```
int cyw43_arch_wifi_connect_blocking(const char * ssid,
        const char * pw, uint32_t auth)
```

Attempt to connect to a wireless access point, blocking until the network is joined or a failure is detected. See also pico_error_codes.

Parameters

ssid

The network name to connect to.

pw

The network password or NULL if there is no password required.

auth

The authorization type to use when the password is enabled. Values are CYW43_AUTH_WPA_TKIP_PSK, CYW43_AUTH_WPA2_AES_PSK, or CYW43_AUTH_WPA2_MIXED_PSK (see CYW43_AUTH_).

Returns

0 if the initialization is successful, an error code otherwise

cyw43_arch_wifi_connect_bssid_async()

```
int cyw43_arch_wifi_connect_bssid_async(const char * ssid,
        const uint8_t * bssid, const char * pw, uint32_t
        auth)
```

Start attempting to connect to a wireless access point specified by SSID and BSSID. This method tells the CYW43 driver to start connecting to an access point. You should subsequently check the status by calling cyw43_wifi_link_status. See also pico_error_codes.

Parameters

ssid

The network name to connect to.

bssid

The network BSSID to connect to or NULL if ignored.

pw

The network password or NULL if there is no password required.

auth

The authorization type to use when the password is enabled. Values are CYW43_AUTH_WPA_TKIP_PSK, CYW43_AUTH_WPA2_AES_PSK, or CYW43_AUTH_WPA2_MIXED_PSK (see CYW43_AUTH_).

Returns

0 if the scan was started successfully, an error code otherwise.

cyw43_arch_wifi_connect_bssid_blocking()

```
int cyw43_arch_wifi_connect_bssid_blocking(const char *
      ssid, const uint8_t * bssid, const char * pw,
      uint32_t auth)
```

Attempt to connect to a wireless access point specified by SSID and BSSID, blocking until the network is joined or a failure is detected. See also pico_error_codes.

Parameters

ssid

The network name to connect to

bssid

The network BSSID to connect to or NULL if ignored.

pw

The network password or NULL if there is no password required.

auth

The authorization type to use when the password is enabled. Values are CYW43_AUTH_WPA_TKIP_PSK, CYW43_AUTH_WPA2_AES_PSK, or CYW43_AUTH_WPA2_MIXED_PSK (see CYW43_AUTH_).

Returns

0 if the initialization is successful, an error code otherwise.

cyw43_arch_wifi_connect_bssid_timeout_ms()

```
int cyw43_arch_wifi_connect_bssid_timeout_ms(const char *
     ssid, const uint8_t * bssid, const char * pw,
     uint32_t auth, uint32_t timeout)
```

Attempt to connect to a wireless access point specified by SSID and BSSID, blocking until the network is joined or a failure is detected or a timeout occurs. See also pico_error_codes.

Parameters

ssid

The network name to connect to.

bssid

The network BSSID to connect to or NULL if ignored.

pw

The network password or NULL if there is no password required.

auth

The authorization type to use when the password is enabled. Values are CYW43_AUTH_WPA_TKIP_PSK, CYW43_AUTH_WPA2_AES_PSK, or CYW43_AUTH_WPA2_MIXED_PSK (see CYW43_AUTH_).

timeout

How long to wait in milliseconds for a connection to succeed before giving up.

Returns

0 if the initialization is successful, an error code otherwise.

cyw43_arch_wifi_connect_timeout_ms()

```
int cyw43_arch_wifi_connect_timeout_ms(const char * ssid,
    const char * pw, uint32_t auth, uint32_t timeout)
```

Attempt to connect to a wireless access point, blocking until the network is joined or a failure is detected or a timeout occurs. See also pico_error_codes.

Parameters

ssid

> The network name to connect to.

pw

> The network password or NULL if there is no password required.

auth

> The authorization type to use when the password is enabled. Values are CYW43_AUTH_WPA_TKIP_PSK, CYW43_AUTH_WPA2_AES_PSK, or CYW43_AUTH_WPA2_MIXED_PSK (see CYW43_AUTH_).

timeout

> How long to wait in milliseconds for a connection to succeed before giving up.

Returns

> 0 if the initialization is successful, an error code otherwise.

cyw43_cb_read_host_interrupt_pin ()

```
int cyw43_cb_read_host_interrupt_pin (void *cb_data)
```

This function is responsible for reading the state of the host interrupt pin and providing the corresponding status. The host interrupt pin is typically connected to a GPIO pin on the microcontroller or system hosting the CYW43 wireless chip. It serves as a signal from the CYW43 chip to the host, indicating that an event or data is available for processing. Defined in cyw43_ctrl.c.

NOTE Very little information is available about the low level driver functions at the time of publication. Therefore some functionality descriptions may not be entirely correct.

Parameters

cb_data

A pointer to user-defined callback data. Callback to be provided by mid-level interface.

Returns

The return value of the function is an integer that represents the status of the host interrupt pin.

cyw43_cb_ensure_awake ()

```
void cyw43_cb_ensure_awake (void *cb_data)
```

This function ensures that the bus is awake. Defined in cyw43_ctrl.c.

NOTE Very little information is available about the low level driver functions at the time of publication. Therefore some functionality descriptions may not be entirely correct.

Parameters

cb_data

A pointer to user-defined callback data. Callback to be provided by mid-level interface.

cyw43_cb_process_async_event ()

```
void cyw43_cb_process_async_event (void *cb_data,
        const cyw43_async_event_t *ev)
```

This function is an event handler for processing various asynchronous events related to the CYW43 WiFi module. The function processes different types of asynchronous events and updates the state of the WiFi module accordingly. It handles events related to WiFi scanning, association, disassociation, authentication, link status, and PSK (Pre-Shared Key) setup. The function checks the status and type of each event and takes appropriate actions, such as starting or stopping WiFi scanning, setting the SSID, handling authentication, and updating link status. When the WiFi module successfully connects to a network (STA connected), it signals the successful link-up to the TCP/IP stack.

Overall, this function plays a crucial role in managing the WiFi functionality of the CYW43 module based on various asynchronous events triggered during WiFi operation.

NOTE Very little information is available about the low level driver functions at the time of publication. Therefore some functionality descriptions may not be entirely correct.

Parameters

cb_data

A pointer to user-defined callback data. Callback to be provided by mid-level interface.

ev

A pointer to a cyw43_async_event_t structure ev that represents the asynchronous event.

cyw43_cb_process_ethernet ()

```
void cyw43_cb_process_ethernet (void *cb_data, int itf,
        size_t len, const uint8_t *buf)
```

The function starts by casting the cb_data parameter to a pointer of type cyw43_t, which represents the CYW43 WiFi module structure. It then accesses the network interface data corresponding to the specified itf index. If the CYW43_NETUTILS macro is defined, the function checks the trace_flags to determine if Ethernet tracing is enabled. If tracing is enabled, it calls the cyw43_ethernet_trace function to log information about the received Ethernet packet. Next, the function checks if the network interface's link is up (NETIF_FLAG_LINK_UP). If the link is up, it allocates a packet buffer (struct pbuf) with the size of the received Ethernet packet using the pbuf_alloc function. If the allocation is successful, the function copies the received packet data to the packet buffer using the pbuf_take function. The packet buffer is then passed to the network interface's input function (netif->input) to be processed further by the network stack. If the input function returns an error, the packet buffer is freed using pbuf_free.

Overall, this function handles received Ethernet packets, checks the link status, and processes the packets by passing them to the appropriate network interface for further processing by the network stack.

Parameters

cb_data

A pointer to user-defined callback data. Callback to be provided by mid-level interface.

itf

An int parameter itf representing the interface which the packet was received. The interface used, either CYW43_ITF_STA or CYW43_ITF_AP.

len

A size_t parameter representing the length of the packet data. The len parameter specifies the length of the packet data in bytes, enabling the function to access and process the correct amount of data from the buffer pointed to by buf.

buf

A const uint8_t* parameter buf pointing to the buffer containing the packet data. The buf parameter is a pointer to the buffer containing the raw Ethernet packet data.

cyw43_cb_tcpip_deinit()

```
void cyw43_cb_tcpip_deinit(cyw43_t * self, int itf)
```

Deinitialize the IP stack. This method must be provided by the network stack interface It is called to close the IP stack and free resources.

Parameters

self

> The driver state object. This should always be &cyw43_state.

itf

> The interface used, either CYW43_ITF_STA or CYW43_ITF_AP.

cyw43_cb_tcpip_init()

```
void cyw43_cb_tcpip_init(cyw43_t * self, int itf)
```

Initialize the IP stack. This method must be provided by the network stack interface It is called to Initialize the IP stack.

Parameters

self

> The driver state object. This should always be &cyw43_state.

itf

> The interface used, either CYW43_ITF_STA or CYW43_ITF_AP.

cyw43_cb_tcpip_set_link_down()

```
void cyw43_cb_tcpip_set_link_down(cyw43_t * self, int itf)
```

Notify the IP stack that the link is down. This method must be provided by the network stack interface It is called to notify the IP stack that the link is down.

Parameters

self

The driver state object. This should always be &cyw43_state.

itf

The interface used, either CYW43_ITF_STA or CYW43_ITF_AP.

cyw43_cb_tcpip_set_link_up()

```
void cyw43_cb_tcpip_set_link_up(cyw43_t * self, int itf)
```

Notify the IP stack that the link is up. This method must be provided by the network stack interface It is called to notify the IP stack that the link is up. This can, for example be used to request an IP address via DHCP.

Parameters

self

The driver state object. This should always be &cyw43_state.

itf

The interface used, either CYW43_ITF_STA or CYW43_ITF_AP.

cyw43_deinit()

```
void cyw43_deinit(cyw43_t * self)
```

Shut the driver down. This method will close the network interfaces, and free up resources

Parameters

self

The driver state object. This should always be &cyw43_state.

cyw43_init()

```
void cyw43_init(cyw43_t * self)
```

Initialize the driver. This method must be called before using the driver

Parameters

self

The driver state object. This should always be &cyw43_state.

cyw43_ioctl()

```
int cyw43_ioctl(cyw43_t * self, uint32_t cmd, size_t len,
        uint8_t * buf, uint32_t iface)
```

Send an ioctl command to cyw43. This method sends a command to cyw43.

Parameters

self	The driver state object. This should always be &cyw43_state.
cmd	The command to send.
len	The amount of data to send with the command.
buf	A buffer containing the data to send.
iface	The interface to use, either CYW43_ITF_STA or CYW43_ITF_AP.

Returns

0 on success.

cyw43_is_initialized()   Inline Static

```
static bool cyw43_is_initialized(cyw43_t * self)
```

Determines if the cyw43 driver been initialized. Returns true if the cyw43 driver has been initialized with a call to cyw43_init.

Parameters

self

> The driver state object. This should always be &cyw43_state.

Returns

> True if the cyw43 driver has been initialized.

cyw43_ll_bt_has_work ()

```
bool cyw43_ll_bt_has_work (cyw43_ll_t *self)
```

The function is used to check if there is any pending work or activity related to the Bluetooth (BT) functionality in the CYW43 chip. It takes a pointer to a cyw43_ll_t structure (self) as a parameter and returns a boolean value indicating whether there is any pending work or not.

Parameters

self

> The driver state object. This should always be &cyw43_state.

Returns

> True if there is pending work in the Bluetooth module, indicating that there are tasks or activities that need to be processed. Conversely, if there is no pending work, the function returns false.

cyw43_ll_bus_init ()

```
int cyw43_ll_bus_init (cyw43_ll_t *self,
          const uint8_t *mac)
```

The function cyw43_ll_bus_init is responsible for initializing the bus communication with the CYW43 chip. It sets up the bus interface and configures various parameters specific to the communication protocol used (SPI or SDIO). It ensures that the communication bus is properly configured before performing any further operations or interactions with the chip.

Parameters

self

The driver state object. This should always be &cyw43_state.

mac

The mac parameter is a pointer to the MAC address assigned to the CYW43 chip. This MAC address is used for identification and communication purposes in network protocols.

Returns

Upon successful initialization, the function returns PICO_OK, indicating that the communication bus has been set up correctly. If there is an error during the initialization process, an appropriate error code is returned.

The Pico C API Functionary

cyw43_ll_bus_sleep ()

```
void cyw43_ll_bus_sleep (cyw43_ll_t *self, bool can_sleep)
```

The function is used to control the sleep mode of the CYW43 chip's communication bus. It takes a pointer to a cyw43_ll_t structure (self) and a boolean parameter (can_sleep) as inputs.

Parameters

self

The driver state object. This should always be &cyw43_state.

can_sleep

The can_sleep parameter indicates whether the communication bus is allowed to enter sleep mode. If can_sleep is set to true, it means the bus can enter sleep mode, indicating a low-power state. If can_sleep is set to false, it means the bus should remain active and not enter sleep mode.

cyw43_ll_deinit ()

```
void cyw43_ll_deinit (cyw43_ll_t *self)
```

The function is used to deinitialize and clean up the resources associated with the CYW43 chip's low-level interface.

Parameters

self

The driver state object. This should always be &cyw43_state.

cyw43_ll_has_work ()

```
bool cyw43_ll_has_work (cyw43_ll_t *self)
```

The purpose of the function is to determine whether there are any pending actions or tasks that need to be processed by the CYW43 chip. This can include tasks such as data transmission, reception, or any other asynchronous operations.

NOTE Very little information is available about the low level driver functions at the time of publication. Therefore some functionality descriptions may not be entirely correct.

Parameters

self

The driver state object. This should always be &cyw43_state.

Returns

A boolean value indicating the presence (true) or absence (false) of pending work.

cyw43_ll_init ()

```
void cyw43_ll_init (cyw43_ll_t *self, void *cb_data)
```

The function is used to initialize the low-level interface for the CYW43 chip.

NOTE Very little information is available about the low level driver functions at the time of publication. Therefore some functionality descriptions may not be entirely correct.

self

The driver state object. This should always be &cyw43_state.

cb_data

This is the registered callback function for the low level driver.

cyw43_ll_ioctl ()

```
int cyw43_ll_ioctl (cyw43_ll_t *self, uint32_t cmd,
        size_t len, uint8_t *buf, uint32_t iface)
```

The cyw43_ll_ioctl function is used to send control commands to the low-level interface of the CYW43 chip. It allows for configuring and interacting with the chip at a low level by executing specific commands and exchanging data with the chip.

NOTE Very little information is available about the low level driver functions at the time of publication. Therefore some functionality descriptions may not be entirely correct.

Parameters

self	The driver state object. This should always be &cyw43_state.
cmd	The command to send.
len	The amount of data to send with the command.
buf	A buffer containing the data to send.
iface	The interface to use, either CYW43_ITF_STA or CYW43_ITF_AP.

Returns

0 on success.

cyw43_ll_process_packets ()

```
void cyw43_ll_process_packets (cyw43_ll_t *self)
```

The cyw43_ll_process_packets function is responsible for processing incoming packets on the low-level interface of the CYW43 chip. It retrieves packets from the chip, performs necessary processing tasks, and facilitates the handling and forwarding of the packets to higher-level software layers or network stacks.

The cyw43_ll_process_packets function typically needs to be called periodically or in response to an interrupt to ensure that incoming packets are processed in a timely manner.

NOTE Very little information is available about the low level driver functions at the time of publication. Therefore some functionality descriptions may not be entirely correct.

cyw43_ll_read_backplane_mem ()

```
int cyw43_ll_read_backplane_mem (cyw43_ll_t *self_in,
     uint32_t addr, uint32_t len, uint8_t *buf)
```

The cyw43_ll_read_backplane_mem function provides an interface to read data from the backplane memory of the CYW43 chip. It utilizes the low-level interface provided by the cyw43_ll_t structure to communicate with the chip and retrieve the requested data.

NOTE Very little information is available about the low level driver functions at the time of publication. Therefore some functionality descriptions may not be entirely correct.

Parameters

self	The driver state object. This should always be &cyw43_state.
addr	The starting address of the memory region to read.
len	The length of the data to read.
buf	A pointer to the buffer where the read data will be stored.

Returns

The function returns an integer value, which can be used to indicate the success or failure of the read operation. A non-zero value typically indicates an error or failure, while a return value of zero indicates a successful read operation.

cyw43_ll_read_backplane_reg ()

```
uint32_t cyw43_ll_read_backplane_reg (cyw43_ll_t *self_in,
        uint32_t addr)
```

The function cyw43_ll_read_backplane_reg in the Pico API is used to read the value of a specific register in the backplane memory of the CYW43 chip.

NOTE Very little information is available about the low level driver functions at the time of publication. Therefore some functionality descriptions may not be entirely correct.

Parameters

self   The driver state object. This should always be &cyw43_state.

addr   The address of the register to read.

Returns

The register value.

cyw43_ll_send_ethernet ()

```
int cyw43_ll_send_ethernet (cyw43_ll_t *self, int itf,
        size_t len, const void *buf, bool is_pbuf)
```

The cyw43_ll_send_ethernet function allows for sending Ethernet packets through the CYW43 chip's Ethernet interface. It utilizes the low-level interface provided by the cyw43_ll_t structure to communicate with the chip and transmit the packet data. The result of the send operation is returned as an integer value.

NOTE Very little information is available about the low level driver functions at the time of publication. Therefore some functionality descriptions may not be entirely correct.

Parameters

self	The driver state object. This should always be &cyw43_state.
itf	The interface number (itf) for the Ethernet interface.
len	The length of the packet.
buf	A pointer to the packet data.
is_pbuf	A flag indicating whether the packet data is in pbuf format.

Returns

The function returns an integer value representing the result of the send operation.

cyw43_ll_wifi_ap_get_stas ()

```
int cyw43_ll_wifi_ap_get_stas (cyw43_ll_t *self, int
      *num_stas, uint8_t *macs)
```

The cyw43_ll_wifi_ap_get_stas function allows for retrieving the MAC addresses of the stations connected to the Wi-Fi access point on the CYW43 chip. It utilizes the low-level interface provided by the cyw43_ll_t structure to communicate with the chip and retrieve the necessary information. The result of the operation, including the count of connected stations and their MAC addresses, is returned and can be used for further processing or analysis.

NOTE Very little information is available about the low level driver functions at the time of publication. Therefore some functionality descriptions may not be entirely correct.

Parameters

self

> The driver state object. This should always be &cyw43_state.

num_stas

> A pointer to an integer variable to store the number of   connected stations.

macs

> A pointer to a buffer (macs) to store the MAC addresses of the connected stations.

Returns

> The function returns an integer value representing the result of the operation.

cyw43_ll_wifi_ap_init ()

```
int cyw43_ll_wifi_ap_init (cyw43_ll_t *self,
        size_t ssid_len, const uint8_t *ssid,
        uint32_t auth, size_t key_len,
        const uint8_t *key, uint32_t channel)
```

The function cyw43_ll_wifi_ap_init in the Pico API is used to initialize the Wi-Fi access point (AP) functionality on the CYW43 chip. It configures the AP with the specified SSID, authentication method, encryption key, and operating channel.

NOTE Very little information is available about the low level driver functions at the time of publication. Therefore some functionality descriptions may not be entirely correct.

Parameters

self

The driver state object. This should always be &cyw43_state.

ssid_len

The length of the SSID.

ssid

A pointer to the SSID data.

auth

This parameter represents the authentication type, such as WPA2 or open network.

key_len

If authentication is required, the function specifies the encryption key by providing the length of the key.

key

A pointer to the key data.

channel

The operating channel for the AP. The channel determines the frequency on which the AP operates.

Returns

The function returns an integer value representing the result of the operation.

The Pico C API Functionary

cyw43_ll_wifi_ap_set_up ()

```
int cyw43_ll_wifi_ap_set_up (cyw43_ll_t *self, bool up)
```

The cyw43_ll_wifi_ap_set_up function is used to control the state of the Wi-Fi access point on the CYW43 chip. It enables or disables the AP functionality based on the up parameter, and returns a result indicating the success or failure of the operation.

NOTE Very little information is available about the low level driver functions at the time of publication. Therefore some functionality descriptions may not be entirely correct.

Parameters

self

The driver state object. This should always be &cyw43_state.

up

This indicates whether to bring up (true) or take down (false) the AP.

Returns

The function returns an integer value representing the result of the operation.

cyw43_ll_wifi_get_bssid ()

```
int cyw43_ll_wifi_get_bssid (cyw43_ll_t *self_in,
          uint8_t *bssid)
```

The function is used to retrieve the BSSID (Basic Service Set Identifier) of the Wi-Fi connection on the CYW43 chip. The BSSID is a unique identifier for a wireless network and represents the MAC address of the access point (AP) the CYW43 chip is connected to.

NOTE Very little information is available about the low level driver functions at the time of publication. Therefore some functionality descriptions may not be entirely correct.

Parameters

self   The driver state object. This should always be &cyw43_state.

bssid   A pointer to a uint8_t array to store the BSSID.

Returns

The function returns an integer value representing the result of the operation.

438

cyw43_ll_wifi_get_mac ()

```
int cyw43_ll_wifi_get_mac (cyw43_ll_t *self_in,
        uint8_t *addr)
```

The function is used to retrieve the MAC address of the Wi-Fi interface on the CYW43 chip. The MAC address is a unique identifier assigned to the network interface, and it consists of six bytes.

NOTE Very little information is available about the low level driver functions at the time of publication. Therefore some functionality descriptions may not be entirely correct.

Parameters

self

The driver state object. This should always be &cyw43_state.

addr

A uint8_t array where the MAC address will be stored. The array should have enough capacity to hold the MAC address, which is typically six bytes.

Returns

The function returns an integer value representing the result of the operation.

The Pico C API Functionary

cyw43_ll_wifi_get_pm ()

```
int cyw43_ll_wifi_get_pm (cyw43_ll_t *self, uint32_t *pm,
        uint32_t *pm_sleep_ret, uint32_t *li_bcn,
        uint32_t *li_dtim, uint32_t *li_assoc)
```

The function retrieves various power management-related parameters and values from the CYW43 Wi-Fi chip.The function then proceeds to read the desired values from the CYW43 chip using various IOVAR commands.

NOTE Very little information is available about the low level driver functions at the time of publication. Therefore some functionality descriptions may not be entirely correct.

Parameters

self

The driver state object. This should always be &cyw43_state.

pm

A pointer to a uint32_t variable to store the retrieved power management value.

pm_sleep_ret

A pointer to a uint32_t variable to store the retrieved sleep return value.

li_ben

A pointer to a uint32_t variable to store the retrieved beacon listen interval value.

li_dtm

A pointer to a uint32_t variable to store the retrieved DTIM listen interval value.

li_assoc

A pointer to a uint32_t variable to store the retrieved association listen value.

Returns

Zero.

cyw43_ll_wifi_join ()

```
int cyw43_ll_wifi_join (cyw43_ll_t *self, size_t ssid_len,
        const uint8_t *ssid, size_t key_len,
        const uint8_t *key, uint32_t auth_type,
        const uint8_t *bssid, uint32_t channel)
```

The cyw43_ll_wifi_join function is responsible for joining a Wi-Fi network using the CYW43 chip. It takes several parameters: self_in (a pointer to the CYW43 chip driver), ssid_len (length of the network SSID), ssid (buffer containing the SSID), key_len (length of the security key), key (buffer containing the security key), auth_type (authentication type), bssid (BSSID of the network), and channel (channel number).

The function configures the necessary parameters for network connection and sends appropriate commands to establish the connection. It sets authentication, encryption, and network mode parameters based on the provided information. If a security key is required, it sets the key using the "wsec_pmk" command. The function also handles the association process by setting the SSID and BSSID parameters.

NOTE Very little information is available about the low level driver functions at the time of publication. Therefore some functionality descriptions may not be entirely correct.

Parameters

self	The driver state object. This should always be &cyw43_state.
ssid_len	The length of the network SSID.
ssid	A buffer containing the SSID of the network.
key_len	The length of the security key.
key	A buffer containing the security key.
auth_type	The authentication type of the network.
bssid	The BSSID (MAC address) of the network.
channel	The channel number of the network.

Returns

The function returns 0 upon successful execution.

cyw43_ll_wifi_on ()

```
int cyw43_ll_wifi_on (cyw43_ll_t *self, uint32_t country)
```

The function cyw43_ll_wifi_on initializes the Wi-Fi functionality of the CYW43 chip. It configures various parameters and settings to enable Wi-Fi communication. Requires cyw43_ll_bus_init to have been called first.

NOTE Very little information is available about the low level driver functions at the time of publication. Therefore some functionality descriptions may not be entirely correct.

Parameters

self

The driver state object. This should always be &cyw43_state.

country

The country code to set for regulatory compliance.

Returns

0 if the initialization is successful.

cyw43_ll_wifi_pm ()

```
int cyw43_ll_wifi_pm (cyw43_ll_t *self, uint32_t pm,
        uint32_t pm_sleep_ret, uint32_t li_bcn,
        uint32_t li_dtim, uint32_t li_assoc)
```

The function cyw43_ll_wifi_pm sets power-saving parameters for the CYW43 chip's Wi-Fi functionality. It configures parameters related to power management and beacon intervals to optimize power consumption.

NOTE Very little information is available about the low level driver functions at the time of publication. Therefore some functionality descriptions may not be entirely correct.

Parameters

self_in: A pointer to the CYW43 chip driver.

pm: Power management mode to set.

pm_sleep_ret: Sleep return time in milliseconds.

li_bcn: Beacon interval.

li_dtim: DTIM (Delivery Traffic Indication Message) interval.

li_assoc: Association listen interval.

Returns

0 if the power-saving configuration is successful.

cyw43_ll_wifi_rejoin ()

```
void cyw43_ll_wifi_rejoin (cyw43_ll_t *self)
```

The function cyw43_ll_wifi_rejoin is used to initiate the rejoining process of a Wi-Fi network using the CYW43 chip. It sets the SSID parameter for reconnection.

NOTE Very little information is available about the low level driver functions at the time of publication. Therefore some functionality descriptions may not be entirely correct.

Parameters

self_in: A pointer to the CYW43 chip driver.

cyw43_ll_wifi_scan ()

```
int cyw43_ll_wifi_scan (cyw43_ll_t *self,
        cyw43_wifi_scan_options_t *opts)
```

The function cyw43_ll_wifi_scan is used to initiate a Wi-Fi scan using the CYW43 chip. It sets the scan options and triggers the scan process.

NOTE Very little information is available about the low level driver functions at the time of publication. Therefore some functionality descriptions may not be entirely correct.

Parameters

self_in

The driver state object. This should always be &cyw43_state.

opts

A pointer to the cyw43_wifi_scan_options_t structure that contains the scan options.

Returns

0: Indicates successful initiation of the Wi-Fi scan.

cyw43_ll_wifi_set_wpa_auth ()

```
void cyw43_ll_wifi_set_wpa_auth (cyw43_ll_t *self)
```

The function cyw43_ll_wifi_set_wpa_auth is used to set the WPA authentication mode for Wi-Fi communication using the CYW43 chip.

NOTE Very little information is available about the low level driver functions at the time of publication. Therefore some functionality descriptions may not be entirely correct.

Parameters

self_in

The driver state object. This should always be &cyw43_state.

cyw43_ll_wifi_update_multicast_filter ()

```
int cyw43_ll_wifi_update_multicast_filter
        (cyw43_ll_t *self_in, uint8_t *addr, bool add)
```

The function cyw43_ll_wifi_update_multicast_filter is used to update the multicast filter in the CYW43 chip. It allows adding or removing multicast addresses from the filter.

NOTE Very little information is available about the low level driver functions at the time of publication. Therefore some functionality descriptions may not be entirely correct.

Parameters:

self_in

A pointer to the CYW43 chip driver.

addr

The multicast address to add or remove.

add

A boolean flag indicating whether to add (true) or remove (false) the multicast address.

Returns

Return 0 to indicate a successful update.

cyw43_ll_write_backplane_mem ()

```
int cyw43_ll_write_backplane_mem (cyw43_ll_t *self_in,
        uint32_t addr, uint32_t len, const uint8_t *buf)
```

The function cyw43_ll_write_backplane_mem is used to write data to the backplane memory of the CYW43 chip. It writes data in chunks to ensure that the data does not exceed the maximum backplane address range.

NOTE Very little information is available about the low level driver functions at the time of publication. Therefore some functionality descriptions may not be entirely correct.

Parameters

self_in	A pointer to the CYW43 chip driver.
addr	The starting address in the backplane memory to write the data.
len	The length of the data to write.
buf	A pointer to the buffer containing the data to write.

Returns

Return 0 to indicate a successful write operation.

cyw43_ll_write_backplane_reg ()

```
void cyw43_ll_write_backplane_reg (cyw43_ll_t *self_in,
        uint32_t addr, uint32_t val)
```

The purpose of this function is to provide a simplified interface for writing a 32-bit value to a backplane register. It encapsulates the low-level details of writing to the backplane memory and allows for easier manipulation of backplane registers by specifying the address and value directly.

NOTE Very little information is available about the low level driver functions at the time of publication. Therefore some functionality descriptions may not be entirely correct.

Parameters

self_in	A pointer to the CYW43 chip driver.
addr	The address of the register in the backplane memory to write the value.
val	The 32-bit value to write.

cyw43_pm_value()   **Inline Static**

```
static uint32_t cyw43_pm_value(uint8_t pm_mode,
        uint16_t pm2_sleep_ret_ms,
        uint8_t li_beacon_period, uint8_t li_dtim_period,
        uint8_t li_assoc)
```

Return a power management value to pass to cyw43_wifi_pm. Generate the power management (PM) value to pass to cyw43_wifi_pm. See also CYW43_DEFAULT_PM CYW43_AGGRESSIVE_PM CYW43_PERFORMANCE_PM.

pm_mode	Meaning
CYW43_NO_POWERSAVE_MODE	No power saving
CYW43_PM1_POWERSAVE_MODE	Aggressive power saving which reduces wifi throughput
CYW43_PM2_POWERSAVE_MODE	Power saving with High throughput (preferred). Saves power when there is no wifi activity for some time.

Parameters

pm_mode

Power management mode.

pm2_sleep_ret_ms

The maximum time to wait before going back to sleep for CYW43_PM2_POWERSAVE_MODE mode. Value measured in milliseconds and must be between 10 and 2000ms and divisible by 10.

li_beacon_period

Wake period is measured in beacon periods.

li_dtim_period

Wake interval measured in DTIMs. If this is set to 0, the wake interval is measured in beacon periods.

li_assoc

Wake interval sent to the access point.

cyw43_send_ethernet()

```
int cyw43_send_ethernet(cyw43_t * self, int itf, size_t
        len, const void * buf, bool is_pbuf)
```

Send a raw ethernet packet. This method sends a raw ethernet packet.

Parameters

self	The driver state object. This should always be &cyw43_state.
itf	Interface to use, either CYW43_ITF_STA or CYW43_ITF_AP.
len	The amount of data to send.
buf	The data to send.
is_pbuf	True if buf points to an lwip struct pbuf.

Returns

0 on success.

cyw43_tcpip_link_status()

```
int cyw43_tcpip_link_status(cyw43_t * self, int itf )
```

Get the link status. Returns the status of the link which is a superset of the wifi link status returned by cyw43_wifi_link_status

NOTE If the link status is negative it indicates an error.

link status	Meaning
CYW43_LINK_DOWN	Wifi down.
CYW43_LINK_JOIN	Connected to wifi.
CYW43_LINK_NOIP	Connected to wifi, but no IP address.
CYW43_LINK_UP	Connect to wifi with an IP address.
CYW43_LINK_FAIL	Connection failed.
CYW43_LINK_NONET	No matching SSID found (could be out of range, or down).
CYW43_LINK_BADAUTH	Authentication failure.

Parameters

self

The driver state object. This should always be &cyw43_state.

itf

The interface for which to return the link status, should be CYW43_ITF_STA or CYW43_ITF_AP.

Returns

A value representing the link status.

cyw43_wifi_ap_get_auth()   Inline Static

```
static uint32_t cyw43_wifi_ap_get_auth(cyw43_t * self)
```

Get the security authorization used in AP mode. For access point (AP) mode, this method can be used to get the security authorization mode.

Parameters

self   The driver state object. This should always be &cyw43_state.

Returns

The current security authorization mode for the access point.

cyw43_wifi_ap_get_max_stas()

```
void cyw43_wifi_ap_get_max_stas(cyw43_t * self, int *
        max_stas)
```

Get the maximum number of devices (STAs) that can be associated with the wifi access point. For access point (AP) mode, this method can be used to get the maximum number of devices that can be connected to the wifi access point.

Parameters

self

> The driver state object. This should always be &cyw43_state.

max_stas

> Returns the maximum number of devices (STAs) that can be connected to the access point.

cyw43_wifi_ap_get_ssid()   Inline Static

```
static void cyw43_wifi_ap_get_ssid(cyw43_t * self,
        size_t * len, const uint8_t ** buf)
```

Get the ssid for the access point. For access point (AP) mode, this method can be used to get the SSID name of the wifi access point.

Parameters

self

> The driver state object. This should always be &cyw43_state.

len

> Returns the length of the AP SSID name

buf

> Returns a pointer to an internal buffer containing the AP SSID name.

cyw43_wifi_ap_get_stas()

```
void cyw43_wifi_ap_get_stas(cyw43_t * self, int * num_stas,
          uint8_t * macs)
```

Get the number of devices (STAs) associated with the wifi access point. For access point (AP) mode, this method can be used to get the number of devices and mac addresses of devices connected to the wifi access point.

Parameters

self

> The driver state object. This should always be &cyw43_state.

num_stas

> Returns the number of devices (STA) connected to the access point

macs

> Returns the mac addresses of devices (STA) connected to the access point. The supplied buffer should have enough room for 6 bytes per mac address. Call cyw43_wifi_ap_get_max_stas to determine how many mac addresses can be returned.

cyw43_wifi_ap_set_auth() Inline Static

```
static void cyw43_wifi_ap_set_auth(cyw43_t * self,
        uint32_t auth)
```

Set the security authorization used in AP mode. For access point (AP) mode, this method can be used to set how access to the access point is authorized.

Auth mode	Meaning
CYW43_AUTH_OPEN	Use an open access point with no authorization required
CYW43_AUTH_WPA_TKIP_PSK	Use WPA authorization
CYW43_AUTH_WPA2_AES_PSK	Use WPA2 (preferred)
CYW43_AUTH_WPA2_MIXED_PSK	Use WPA2/WPA mixed (currently treated the same as CYW43_AUTH_WPA2_AES_PSK)

Parameters

self	The driver state object. This should always be &cyw43_state.
auth	Auth mode for the access point.

cyw43_wifi_ap_set_channel() Inline Static

```
static void cyw43_wifi_ap_set_channel(cyw43_t * self,
        uint32_t channel)
```

Set the the channel for the access point. For access point (AP) mode, this method can be used to set the channel used for the wifi access point.

Parameters

self	The driver state object. This should always be &cyw43_state.
channel	Wifi channel to use for the wifi access point.

cyw43_wifi_ap_set_password()   Inline Static

```
static void cyw43_wifi_ap_set_password(cyw43_t * self,
        size_t len, const uint8_t * buf)
```

Set the password for the wifi access point. For access point (AP) mode, this method can be used to set the password for the wifi access point.

Parameters

self	The driver state object. This should always be &cyw43_state.
len	The length of the AP password.
buf	A buffer containing the AP password.

cyw43_wifi_ap_set_ssid()   Inline Static

```
static void cyw43_wifi_ap_set_ssid(cyw43_t * self,
        size_t len, const uint8_t * buf)
```

Set the ssid for the access point. For access point (AP) mode, this method can be used to set the SSID name of the wifi access point.

Parameters

self	The driver state object. This should always be &cyw43_state.
len	The length of the AP SSID name.
buf	A buffer containing the AP SSID name.

cyw43_wifi_get_bssid()

```
int cyw43_wifi_get_bssid(cyw43_t * self, uint8_t bssid[6])
```

Get the BSSID of the connected wifi network.

Parameters

self	The driver state object. This should always be &cyw43_state.
bssid	A buffer to receive the BSSID.

Returns

0 on success.

cyw43_wifi_get_mac()

```
int cyw43_wifi_get_mac(cyw43_t * self, int itf,
        uint8_t mac[6])
```

Get the mac address of the device. This method returns the mac address of the interface.

Parameters

self	The driver state object. This should always be &cyw43_state.
itf	The interface to use, either CYW43_ITF_STA or CYW43_ITF_AP.
mac	A buffer to receive the mac address.

Returns

0 on success.

cyw43_wifi_get_pm()

```
int cyw43_wifi_get_pm(cyw43_t * self, uint32_t * pm)
```

Get the wifi power management mode. This method gets the power management mode used by cyw43. The value is expressed as an unsigned integer 0x00adbrrm where, m = pm_mode Power management mode rr = pm2_sleep_ret (in units of 10ms) b = li_beacon_period d = li_dtim_period a = li_assoc.

See also cyw43_pm_value for an explanation of these values This should be called after cyw43_wifi_set_up.

Parameters

self	The driver state object. This should always be &cyw43_state.
pm	Power management value.

Returns

0 on success.

cyw43_wifi_get_rssi()

```
int cyw43_wifi_get_rssi(cyw43_t * self, int32_t * rssi)
```

Get the signal strength (RSSI) of the wifi network. For STA (client) mode, returns the signal strength or RSSI of the wifi network. An RSSI value of zero is returned if you call this function before a network is connected.

Parameters

self	The driver state object. This should always be &cyw43_state.
rssi	A pointer to which the returned RSSI value is stored.

Returns

0 on success.

cyw43_wifi_join()

```
int cyw43_wifi_join(cyw43_t * self, size_t ssid_len,
        const uint8_t * ssid, size_t key_len,
        const uint8_t * key, uint32_t auth_type,
        const uint8_t * bssid, uint32_t channel)
```

Connect or join a wifi network. Connect to a wifi network in STA (client) mode After success is returned, periodically call cyw43_wifi_link_status or cyw43_tcpip_link_status, to query the status of the link. It can take a many seconds to connect to fully join a network.

NOTE Call cyw43_wifi_leave to disassociate from a wifi network.

Parameters

self	The driver state object. This should always be &cyw43_state.
ssid_len	The length of the wifi network name.
ssid	A buffer containing the wifi network name.
key_len	The length of the wifi password.
key	A buffer containing the wifi password.
auth_type	Auth type, See also CYW43_AUTH_
bssid	The mac address of the access point to connect to. This can be NULL.
channel	Used to set the band of the connection. This is only used if bssid is non NULL.

Returns

0 on success.

cyw43_wifi_leave()

```
int cyw43 wifi leave(cyw43 t * self, int itf)
```

Disassociate from a wifi network. This method disassociates from a wifi network.

Parameters

self	The driver state object. This should always be &cyw43_state.
itf	The interface to disconnect, either CYW43_ITF_STA or CYW43_ITF_AP.

Returns

0 on success.

cyw43_wifi_link_status()

```
int cyw43 wifi link status(cyw43 t * self, int itf)
```

Get the wifi link status. Returns the status of the wifi link.

link status	Meaning
CYW43_LINK_DOWN	Wifi down.
CYW43_LINK_JOIN	Connected to wifi.
CYW43_LINK_FAIL	Connection failed.
CYW43_LINK_NONET	No matching SSID found (could be out of range, or down).
CYW43_LINK_BADAUTH	Authentication failure.

NOTE If the link status is negative it indicates an error The wifi link status for the interface CYW43_ITF_AP is always CYW43_LINK_DOWN.

Parameters

self	The driver state object. This should always be &cyw43_state.
itf	The interface to use, should be CYW43_ITF_STA or CYW43_ITF_AP.

Returns

A integer value representing the link status.

cyw43_wifi_pm()

```
int cyw43_wifi_pm(cyw43_t * self, uint32_t pm)
```

Set the wifi power management mode. This method sets the power management mode used by cyw43. This should be called after cyw43_wifi_set_up. See also cyw43_pm_value CYW43_DEFAULT_PM CYW43_AGGRESSIVE_PM CYW43_PERFORMANCE_PM.

Parameters

self	The driver state object. This should always be &cyw43_state.
pm	Power management value.

Returns

0 on success.

cyw43_wifi_scan()

```
int cyw43_wifi_scan(cyw43_t * self,
        cyw43_wifi_scan_options_t * opts, void * env,
        int(*)(void *, const cyw43_ev_scan_result_t *)
        result_cb)
```

Perform a wifi scan for wifi networks. Start a scan for wifi networks. Results are returned via the callback.

NOTE The scan is complete when cyw43_wifi_scan_active return false.

Parameters

self	The driver state object. This should always be &cyw43_state.
opts	An instance of cyw43_wifi_scan_options_t. Values in here are currently ignored.
env	Pointer passed back in the callback
result_cb	Callback for wifi scan results, see cyw43_ev_scan_result_t

Returns

0 on success.

cyw43_wifi_scan_active()   **Inline Static**

```
static bool cyw43_wifi_scan_active(cyw43_t * self)
```

Determine if a wifi scan is in progress. This method tells you if the scan is still in progress.

Parameters

self   The driver state object. This should always be &cyw43_state.

Returns

True if a wifi scan is in progress.

cyw43_wifi_set_up()

```
void cyw43_wifi_set_up(cyw43_t * self, int itf, bool up,
        uint32_t country)
```

Set up and Initialize wifi. This method turns on wifi and sets the country for regulation purposes. The power management mode is initialized to CYW43_DEFAULT_PM For CYW43_ITF_AP, the access point is enabled. For CYW43_ITF_STA, the TCP/IP stack is reinitialized.

Parameters

self

The driver state object. This should always be &cyw43_state.

itf

The interface to use either CYW43_ITF_STA or CYW43_ITF_AP.

up

True to enable the link. Set to false to disable AP mode. Setting the up parameter to false for CYW43_ITF_STA is ignored.

country

The country code, see CYW43_COUNTRY_.

cyw43_wifi_update_multicast_filter()

```
int cyw43_wifi_update_multicast_filter(cyw43_t * self,
        uint8_t * addr, bool add)
```

Add/remove multicast group address. This method adds/removes an address from the multicast filter, allowing frames sent to this group to be received.

Parameters

self

The driver state object. This should always be &cyw43_state.

addr

A buffer containing a group mac address.

add

Tue to add the address, false to remove it.

Returns

0 on success.

INDEX OF FUNCTIONS

PLL - Phase Lock Loop

PWM - Pulse Width Modulation

Index of Non Function Types

Definitions (#define)

Enumerations

Macros

OTHER DIENSTNET PUBLICATIONS

Raspberry Pi Pico W Documentation Compilation

A compilation of the Raspberry Pi Pico W Pinout PDF, the Raspberry Pi Pico W Product Brief PDF, and the Raspberry Pi Pico W Datasheet PDF. For people that enjoy using and working with printed manuals. The information in this compilation is available for free in PDF format directly from Raspberry Pi. 33 full color pages.

Available at www.Lulu.com/shop

The RP2040 Documentation Compilation

This is a printed compilation of the RP2040 Product Brief PDF, the RP2040 Datasheet PDF, and the Hardware Design with RP2040 PDF from the Raspberry Pi foundation. The information in this compilation is available for free in PDF format directly from Raspberry Pi. 683 full color pages.

Available at www.Lulu.com/shop

Quester's Keep - A Competitive RPG Board Game

Quester's Keep is a board game for 1 to 6 players. A game of exploration, character development, engaging combat, survival, and suspense! Where everyone is in a race to complete their secret quests and survive long enough to get their treasures back to the keep.

Available at www.Amazon.com

www.ingramcontent.com/pod-product-compliance
Lightning Source LLC
LaVergne TN
LVHW081328050326
832903LV00024B/1062